D0792647

Advance Praise for R
Rising from the Shadow of the Sun

This fascinating chronicle of a Dutch mother and daughter records an agonizing, but eventually triumphant, journey from the horrors of life in a WW II Japanese prison camp in the 1940s to peace and prosperity in the United States in the 21st century.

The description of Indonesian Dutch in the Japanese prison camp enriches the historical record. It's a part of WW II history too little appreciated in the U.S. And, Ms de Jong's reliance on her mother's diary satisfies the scholar's search for valid, primary resources.

The tale of a loving and infinitely resourceful mother elevates the human spirit. It's a part of the story capturing the novelist's search for the elusive nobility of the human psyche and soul.

And, the final chapters celebrate the heart-warming success of Dutch immigrants in the US and the contributions they make to their adopted country.

—Ed Williams, PhD
Professor Emeritus of Comparative Politics
University of Arizona

Rising from the Shadow of the Sun is the story of Ronny Herman de Jong and her mother, Netty Herman, who not only survived the Japanese occupation of Java during World War II, but emerged as women with indomitable spirits. Through Netty's diary and memoirs, readers learn how Netty and the other women imprisoned in Japanese camps lived and fought in their own ways to keep their dignity, protect themselves and their children, and ultimately triumph over their captors. De Jong has a strong and engaging voice which brings clear understanding of the reality and depth of the physical and psychological suffering that interned women endured during the Japanese occupation.

Netty's memories of life in the prison camp show not only the brutality of the Japanese, but also the solidarity of the women who had to endure daily humiliation and life-threatening fear. De Jong uses such stark language that the reader cannot help but experience the haunting images of malnutrition grinding so many into death by starvation. De Jong goes on to describe the war's end and its aftermath in sharp, sometimes happy, sometimes frightening contrasts.

De Jong sees her life after the war as a roller coaster ride. Readers will be delighted that she has invited them along. In a book that reflects the strength and hope of the human spirit, much like *The Diary of a Young Girl* by Anne Frank, the young women in this story survive and go on to live among us and inspire us with their courage.

—Virginia Colangelo, MA
Instructor in English and Writing.

Any war is always two wars: one a headline war in which brave soldiers, free civilians, prominent politicians and generals work tirelessly for "victory"; the other a hidden war in which cowardly, uniformed brutes inflict unspeakable savagery on imprisoned, defenseless men and innocent women and children. Both wars reveal the full dimensions and contradictions of human greatness and human depravity.

Ronny Herman de Jong's <u>Rising from the Shadow of the Sun</u> *reveals human greatness and depravity through the eyes of a little girl and the diary entries of her courageous and determined mother Netty, who kept both Ronny and her younger sister Paula alive through nearly four years of captivity and hardship in a Japanese concentration camp. The book is a rhapsody in courage; read it not only to learn about the hidden war in the concentration camps of World War II Dutch East Indies, but also to learn about the beautiful lives Ronny and her*

family miraculously pieced together after the war ended. Ronny's life glows like a "lunar rainbow" of perseverance and hope, and is a testimony to the abiding strength of family and love.
—James M. Williams, MAT

Only a few books have detailed the horrors of the Japanese concentration camps for civilians in Southeast Asia during World War II. The graphic story de Jong tells of her mother's dedication to survive with her two little girls will touch the heart of anyone who reads it.

In Part Two of Rising from the Shadow of the Sun *de Jong recalls her life after the camps. Her direct, matter-of-fact narrative is optimistic, revealing her abiding faith that love, determination and positive willpower can overcome adversity. I enthusiastically recommend this book.*
—Ray Newton, PhD
Professor-Administrator Emeritus
University of Northern Arizona

Rising from the Shadow of the Sun

A Story of Love, Survival and Joy

Ronny Herman de Jong

To Jack: Celebrate life!
Ronny Herman de Jong
Prescott, 17 September 2011

**IN MEMORY OF ALL THE WOMEN AND CHILDREN
WHO NEVER HAD A CHANCE**

Acknowledgements

First and foremost, my heartfelt thanks go to my wonderful editor Harvey Stanbrough. A writer, poet and freelance editor, his knowledge and expertise were invaluable and he was a joy to work with: enthusiastic, fast, informative and always supportive.

My eternal thanks to the late Roger Mansell, Founder of the Center for Research, Allied POWs under the Japanese for encouraging me to publish my mother's story. It saddened me to hear that Roger passed away on October 25, 2010.

Many thanks to Ray Newton, Professor Emeritus of Northern Arizona University with an extensive journalism background, for always being available and for supplying me with contacts in many areas.

Last but not least, I am very grateful for the support of my wonderful family, my husband Mike and my children Annemieke, Jacqueline and Dennis.

Table of Contents

Author's Note

With permission of the people in question, where possible, I have used the original names, sometimes abbreviated them. All times are given as they were locally. For instance, Sunday, December 7, 1941 at Pearl Harbor was Monday, December 8 on Java.

I have used spellings of place names and islands from the period. For instance, Soerabaja, not Surabaya; Batavia, not Jakarta; Halmahera, not Halmaheira, and so on. The official name for Holland is the Netherlands. I have used both names indiscriminately.

Numbers of prisoners given often vary depending on the source. Large numbers I have indicated in orders of magnitude.

Part One

In the Shadow of the Sun

Based on

The Diary and Memoirs of
Jeannette Herman-Louwerse

Eluding Death

Sticking his bayonet through the *gedèk* (bamboo fence), the Japanese soldier aimed to kill me. He missed. A little girl with blond braids, I was only five years old in March of 1944. The bayonet sliced through the air over my head. "Mamma!" I cried.

"Ronny, come here!" cried Mamma.

Dropping my flowers I scrambled across the *slokan* (ditch) and into Mamma's arms. "Oh Ron!" said Mamma. "I am so glad you could run so fast through the *slokan*! You're such a big girl!"

"What was that, Mamma?"

"You probably came too close to the *gedèk*. On the other side is a soldier. He thought you were running away and put a stick through the *gedèk* to scare you."

"Can you get my flowers, Mam? They are for you."

Mamma took my hand. "We will get them later, when the soldier is gone. All right?"

That morning, Mamma and I were walking along the edge of the camp. I was picking wildflowers for Mamma across the *slokan*. On the other side of the *gedèk*, a Japanese guard heard voices and intended to kill me. It is one of the bad memories I have of those three and a half years in Japanese concentration camps. At that time, Mamma, my little sister Paula and I were incarcerated in Halmahera, a Japanese concentration camp outside of Semarang, on the island of Java in the Dutch East Indies. The war had gone on for two years.

The Japanese Army had conquered our island in March of 1942. Civilians—men, women and children—were put into concentration camps. Our captors withheld food and medication and treated the prisoners in the most inhumane way. Many were tortured and raped and beheaded. The Imperial Japanese Army's instructions were to exterminate the Western Race in the islands at all costs so Japan could achieve a monopoly in Southeast Asia.

It was a near miss. I did not die at the hands of that Japanese soldier in 1944 because I was too small. I could have died a year later from hunger edema. In August of 1945, I was six. My legs were like sticks, my tummy was bloated and my cheeks were puffy. I was in the last stages of *beri-beri*, hunger edema. Paula, then four years old, had dry edema and was a mere skeleton. She could not walk or sit anymore. I imagined how it would happen. Paula would die first. Mamma had "wet" edema, like me, and she would die soon after Paula. I would have a month, perhaps two, before it was my turn. The Japanese would throw me into a mass grave outside the camp; a large hole in the ground dug especially for this purpose. When the war was over, allied rescue troops would unearth my body with all the others and bury it properly in the cemetery outside of town. They would top my grave with a nameless white cross. They put white crosses on thousands of graves in memory of the women and children who perished under the cruel treatment of the Japanese.

Forty-nine years later, I stood at that cemetery and wept. I wept tears of sorrow for all those mothers and children who had perished, and I wept tears of joy because I was alive.

I did not die in 1945 from hunger edema, because on August 15, 1945, the Japanese Empire abruptly surrendered and the war was over. With perseverance, great love for her little girls, faith in God, trust in the ultimate victory of the Allied Forces, and hope to be reunited with Fokko, our Pappa, Mamma kept the three of us alive for almost four years. During our time in captivity, she wrote letters to her parents in the Netherlands, which was occupied by Germany, in a thick, black diary. Initially she wrote how we little ones grew up, then how Fokko, our Pappa, had to leave when the Japanese army invaded our island, and then about all the things that happened to us during those grueling years under Japanese occupation. When the war was over in Europe as well as in Asia, we returned to the Netherlands for a six-month furlough and she gave the letter diary to her parents in Middelburg.

The world knows a lot about the war in Europe, the German occupation and the Holocaust. This book captures an aspect of WWII that is unknown to many: the torture and deaths that took place in civilian concentration camps all over Asia under Japanese occupation.

Following are the experiences of my family during the war in the Pacific. Thanks to my mother's love and courage I was given a second chance on life. To understand the full scope of the effects of the murderous invasion and four years of captivity on the lives of civilians it is important to begin with a description of their lives in the tropics some seventy years ago.

Figure 1 - Fokko, dressed for take-off

My Parents

My father, Fokko Herman, blond and blue-eyed, was born in August of 1913. He lived in Amsterdam with his parents and his little brother, Rudy. My mother, Jeannette Louwerse, Netty for short, was the middle child in her family, with chestnut brown hair. Born in January 1910, she lived with her parents, her father Kees and her mother, two older siblings Willy and Piet, and her little sister Jan in Middelburg.

On a beautiful evening in August 1933, strolling through town, their paths crossed, their eyes met, and they fell in love. Fokko was drafted for the army, as was customary in the Netherlands, and garrisoned in Middelburg for six months of military training. After the initial six months they didn't see each other often, but wrote long letters while Fokko finished his military training in another city. Soon thereafter, Fokko started looking for a job. In the 1930s, during the Depression, finding a job was not easy.

In 1935, the local newspaper was calling on young men for pilot training in the Dutch Naval Air Force. After training they would be sent to the Dutch East Indies, a Dutch colony at that time. Fokko applied and was selected together with fifteen other young men out of six hundred applicants. Of those sixteen, eight, one of them Fokko, were selected to serve. He wrote Netty all about the training, and his stories were so interesting that she became an avid aviation fan. On the day he took his first solo overland flight, a milestone, Netty received a telegram reading *Los!* (Airborne). The airplanes at that time were open, had one propeller, and could fly only at low altitudes. Netty clearly remembers where she stood, waving her arms at her pilot up above, who waved back at her. Happy memories. Fokko, the first one to move to the seaplane base on the Island of Texel, in the north of Holland, was trained to fly seaplanes.

Figure 2 - May 26, 1937

In May of 1937 they married. Of the eight young men originally selected, one had crashed with his plane on a solo flight, and two others hadn't met the final requirements. Early in July, Fokko left for the Indies with his group of five. Netty followed three weeks later. Two steamship companies, *Rotterdam Lloyd* and *Steamship Cie Netherlands*, transported passengers to the Dutch East Indies and other destinations on the way. It was a five-week voyage with stops in Southampton, Lisbon, Tangiers, Marseilles, Genoa, Port Said, Suez, Aden,

Colombo, Sabang, Medan, Batavia and Soerabaja. Those liners, each carrying about eight hundred passengers and four hundred crewmembers, left once a week from Holland for the Indies and vice versa. Netty's ship, *Dempo*, now rests on the bottom of the ocean near Algiers, torpedoed during World War II.

When Netty left to join Fokko on the 28th of July, her parents and little sister Jan accompanied her to the harbor of Rotterdam where the beautiful *Dempo* awaited her passengers. It was Father Kees' birthday, and having to say goodbye to his Netty for a long time made it a very sad day for him. It was a sad farewell for all of them. Yet when the steam whistle sounded three times, a sign that all visitors had to leave the ship, Netty waved at them and shouted, full of joy, "I'm so happy I'm going to Fokko!" On board she met several young people, some of whom were returning to their parents after graduating from college in Holland. For others, like Netty, it was their first trip to the Indies. They all went sightseeing together in the different ports.

Returning on board in Colombo, Netty received a letter from Fokko, mailed from Batavia, with bad news. Upon his arrival in Batavia three weeks earlier, Fokko had been taken to a hospital because of a persistent fever. He asked Netty to come to the hospital as soon as she arrived. When she landed in Batavia, she collected her footlocker and other luggage and took a taxi to the military hospital. She left her luggage in the hallway, walked over to the reception desk, and asked to see her husband. It was a happy, albeit short reunion.

The Naval Air Force had reserved a room for Netty at a hotel for navy personnel. A spacious room, one of three rooms on the left side of the main corridor, it sported a brass Singapore bed with a *klamboe* (mosquito net). The large window had no glass, only iron bars and wooden shutters. It was cool inside. Wide marble pillars supported the roof of the hotel, a beautiful old-fashioned building in colonial style. A few steps led up to a white marble front porch as wide as the building itself. Breakfast was served at a long table in the dining room. For lunch and dinner, both hot meals, Netty sat by herself.

Excited to finally be on Java, the most important and most densely populated island of the Archipelago, Netty soon experienced the humid heat of the tropics, and walking with her quick Dutch pace caused palpitations and perspiration she had never felt back home. Twice a day she walked to the hospital with flowers or fruit for Fokko, and enjoyed speaking her first words in Malay, which she had begun to learn while still in Holland. After two weeks, when Fokko was finally released from the hospital, they left for Soerabaja.

The interesting train voyage took a whole day. Views of beautiful Java passed by the windows: volcanoes, rice fields and woodlands. At each station, native children sold tropical fruit that Fokko and Netty had never seen before. In the evening they arrived in Soerabaja where their friend, Jos Vermeulen, welcomed them at the station. He took them to a well-known apartment hotel, Embong Woengoe, where he had rented a studio for them. Several young people lived in similar studio apartments around a rectangular garden. Other couples lived in large rooms in the main building. A covered corridor led to a spacious dining room. People in the hotel were coming and going on a regular basis. Some were going home on furlough, and some had come back from the Netherlands. Many young men, after graduating from high school or college, made a career oversees in trade or banking with the big oil or estate companies as government officials, doctors, ministers, priests, teachers, and army or navy personnel. Life was good in the tropics. After six years of work, they enjoyed a six months' paid furlough. Everyone always liked to return to the Netherlands to renew old friendships and enjoy good times with their relatives.

But they were all happy to come back to the Emerald Girdle, to smell again the familiar scents of the flowers, herbs and fruit when they set foot ashore in Sabang, the first port in the Indies.

The naval base was situated in Soerabaja. While Fokko was being trained to fly different types of seaplanes, Netty discovered the differences of life in the tropics. She heard from her two cousins in Batavia that she needed to hire at least one female servant, a Baboe, to clean the house and do the daily laundry. It was impossible to do all the normal housework herself in the exhausting heat of the tropics. Washing machines didn't exist in those days. So Netty hired Baboe Aida, who came very early every morning. Everyone went to work early in the morning, when it was relatively cool, and went home early in the afternoon. On the walled-in patio with a tiled floor, a tap and a drain, all the Baboes squatted to do the laundry with cold water from the tap, which was not really cold. (Nothing was really cold.) They rubbed the clothes with a piece of soap they were given when they came to pick up the laundry, and beat the wet garments on the slab for a while. They rinsed them, and hung everything on the clothesline. Since they were cotton or

Figure 3 - Baboes doing the laundry

11

linen, all clothes had to be ironed. The Baboes used a large iron with glowing charcoal inside.

Netty had plenty of time to sew, embroider, and write long letters to her parents in Holland. The letters took five or six weeks to reach their destination. Since airmail didn't exist in those days, the answers from Holland ten to twelve weeks later contained old news.

The apartment hotel was not far from *Toendjoengan*, the main street with most of the shops. Early in the morning, keeping in the shade of the trees, Netty could walk there. Transportation with the electric or the steam tram, with *betjaks* (bicycle-taxis), *sados* (small horse-drawn carriages), or taxicabs was inexpensive. Very few people owned a car. Fokko bought a bike to go to the naval base, and when his best friend Jos Vermeulen (one of the five pilots selected) bought a second-hand Ford, he sometimes got a ride.

To her great joy Netty became pregnant in the spring of the following year, and the day after Christmas in 1938 baby Ronny was born. They sent pictures to Holland, and one day decided that Mother and Father Kees should hear my voice. In the early thirties, telephone communications had been established between Holland and the Dutch East Indies. Hundreds of wires ran through long vacuum tubes across many countries and along the bottoms of many oceans. Special "call boxes"—booths, where several people, seated around a table, could take part in a conversation—were built in the post offices. On the designated day, Mother and Father Kees went to the post office in Middelburg, and Fokko and Netty to the one in Soerabaja, and they actually talked to each other. It was wonderful for all of them to hear each other's voices again after more than two years, but the whole experience was only a partial success, because baby Ronny didn't want to utter a sound, and grandmother was so overwhelmed with emotion, she could hardly speak at all.

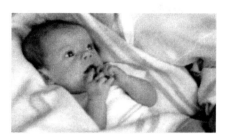

Figure 4 – Ronny

When I was about a year old, Mamma obtained a list of houses for rent from a registration office, and they went house hunting. They rented one of the first homes they saw, a house on Brouwerstreet. A front yard with a terrace on the left opened up to a living room, a dining room and two bedrooms, all in a row. On the right side of the garden, a garage, a bathroom, a toilet (the shower room and the toilet were separate rooms), a *goedang (*storage room) and the kitchen were lined up. A patio with a tiled floor, where the Baboe did the laundry, separated both sides of the place. Baboe Adia of Hotel Embong Woengoe preferred to continue working at the hotel, so she brought a friend along to work for us.

When Mamma was pregnant again in the spring of 1940, she could still write her parents the good news, but dark clouds were already gathering over Europe. In May all contact with Holland was broken. My sister Paula was born in November 1940, and Mamma decided to write down in a thick black book how we little ones grew up. She wrote in detail about our daily events, hoping that the new grandparents in Holland would be able to read her "letter diary" when the war was over.

Figure 5 - Mamma's Diary

In 1985, after her parents died and Mamma recovered the diary, she gave it to me. When I read it, I was moved to tears. Mamma's diary contained a fascinating story, the story of my early years. Mamma told me about all the things that happened during the last years we were in the camps, things she could not record because writing was strictly forbidden, but which she still remembered vividly. Over the next six months she sent me weekly letters from Holland that described in detail our lives in the camps during 1944 and 1945. To her stories I added the memoirs of my father, who was "on the outside" during most of the war. Following the historical setting of the years preceding the war is my parents' story.

Historical Setting

Figure 6 - Map of Southeast Asia with current names
Courtesy of mapcruzin.com

As early as the fourteenth and fifteenth centuries, explorers from different nations traveled the world in search of new territories to exploit for trading purposes. Trading companies in the Netherlands focused their attention primarily on the Far East. Southeast of Malaysia, west of the nation of Papua New Guinea, northwest of Australia, and bordered by the Indian Ocean in the west and the Pacific in the east, they discovered a tropical island empire, the world's largest archipelagic nation, consisting of 18,110 islands rich in oil, tin, copra and spices. The region also was an important trade route to China, thriving in trade of spices.

Initially, the Dutch traders settled only on Java, the most densely populated island, where they occupied several seaports with a small number of soldiers. Over centuries, Holland increased its influence. It established an army with Dutch and locally recruited soldiers, gradually placing the whole archipelago under its authority and calling the new colony the Dutch East Indies. The number of businesses grew. So did the European population, resulting in better education for Europeans and natives alike. The bond between the countries became stronger, and interracial marriages took place. The Eurasians, people who are part European and part native, are called *Indos.*

The expansion of education instilled in the natives a growing national awareness and a desire for independence. In 1918, Governor-General of the Dutch East Indies, Van Limburg Stirum, declared that the goal of the Dutch foreign policy was to make the Dutch East Indies independent in the future, while still maintaining close relationships with the Netherlands. When those plans didn't materialize during the following years, the Nationalists didn't believe in cooperation with Holland any more, but wanted total separation and radical independence. In 1927, Sukarno, one of their leaders who had been educated in the Netherlands, founded what was to become the *Partai Nasional Indonesia.* The worldwide economic crisis of the thirties brought more unrest and revolt against Dutch authority. The Dutch government took strong action and exiled three Nationalist leaders.

Meanwhile, Japan was making plans to conquer Asia. In 1931 and 1932 it conquered Manchuria, continued to fight in China, and in 1937 occupied the city of Nanking (currently Peking), brutally murdering 150,000 to 200,000 residents. International tensions in Europe increased. On September 1, 1939, the Germans invaded Poland without having declared war. On May 10, 1940, they invaded the Netherlands. The Dutch Government became a government-in-exile in London. France surrendered also. Japan would get absolute monarchy in Southeast Asia, as was decided in the Tripartite Treaty between Japan, Germany and Italy, and it was given permission to occupy bases in Indochina, a French colony at the time.

Since oil was the driving force for the Japanese economy and expansion in Southeast Asia, occupation of the Dutch East Indies was its next goal. Great Britain, the Dutch Colonial Government in Batavia (currently Jakarta), and the U.S.A. took action against this threat. In October 1941, they cut off Japan's oil supplies and delivered an ultimatum to get out of China and Indochina, renounce its alliance with Germany and Italy, and sign a non-aggression pact with its neighbors. Japan ignored the ultimatum and forged ahead. First, Japanese forces attacked Pearl Harbor where the whole U.S. Fleet lay at anchor. The unexpected attack took place in the early morning hours of December 7, 1941. A few hours later they destroyed a large part of the American Air Force on the ground in the Philippines. The last barricade was the seemingly impregnable fortress near the southernmost tip of Malaysia: the island of Singapore. The surrender of Singapore, a British stronghold, on February 15, 1942, opened the door for Japan to Southeast Asia.

The enormous archipelago, larger than Europe, could not be defended successfully by its armed forces without allied support. On March 1, 1942 the Japanese landed in three different places on the north coast of Java. Vice-Admiral Helfrich, commander of the naval forces in the Dutch East Indies, departed on the same day with his staff for Colombo on Ceylon (currently Sri-Lanka), in order to continue to lead the Dutch Navy from there. On March 8, almost 100,000 Dutch and native troops surrendered, along with 5,000 Australians, British and Americans. Throughout the islands, large groups of civilians, men, women and children, Dutch as well as *Indos*, were locked up in concentration camps, where many perished from malnutrition, exhaustion, and extremely cruel treatment by the Japanese. Military personnel were put in prisoner-of-war camps and experienced similar treatment. Outside the camps, natives lived under Japanese law.

Mamma's Diary

Figure 7 - The Diary

Preface

This Diary is dedicated to Mother and Father Kees,
And All Other Members of the Household.

Soerabaja

It all began with World War II in Europe. The Nazis had occupied Poland in 1939. After the bombardments, huge fires erupted all over Warsaw. We read about it in the newspaper and we met a Polish friend who was crying because she was worried about all her relatives living in Poland. Before long we would feel the same anxiety about the Netherlands and our own relatives.

On the 10th of May 1940, a beautiful morning, the people of Holland were rudely awakened by the roaring sound of hundreds of airplanes trespassing the Eastern border with

Germany. It was a totally unexpected attack. After heavy bombing that almost totally destroyed the city of Rotterdam, the Dutch Army and Air Force, after five days of heavy combat with their backs to the wall, capitulated. Queen Wilhelmina, her family and part of the government fled the country and formed a Dutch government-in-exile in London.

At that time, Fokko and I, together with our daughters Ronny and Paula, lived in Soerabaja, on the island of Java, in what was then called the Dutch East Indies, a Colony of Holland for 300 years. Fokko, who was a pilot with the Dutch East Indies Naval Airforce, worked at the naval base. We corresponded regularly with our parents in Holland until that May morning in 1940, when all contact with Holland was discontinued. It was then that I decided to write down our daily news in a diary so my parents would know later how their two granddaughters grew up.

Figure 8 - Mamma with Paula and Ronny

My story begins when we were still in our own home, when Fokko was still with us. The strange thing is, when I reread all the things I wrote about during those first years of the war, things I thought unbearable at the time, I came to the conclusion that they were child's play, absolutely unimportant in comparison with what happened to us later in the camp in Semarang. Therefore, please read this with that thought in the back of your mind. There are things that I took too seriously, elaborated too much on, compared to life in the prison camp in Semarang. It shows, however, how the Japanese entered our lives: only threatening at first, then slowly but surely, in a cruel, devilish way, achieving their goal: to exterminate all of us by starvation. They just let us die from the most terrible diseases of malnutrition like beriberi, and epidemic diseases like malaria, dysentery, cholera, and tropical ulcers.

The bomb on Hiroshima prevented this for many of us, for my girls and me, but many, many women and children died in these camps. I am very grateful that we are still alive, and that I could send this diary "because the war is over" to my dear family in Middelburg.

Netty Herman-Louwerse

The First Year

Saturday, November 1, 1941
Soerabaja

I think my little sister's birthday is a nice day to start my diary. All day long I've been thinking about our Jan turning 20 already. How is it possible? I would love to see how she has changed. I can still see her in her orange-speckled sweater that day she came along to wave goodbye to me at the harbor four and a half years ago.

It is Saturday night about seven o'clock. Both girls are in bed. Nineteen days before Paula's first birthday, she has a bad cough. She frequently has one thing or another, just like Ronny during her first two years. She is a cute little baby with big blue eyes and short, silky blond hair. Ronny will be three in two months, as you know. You should see her! Last year in November we gave her a short haircut, like a boy's, because it is so hot and humid during these three months before the monsoon arrives in December. Her hair has grown since, so I can part it in the middle with a little bow on each side. We'll take pictures of them while they are growing up so you will be able to see how they looked at the time I am writing this down.

What a great idea of Mother's to start a diary. I often wish we could write to each other regularly again, and by that I mean a lot, and whatever we want. After the invasion of Holland one and a half years ago you couldn't write at all for several months. We were so worried about you. Thank God we received Mother's October 1940 letter from Domburg. We were so grateful. For a few months many people tried to get in touch with their relatives in Holland through the Red Cross in Switzerland. Others didn't, afraid the Germans would find out who had relatives in the Dutch East Indies and would use it against them in some devious way. As far as the Germans over here are concerned, shortly after the invasion of Holland, Fokko came home one day with the news that the Germans working at the naval base had been interned. In October, the Postal Services supplied "legal" writing forms, but then, because everyone wrote, we were asked to limit ourselves to one letter a month and it took four months to get to you. Now we are allowed only one page, on one side only, and we have to be very careful not to write things that aren't permitted. All mail is being censored. The Postal Services are extremely strict and you'd get your letter back immediately if it doesn't pass inspection. Sending photographs is totally out of the question, so I can't send you any of Paula's first few weeks.

Because I will be "visiting" with you every day now, or almost every day, I will quit for now. My heart aches when I think of all the misery that has been brought upon our country and upon the whole world. It is such a blessing that all of you at least have been spared so far.

Tuesday Night, November 4, 1941
Air Raid Exercises

We have been sitting in the dark from Sunday 6 p.m. until Friday 6 a.m., because of possible Japanese air raids. Once in a while we get a simulated air raid warning. The sirens go on and on, much too long I think. It wakes Ronny and scares her. It is frightening, especially at night. I remember, Mother, you wrote you had those too, and you said, "Let's not complain; they are only exercises." Initially, we had them once every two or three months for two nights in a row. Now we have them four nights in a row. A lot of people taped their windows shut with blue paper to be able to continue with their work, but that makes it so incredibly hot that perspiration streams down your body. We can't stand that, and have kept everything open, leaving only the table lamp on with a 15-watt bulb, screened by a blue carton cylinder. During air raid drills we have to switch it off. Tonight, a beautiful full moon shines outside, brighter than the light inside.

We are always so happy when it's over and all the lights are on again. It must be a terrible ordeal for you back in Holland to be in the dark for months, as you wrote in your letter of October 1940. We can understand that now, being in a similar situation. To have evening curfews, no stores with lighted windows, a mandatory I.D. for everyone and now, on top of that, small rations and a fuel shortage just as winter approaches must be difficult for you. Compared to you we live in paradise, only we don't realize it. I wish we could do something to help you.

Since the invasion of Holland, Fokko has worked overtime every day. When we lived in Hotel Embong Woengoe, I wrote you that Fokko had a bad physical at the semi-annual pilot's checkup and was temporarily grounded until a re-check could be done. To our great disappointment he was disqualified. The requirements are extremely strict. He could have been sent back to Holland, but instead he was given a job at one of the offices at the naval base.

In order to be prepared for the worst, we heard they take preventive measures in the whole country. Army and Navy reserves are drafted for a month or longer for training, and their wives are alone from time to time. Fokko doesn't have to serve in the military because he is needed in the office, which is very nice for me. Today he was promoted to head of the department and is now Fire-watch with about 20 men under him. In case of fire after a bombardment, or in order to prevent fires, special precautions were taken in the homes. They informed us about those during a radio broadcast by the Government in Batavia. Fokko is on watch today and won't be home until 10:30 p.m. It is now 8 p.m. and I'm writing in the bedroom, now an inner room. The windows are closed with the shutters. I dressed lightly, wearing only my panties; my hair's in a bun. I have never been alone, and I'm a little scared. This is such a strange country. Who knows how someone might take advantage of this darkness. In the yard the palm trees are rustling. We have just had our monthly salary, in cash as usual, in a small brown envelope, which I hid in the medicine cabinet in the bedroom. So here I am, the whole house closed up and sitting in the bedroom, the chicken!

As far as air raid protection goes, a lot of places in town have shelters. They look like trenches, often without a roof, just thick walls as protection against flying shrapnel. There are none in our area. I wouldn't even know where to go during a real air raid. Private underground shelters in a lot of yards around here are very expensive. If things get really serious, they may evacuate us to the mountains. Let's hope it will never get that bad.

Starting in November we expect the rainy season again. The preceding months are the hottest months of the year. At the end of October, a sudden rainstorm lasted four days. After that it became humid and muggy. That will continue until the rains fully start, perhaps in another four to five weeks. The bougainvillea, overhanging the patio like a roof, has grown so much; I can sit in the shade and still catch the breeze, if there is one. It blooms profusely almost all year 'round, with gorgeous purple-red flowers. Against the house we have a pink one, really beautiful.

It's time to stop. When Fokko comes home he'll be thirsty. I'll fix him a glass of ice-cold lemonade, or *stroop* as they call it here. I won't have to cook dinner for him. He had a sandwich and coffee for dinner at the office, and he can finish the leftover chocolate pudding. It'll be late tonight, because when he comes home he still has to take a shower and shave. Until next time!

Monday Afternoon, November 10, 1941
A Visit to Aunt Jopie

Mother, do you remember Jopie van Puffelen? I went to kindergarten and elementary school with her in Middelburg, after which our ways separated. She married Henk Esser. We met them again here in Soerabaja. Henk is a Civil Engineer with the Submarine Service. The children call them Aunt and Uncle. They have moved to the other side of town. Soerabaja begins at the ocean and runs inward in a long, narrow strip for about fifteen kilometers. Initially, the Essers lived close to the ocean, on Perak Boulevard, a long road leading from the harbor to the center of town. Most of the navy people live on Perak Boulevard in rather small homes. The Essers really wanted to live in the countryside. They moved to Waroe, a little village along the railroad tracks, with a sugar factory and about eight homes. Rent is very low there, Fl.25 per month for a large—but old—colonial style house. The train stops in Waroe only once in a blue moon. There is a bus stop close to their house. They have a little Ford and come to town whenever they want for shopping, or to visit the doctor or the dentist. Waroe, about nine kilometers from our house, is too far to visit on a regular basis. Jopie feels rather lonely there. It would be too lonely for me too, and too hot. Besides, there is no doctor in Waroe. I need a doctor for the little ones, and we don't have a car!

Well, we planned a visit for Friday, and on that particular day we left the house around 8 a.m. First, we had to take the tram, and then walk to the bus stop. I piled both kids into the stroller. Kokki, the cook, came along to the bus stop to carry our luggage, a small suitcase. The tram was twenty minutes late and the first bus too full, but finally we got on. There wasn't a whole lot of room in the second bus either, but we sat close together, for 15 cents each. We arrived at 9. Jopie was already on the lookout. An upside-down coffee table with a sheet around the legs and a blanket on the bottom served as a playpen for Paula. In her own playpen at home she has more room of course, but this served the purpose temporarily.

Jopie, always very friendly and thoughtful, had made *drie-in-the-pan* (dollar size pancakes) and had a basketful of domino pieces for Ronny to play with. When Paula pulled the sheets down from around her, I let her crawl on the floor. She loved it. It was noon before we knew it. We had a sandwich and the girls took a nap in the bedroom while we sat and talked. Our conversation made time pass so quickly that I didn't get any embroidery done. I took a quick shower at 3 and at 3:30 Henk came home from the office. After a cup of tea they took us home in the Ford. We had a very nice visit.

Thursday, November 13, 1941
East Is East And West Is West And Never The Twain Shall Meet (Kipling)

Peng, our *katjong* (a teenage boy, which most families here employ to do odd jobs around the house) asked for three or four days off to go to Modjokerto, a town 44 kilometers from here. I don't like it very much when servants ask for a leave of absence. Usually they are lazy and stubborn when they get back. But if you don't give them permission they'll go anyway, so we did. Four days later he still hadn't returned. His brother, Tjoh, whom he had sent as a replacement, did not work as well, so we kept asking him when Peng would be back. Another thing that worried us was that things kept disappearing from the house over the last few months: 5 silver teaspoons and a pillowcase. When we asked Tjoh whether his brother had sometimes brought things home, he said he didn't know. Baboe told me they live in a small home and have hardly any possessions. They have no plates and they use empty cans for cups. The boys' parents are old. The father earns a few pennies as a water carrier. The mother is too old to work. It is the custom here for the children to take the parents in when they get married, and take care of them in their later years. Our boy, who earns 5 guilders per month, apparently never gives much money to his parents. Once in a while he contributes 1 or 2 guilders. The oldest daughter doesn't give anything at all and the youngest child is 6 or 7. They must have a very hard time to make ends meet. I'd like to go to their *kampong* soon (a part of town where the natives live in bamboo huts) to see what I can do for them.

One night the father came to our house, a little man with a shriveled face. He said that if Peng did not return the next day, he himself would go to Modjokerto to send him back. When he had left, Fokko and I decided we'd round up some clothes for the family. The next day we heard that the father had indeed gone to Modjokerto, on foot because he had no money for transportation. The next morning at 10, Peng arrived. We asked why he had not come back sooner. He said that he had no money. He had sold his new sarong, which we had given him for New Year's, to take the bus.

"And your father?"

"Oh, he is coming on foot."

Well, that did it! We gave him a piece of our mind. He should be ashamed of himself, we told him. His old father should have taken the bus. He didn't feel much like working, it seemed, and then said that his mother thought he wasn't earning enough and shouldn't work for us any more. We asked him to get his mother. She came a little later, a troubled, wrinkled little woman. I felt so sorry for her having all those insensitive children. We heard how little Peng contributed at home and suggested that *she* should come to get the wages, Fl.3.50 for her and Fl. 1.50 for the boy. She was very hesitant. When the children are so much stronger, they actually boss the parents around, so his parents are afraid of this belligerent fifteen year old! We gave her some clothes and other things and called the boy, who had been waiting outside during our conversation. He didn't agree at all with this settlement and asked for a raise, which we refused. He then wanted to leave and we said, "The sooner the better." Too bad actually, because he was a good worker and we had planned to give him a raise later in the year.

After all my meddling with the affairs of that family in the *kampong*, I met Aunt Rita at the clubhouse of the Women's Association, a club I joined because they give advice to newcomers. They also organize field trips and lectures about interesting subjects pertaining to this country. While I was waiting at the front desk, Mrs. Rood came to stand next to me and started a conversation. Ten years older than I, she has had ten years of experience with servants and the way of life in the Far East. After talking for a while she invited me to come and visit her at her house. I gladly accepted. Her family consists of a husband and two daughters, two and eight years old. Mrs. Rood asked me to call her Rita, and my girls have been calling her Aunt Rita ever since.

I told Rita the story about the *katjong*. She laughed. "He will not be your last one; they come and go. It takes quite a while before you will begin to understand the character traits of the people in the Far East. They are totally different from ours. Europeans are straightforward. Natives tend to beat around the bush all the time, and they don't like our ways. It also amazes us how extremely slow they work, which is why it takes them three times as long to do a job as it takes us. But you will slow down soon enough yourself. Otherwise, the climate with its never-ending heat will soon take its toll. You'll realize soon enough you simply cannot keep going at the pace you are used to. Neither can you interfere with the way of life of a family in the *kampong*. They have their own ways, and they survive. Things will keep disappearing from your house. We all have that problem. But when you, after changing servants a few times, meet a good one—and there are many good ones—she will be faithful, and the faithful ones won't steal. Don't forget, the natives consider us very wealthy people and, in comparison, we are."

What she had said made everything more clear to me, and somehow a little bit easier to accept.

Monday, November 17, 1941
Ronny and the Rooster

I had promised the old mother that I would visit her sometime soon. I went this morning, with Ronny in the stroller and Baboe to show me the way. The *kampongs* have narrow dirt roads with bamboo huts on both sides. A few scrawny chickens wandered around and a lot of children followed us from the entrance to number 10. The house, with a total area of about 15 square yards, was divided into two equal parts by a wall with a doorway. It had a dirt floor, twined fiber walls with lots of holes, and a roof made of overlapping sheets of flattened metal gasoline cans. I ducked and went inside. The stroller, Baboe and I filled the entire front room. I sat down on a bamboo bench against the wall. An *anglo*, a clay pot used to burn charcoal for cooking, stood empty on the floor in the corner. The father and mother huddled in the back room with the youngest child. I had brought a strand of beads for the little girl and put it around her neck. I was delighted to see how she loved it. I also brought some of Fokko's T-shirts and shorts and a few yards of silk, faded but still strong, for a blouse for the mother.

When I asked her if she knew a seamstress in the area to have a blouse made, I heard voices behind me, yet I was sitting with my back against the wall. I looked around and saw a few native women peeking through a hole in the wall, enjoying what they saw and discussing the things we were discussing. I asked the old mother if there were any holes in the roof. "Does it leak when it rains?"

"Oh yes, it leaks plenty!" Can you imagine living under a roof like this one, with the incredibly heavy rains we get here, so heavy that even *we* have leaks all the time? Other than the bench, neither pillows nor other furniture were visible. I thought, *I'm sure I won't find my pillowcase here!* They had one enamel dish, one enamel mug, two clay dishes and one cup and saucer. That was all there was in the whole house.

Our visit was coming to an end when a scrawny baby rooster walked in, which Peng had apparently brought home from Modjokerto together with a few hens—precious possessions. Ronny asked if she could hold the chick, and the father put it in her lap. Delighted, Ronny kept petting it with all the love she could give. The old man said she could keep it. I couldn't accept that of course, but I had to, for Ronny just stood there with the rooster in her arms and wouldn't let go. I was moved beyond words. These people had nothing and still gave away the little they had. I gave the old mother a guilder, for which she would be able to buy five other chickens. We thanked them, said goodbye and went home. Ron and the rooster were inseparable. When she took a shower she took him into the bathroom with her, and when she went to bed he joined her there. We put a basket with a lot of holes over him and Ron closed all the doors so he couldn't run away. Once in a while she would pick him up and hug him, saying, "Oh, how I love this little chickee!" When I heard she didn't go to sleep, I took the rooster out of her room and tried to persuade her to let me take him to Aunt Jopie's because she had such a large henhouse and no chickens. I didn't have a chance. Later that night Kokki (the cook) took him back to the kampong. We can't very well keep a rooster at this time. Maybe we can have a few hens and a rooster in the future. It seems nice to be able to have fresh eggs every day. The next morning I told Ron her chickee had run away because he missed his little chicken friends so much.

November 19, 1941
Paula's First Birthday

Little Paula wasn't even awake yet when our first visitors arrived. We were still having breakfast when Henk Esser, on his way to the office before 6 a.m., dropped off Jopie, who came for the day. She brought some beautiful purple orchids. Fokko hugged his little one year old before he left, and Ronny carried his lunch pail to the motorcycle and waved goodbye with both arms. When he disappeared around the corner she yelled at the top of her voice, "Bye, Pappaaa!" as she does every morning. She wakes up all the neighbors at that time, she yells so loud.

Ronny unwrapped the gifts for Paula: a wooden truck with seven reels in the back that turn with the red wheels, from us; a wooden doll from Ron, and three little handkerchiefs from Jopie. From 8 to 10, Jopie and I went shopping. The girls stayed home with Baboe and Kokki. After 10 a.m. other guests arrived with their little children and more gifts. Paula loved the birthday cake I had made, and it was delicious, I must say: fluffy cake with a filling of vanilla custard, glazed, with apricots around the edge and almonds on top. It cost less than 50 cents. It is economical to bake your own goodies. I don't have an oven, but I bake everything in my *pan bakaran*, my pan oven, with 3 cents' worth of *arang* (charcoal). A *pan bakaran* is a round metal pan with three legs and a lid. You have to keep the charcoal underneath the pan and on top of the lid glowing by fanning. It isn't easy to keep a constant temperature inside. We also had cookies and fudge. I am glad you will be reading this after the war, when everything in Holland will no longer be rationed; otherwise I wouldn't tell you about all these tempting delicacies.

After tea, the men came home, and over dinner we talked about you a lot. Some very refreshing rain fell later, and around 8:30 p.m. the Essers left. I wish you could see our little doll. I hope she won't be too big when we come back to Holland, although at this time we don't know when that will be. Things may change because Fokko has changed jobs. This war is spoiling everything, but we'll keep heart!

November 26, 1941
Ronny Meets Saint Nicholas

It's that time of year again. On December 5th, St. Nicholas comes from Spain on his white horse to bring gifts to all the children who have been good for a whole year. It will always be a joyous day in my memory. I read a little while ago where this celebration originated. This is how the story goes: Wodan, the Upper God of the Germanic Tribes, came by the huts of the people in December, riding a white horse. The huts had smoke holes in the roof through which his assistant collected the offerings the people had put down for Wodan. In exchange for the offerings, parts of their harvests and food for Wodan's horse, like carrots and hay, Wodan gave the people seeds, which they could sow on their land the following spring. Because of all his work over the smoke holes, Wodan's helper's face turned black. When Christianity reached the Germanic countries, the Church changed the Wodan figure to a Bishop called Saint Nicholas, or *Sinterklaas*, who arrived from Spain by boat, riding a white horse. Dressed in a red robe, a mitre on his head, he rode on the rooftops with *Black Piet*, (Black, because of his charcoal-blackened face) his helper, and stopped by every chimney. The children put their shoes by the fireplace the night before the 5th, filled with a carrot or some grass for the horse. Candy and toys replaced the seeds over the years. Most people in Holland won't know this story, I think—at least I didn't.

We read in the paper that St. Nicholas would be in a particular store every morning and evening until the 5th. Since I had to do an errand in that neighborhood anyway, I decided to take Ronny, almost three years old now, with me and let her have a peek at him. These days she rides on the back of my bike on a pillow, so we went to town, into the store, and up to St. Nicholas. I was just as excited as Ronny. She shook hands with St. Nicholas, who asked, "Well, well... how are you today?"

"Fine," Ronny said promptly.

"And what's your name?"

"Ronny Herman."

"Oh, and are you always a good girl, Ronny?"

I told her to say that she was, but that she still sucked her thumb once in a while.

"Oh," said St. Nicholas. "You should never do that again, or you won't get any toys."

"No, *Sinterklaas*, I won't ever do it again, and I always eat my yogurt all by myself."

"Good girl! Why don't you go to *Black Piet* for some candy?" She shook hands with *Black Piet*, who gave her three candies. She said "Thank you" and we left, enchanted.

St. Nicholas 1940
One Year Ago—Memories of Last Year

I must tell you what we did last year. A few hours before the evening of December 5th, Fokko decided I should dress up as St. Nicholas. He would make a mitre for me and drape a sheet around me. I said, "It has to be red, Fokko. Otherwise I'll look like a ghost or a member of the Ku Klux Klan."

Fokko didn't think that was necessary. I thought I would at least have a real mitre, but when the time came, do you know what I got? A hat made of newspapers like the boys here wear! Just imagine a very large newspaper hat to cover almost all of my face, a piece of cotton around my chin, held in place by one of Fokko's garters, and dark sunglasses! In front, a reddish-brown *sarong* partially covered by a white sheet was wrapped around me. A *sarong* is a floor-length rectangular piece of batiked material, which the native women wear, wrapped around for a narrow skirt. I carried the presents in a gingham pillowcase.

Ronny, almost two years old, sat at the table in her high chair with Fokko next to her. He gave me a sign that we could start. I stood behind the door with my pillowcase but I couldn't start. I felt like such a silly character in my hat and sunglasses, which hid me completely, that I laughed and laughed and almost wet my pants. All before we had even started! Fokko kept telling Ronny that *Sinterklaas* would get there soon. I doubled over against the door. Finally, I pulled myself together and went inside. Before I said anything, Fokko took one look at me and started roaring with laughter. I joined him again and for minutes we couldn't say a word. Ronny looked from Fokko to me and then laughed with us.

Well, I had to go on with the show, so I let Ronny, who was not at all afraid of this scarecrow, open the presents. Each time I laughed, I tried to make it sound like a sneeze, upon which Fokko commented that *Sinterklaas* must have a bad cold, and there I went again. In the end, when Ronny had looked me over from top to toe and it was time for her to say "thank you" for all the presents, she said with a serious look on her face, "Thank you, Aunt." Well, then Sinterklaas ran out the door. I have never been able to think about that evening without laughing out loud again. I wonder what we will do this year. I think Fokko wants to dress up this time. We'll have to have a better costume because Ronny is very smart, and this year she has seen the real one!

November 29, 1941
Water

The last weeks of November have been muggy and warm. A few times, dark clouds promised rain, but they didn't deliver. Earlier this afternoon it looked promising again. Fokko just came home in a gush of wind, and hooray, there it is! The palm trees in the garden are swaying in the wind and raindrops as big as silver guilders are starting to fall. Everyone watches when it starts pouring down, because it is so refreshing. Rain at last! The servants put tubs and buckets under the gutter spouts to collect the water from the roof. When they are full, they empty them into the *mandi bak*, the large tiled container in the bathroom, which is about 2x2x3 feet. It contains water for our daily showers. When it is full, they fill up all other available pots, pans and containers, and all that within fifteen minutes. We can't store more water. It still pours down the spouts in bucketfuls. Now Baboe has a two to three day supply of soft water for the laundry.

By the way, I don't think I've told you the purpose of a *mandi bak*. There are no warm water showers in the colonial style homes over here. After soaping, we use a metal dip bucket with a wooden crossbar to throw cold water from the *mandi bak* over our bodies to rinse off. The first bucketful is freezing, but the more water you use, the better it feels. When it rains, we look for leaks inside the house. Usually we find a few, but not this time. The wind is dying and the worst is over. Ronny is outside in her bare feet, dancing in the deepest puddle, singing and splashing to her heart's content. We let her; she, too, is dried out. The yard loves it, the children love it and we love it. What would we do here without rain!

December 8, 1941
War—Closer to Home

On Mondays I always enjoy an exercise program on the radio at 5:45 a.m. When I switched on the radio on Monday, December 8, I heard the announcer say that after the exercise program the Dutch Governor-General would give a speech. I thought immediately, *that's it.* It really scared me. The Governor-General solemnly announced that Japanese air and naval forces had treacherously attacked the American naval base in Pearl Harbor during the early morning hours of December 7th, and the Dutch East Indies had declared war on Japan. Then they played our Dutch National Anthem, "Wilhelmus."

At first the unknown aspect of it frightened and depressed me. I didn't know what to expect. After a while I thought, *Oh well, let's have it. Mother and Father Kees have had to suffer. Finally it's our turn to be afraid.* We've had it so good all this time. We've had plenty of food while you've had none. In a way it is satisfying to know that now we'll have to sacrifice too. Of course the children are foremost on my mind in case of an attack. I have no fear for myself. I can always quickly duck underneath something, but these two little ones have to be protected. I don't really know what a bombardment will actually be like, so I'd better not boast too loudly about my own lack of fear. The air raid protection exercises were not in vain after all.

That particular Monday was different. Neighbors, naval officers' wives, were crying, because their husbands were at sea. I thought of Jos Vermeulen, Fokko's best friend, who was away on a practice flight. Fokko called to remind me to get the house ready for blackout. Everyone was buying blue cloth, which is much stronger than paper, because all of a sudden everyone realized that we were at war and it looked like it could take a long time. I still had a roll of blue paper, but decided to buy material as well. I started in the bedrooms. I nailed blue cloth and paper in front of the small glass windows high up on the wall, blue paper against the ventilation holes underneath those small windows, and a piece of material against the wooden blinds of the large windows in the bedrooms. The last piece had to be removable during the day; otherwise the heat would be too oppressive. I worked throughout the afternoon, for I wanted to finish it before Fokko came home. He has to stand guard for 24 hours every three days as head of the Air Raid Protection Service. I am so grateful that he hasn't been called for duty yet. He is in a dangerous spot. The dockyards, offices and workshops, all part of the naval base, are prime targets in Soerabaja. When it comes to that, we'll hope for the best.

Fokko didn't like to close everything off with blue paper or cloth, like most people do, in order to be able to have the lights on. He thought it would be too hot. However, after a few evenings of huddling together with the newspaper beneath a 15-watt screened bulb, while occasional visitors couldn't see anything at all, I suggested to at least try it. We opened most of the windows and closed off the openings with blue cloth so we could have the lights on and read normally. It is still very hot, and you wouldn't believe the swarms of mosquitoes in here. We always rub our arms and legs with citronella oil, and have the *flitspuit*, the spraycan with insecticide, handy. The evenings are no fun, although better than before.

All that covering-up took about a week. In the mean time we thought about a hiding place. I wanted to hide under the table, but Fokko suggested the *goedang*, which is a walk-in closet next to the bathroom, away from the main house, along the verandah. If the house collapsed, we wouldn't get the whole roof on top of us. I emptied the *goedang* and put a large wooden crate in it with a little mattress for the children, and a suitcase with some medical supplies.

Every Saturday afternoon they tested the sirens. To make it less scary for the children I made funny faces each time. I also showed Ronny the nice bed I had made for her and Paula in the *goedang* and promised her she could get in there when the *toet-toet* would go. Yesterday morning at ten o'clock we had our first air raid alarm, and Ronny, who was outside, ran into the *goedang* and was already lying down with her thumb in her mouth when I came in with Paula, wrapped in a towel after her morning bath. I was very calm. There seemed nothing to be afraid of in broad daylight. It will be scarier at night. Kokki continued her work in the kitchen, and Baboe kept hanging the laundry on the line. I told them to join us in the *goedang* if they saw airplanes overhead. We did hear airplanes, but no shooting. Later, when everything was declared safe again, we heard that the planes had been our own, thank goodness, but hadn't been identified in time to prevent the alarm.

The war has been going on for two weeks now near Singapore, in the Philippines, and even on British Borneo. The Japs are getting closer. We don't know whether or not to expect them soon in Soerabaja, a very desirable location. They advised us not to move away. Besides, we don't have the money, and I don't want to be in the mountains where there are no pediatricians. We could take the two-hour walk to Jopie Esser's if we had to, but that road, although very well defended, is the main road into the country, and I doubt that it would be safe. I am alone one night out of three and really have to get used to it. Everything is pitch dark outside. Fokko works weekends and holidays too. He takes a gas mask and helmet to work and wants me to buy one too, but they are sold out. We anxiously read the news reports and just have to wait and see how all this will develop.

New Year's Eve, 1941
Thoughts

It is unthinkable that it is New Year's Eve. Almost all men have been mobilized. The women are alone, and any kind of celebration is out of the question. It is dark outside. The rain trickles down softly. The girls are asleep. Fokko is at his post tonight and won't be home until tomorrow afternoon, so here I am, "talking" to you. When will we be able to write real letters again? The arrival of a delivery boy with a basketful of gifts from one of our Chinese friends was the only thing indicating that it is New Year's Eve. A can of biscuits, a tin of cigarettes, six large bottles of beer and a bottle of liqueur: enough to throw a nice party!

The year ahead looks bleak. People think it will be tough. Many battles will require sacrifices and cause hardships. We heard that America and Great Britain are getting ready to come to our rescue. The Japanese are bombing different cities on other islands. Slowly but surely they are approaching Java.

Fokko thought that the *goedang* for a shelter would not be safe enough after all, and he ordered a special table like they have in England, constructed of very strong wood and made to hide and even sleep under. We will take the children between the two of us underneath the table and will be protected inside the house, much nicer than the *goedang* in case of rain or darkness. I pray that we may stay together and I trust that when the danger becomes real we'll be calm, because we'll have to reassure the children. If we listen to Churchill, calling the year 1943 "The Year of The Great Offensive," I'm happy I chose such a thick book to write my letters in. There'll be a lot of things to write about until all danger is past.

We thought of you when Ronny turned three. We know how much you would have liked to be here, but understand you couldn't even write. Fokko had to work, but we had three children and two of their mothers over to play, and of course Jopie Esser, who always gets here for a party at six in the morning. The day ended on a very sad note when we heard of the loss of a submarine, which had some of our friends on board. We rejoiced when we heard our friend Jos had returned unscathed from an encounter with the enemy, during which all except one of our airplanes, including the men, were lost. All those scattered bases with only a few of our planes per base are indefensible. We are losing them one by one, men and material. I was planning to talk to you about something else, but the war is dominating all of our thoughts. I am getting ready for bed. I know you are thinking about us tonight, and hope you won't worry too much. I know that you will find strength and comfort when you pray that God may keep us safe, and I am praying the same for you every night. I hope all of those prayers will be answered.

January 18, 1942
This and That

Our hiding table was delivered yesterday. It looks very solid with a 4" thick top and six 5" square legs, a wooden floor and six panels covered with chickenwire and mosquito-netting to close it off. The dining room is large enough to leave about three feet of space around it, and it has the same color as the rest of the furniture. It doesn't look bad at all. We use it as a dining room table. It would be great for playing ping-pong too, if it wasn't too dark at night and too hot during the day.

Now, let me tell you about my typical day. The alarm rings at 5 a.m. Fokko takes the flashlight and goes out to close the shutters, and then I switch on the lights. While Fokko takes a cold shower, I fix breakfast and sandwiches and a thermos of coffee for his lunch. We have breakfast together, after which Fokko goes out for about five minutes to look at his garden, which he loves, just like Father Kees. Often, Ronny is awake to wave goodbye to him. She holds his sunglasses for him, stands on the little wall by the gate and yells, "Bye, Pappaaa!" which wakes up the neighbors, of course, but they don't mind. It is time for them to get up anyway. Then she and I walk back inside to put Paula on the potty. When she was a year old and could sit up straight, I started potty training Paula, and she loves it. She cries when I take her off after half an hour. Fourteen months old, and except for an occasional accident she is potty trained. How about that? Well, with Paula next to a basket of toys and Ronny playing, I put the oatmeal on the stove and get dressed. Next, I get Ronny washed and dressed. I part her hair in the middle and roll a little braid on each side, tied with a ribbon. It looks so cute.

After breakfast, Ronny usually goes to play with her friend across the street and Paula is put in the playpen outside in the yard. It is then about 7:30 and I have about two hours before Paula's bath, during which I do a variety of things. If it is cool, I take the girls for a walk or an errand, or I buy flowers from a peddler who comes by and arrange them; but more often, I sew. Kokki arrives around 8 a.m. and I check her purchases. Usually, there is something to do in the house, and before long it is time for Paula's bath. She has a glass of juice, the rest of her oatmeal if she didn't eat it all that morning, and a cookie. Then she goes back to bed for about an hour. In the meantime Kokki has mopped the floor and made the beds.

I do some mending or alterations (I have lost some weight, am now about 121 pounds), get visitors or run errands. At 11:30 it is time for Paula to go on her potty and for Ronny to have her bath together with her plastic dolls. Around noon I cut the bread, two slices for each one of us. Ronny loves homemade peanut butter; Paula likes plain butter better. Lunch usually takes an hour. They both eat with a fork, but slowly. After lunch, they are ready for their nap until about 3:30. I balance my checkbook or do some writing, then take a little nap between the cool sheets in the darkened room. At 3:30 we all wake up and Ron and I take a cold, refreshing shower together and get dressed. We take a walk until Fokko comes home, and after he has put away his gas mask, helmet and revolver, Kokki serves dinner and takes the girls out to play. After dinner, the girls get fed and play while Fokko takes a shower and shaves.

The original dining room table is in the girls' bedroom now, against the wall. Your pictures, Opa and Oma, and the other grandparents' pictures hang on that wall, so that you can "see" everything they do. Usually I put flowers near the pictures as homage to their grandparents, and they often talk to you before going to bed or when they wake up. They love to climb on the table and press their little fingers to your faces. After dinner it's a bath and bed for Paula, while Ronny stays up till seven. I tell her a story and tuck her in, after which Fokko and I enjoy a few more hours of tea and a cookie, the newspaper and each other's company. At nine o'clock we close up (or rather, open up) the shutters and go to bed.

January 29, 1942
An Old Friend

For my 32nd birthday two days ago, I only had a couple of neighbors over for coffee in the morning. No one wants to drive around at night if it isn't absolutely necessary. Today I went into town to buy my birthday present from Fokko. I had decided on an English book. While Paula was taking her mid-morning nap, I took Ronny with me on my bike. She loved it. We went to a large bookstore, and when I had parked my bike and was ready to go inside with Ronny, Bob, an old boyfriend, was standing in front of me, wearing the white uniform of the Navy. "Hello Jeannette," he said.

I felt butterflies in my stomach and my heart raced. How handsome he looked! In a flash I remembered our high school years, the many love poems he sent me, and my own coyness. After high school we lost track of each other. I always felt a vague dissatisfaction that I had dumped him and hurt his feelings. Now, looking into his eyes, I saw no trace of reproach. Smiling, I listened, as Bob told me that before the war he was a high government official in Batavia, where he was living with his wife. Now, he was a Reserve Officer on Her Majesty's Cruiser *de Ruyter*, the Flagship of our Navy, and had to be on board again that afternoon. After a few more minutes we said goodbye. I told him how happy I was to have met him again and wished him a good voyage and a safe return. We both realized the danger of the situation. We knew the Japanese had already

44

invaded Celebes, and that both their Navy and Air Force were much stronger than ours, and closing in....

February 5, 1942
The First Bombardments

I wanted to tell you about the first bombardment, but by that time we had already had another. Thank goodness we're unharmed. On February 3rd, after coming home from shopping and bathing Paula, I heard the sirens. Immediately, I took the girls to the dining room, called the servants, and we all crawled underneath the hiding table. I was quite calm, and we were all laughing for a while, because we didn't hear a thing for half an hour. Paula was being a clown and played peek-a-boo with the Baboes, and Ronny was making faces with the rubber mouthpiece in her mouth. We all had a piece of rubber to bite on to protect our lungs in case of a close bombing attack. Then it started. The heavy sound of the explosions really scared me. I put cotton balls in the kids' ears. We had done everything possible for our safety and could do nothing else but wait. It took two and a half hours. Since the table is only five by seven feet, and we were three adults and two children, it became extremely hot underneath. We were relieved when at last the "all clear" signal was given and we could get out.

I thought of Fokko, but couldn't call because the telephone lines were needed for emergencies. In the afternoon, when Fokko came home, I heard that the naval base had not been hit, but the inner city had, where he happened to be that morning to purchase supplies. He told me it was frightening and the noise deafening. He dropped down flat on the grass and watched the airplanes overhead. Many buildings in the inner city were destroyed.

Today, the 5th, I planned to go to the hospital with the children for our annual typhoid shots. I sent the *katjong* out to find a taxicab while I got the children dressed. After an hour, we still didn't see a cab. I hesitated between postponing the whole thing and going on foot (about 20 minutes). Although I feared another alarm, I decided to go with both kids in the stroller. I could walk fast, but went with a fearful heart. The heat was stifling. We were treated right away, and we went home in a hurry. Fifteen minutes after getting home, there they were: air raid sirens! I was exhausted, but so happy that I had made it home in time. I'm not going out any more. We hid underneath the table again, and the explosions started almost immediately. There were more of them this time and they came more frequently. At 11:45 it was safe again. So here we are, right in the middle of it. I hope we won't get any during the night, but we must expect and will have to be prepared for anything.

February 11, 1942
Soerabaja During War Time

It would be a daily chore to write about each air raid attack. We have had them every day. They choose quite convenient hours for them, between 8:30 a.m. and noon. I make the mattress underneath the table every night just to be prepared at all times. We heard the Japanese landed near Singapore. They will conquer the islands in no time, and soon Soerabaja won't be safe anymore. Everything depends on the help we will get from the Allies. The attacks are different now than the first ones. They are over the harbor, about nine kilometres from here, so we feel safer. I am bored underneath the table and cannot sit up straight. Otherwise, I would do some sewing. We waste a few hours each morning because of "those bad Japanese," as Ronny says. The result of this whole situation is that hordes of natives have left town to return to their *dessas*, their home villages, scared to death after all the destruction during that first attack. My most faithful servant, Baboe Atikah, asked for an advance last week. She is very poor and does that often, so I gave it to her. The next morning she was gone. I was so disappointed. You can't trust anyone in this country. She could have at least told me she wanted to leave and sent a replacement. The next day Kokki brought a replacement, but she is not half as good. We promised the others a raise of a guilder in an effort to persuade them to stay, but *katjong* Boeng asked for a two-day leave. We'll see if he comes back on Monday. Fokko said that at work four thousand *koelies* (laborers) had run off. How in the world are they going to get all the work done?

There are no more flower peddlers around, no more home deliveries from the grocery stores, and supplies are getting low. I couldn't get any milk for two days, there is no fish or shrimp at the market, and prices are soaring. I am going to get a few extra cans of milk, oatmeal, and butter to have a supply just in case; although, to prevent hoarding, the Department of Municipal Services allows each shopper to buy only limited quantities of everything. This week we received a letter from the Department of War and my legs gave way as I opened it, thinking it was a call to duty for Fokko, but instead they want him to turn in his motorcycle—his nice little motorcycle which he has had for almost three years, which looks like new because he takes such excellent care of it whenever he has a spare moment. How sad he will be. When Fokko came home my worries were over, because he said he and his motorcycle are considered indispensable at the naval base.

I couldn't believe it, but it was true! Yesterday Mrs. S gave me your letter. I am so happy! Dated October 17, you wrote that our Wim is getting married when he gets a house. I'm so sad that we can't send a gift, not even a letter. We bought six cubic feet of sand and a hundred bags, and are in the process of drying the sand bit by bit, an enormous job since this is the rainy season and there isn't much sun these days. After drying the sand, we fill the bags, about two a day, and pile them up outside the glass dining room doors as protection for the table inside. We'll use the bags around the house too. *Katjong* Boeng came back on Monday and I have a better Baboe now. Hopefully they'll stay.

February 27, 1942
More About Our Daily Life

Fokko didn't have Sunday off this week. He had to work again all day, and said that is to be expected at times like these. We are so grateful that we are still together while so many others have been separated a long time already. We have had about forty air raid attacks. They happen four to five times a day, and they start earlier now, around 7 a.m. Fokko gets them really close to his work and can feel the strong air pressure going like a wind through the hiding trench, while everything in the vicinity shakes vigorously. Our dining room is now prepared for war. We moved the hiding table as close as possible against the two inside walls, with just enough room left to crawl in and out. We barricaded the other two sides with sandbags. These sand walls are about five feet wide, and very sturdy, with a layer of bags on top of the table too, as protection against shrapnel and flying bullets that might penetrate the wood. I feel safe in there. Nothing can protect us in case of a direct hit, but if that should happen none of us will know about it and we'll all be gone at the same time. At the sound of sirens, Ronny comes running and Paula starts jumping up and down in her bed or playpen. When it is over and they get out from under the table, Ronny yells "Hooray!" at the top of her voice, and Paula crawls out through one of the openings as fast as she can.

It's hard to decide when to go shopping. This morning, for instance, I decided on 8:30 and thought I'd wait for the alarm and go right afterwards when it is safe again. But then we didn't get it until 10:30! I had just said to Kokki, "Where are those Japs?" when the sirens went off. She said, "Well, you called them; there they are!"

Paula can finally stand, and takes little steps along the edge of the playpen. She loves to stand next to the dripping faucet with a teaspoon, drinking water. She does it for an hour at a time. Before the spoon reaches her mouth, all the water has spilled, but she thinks she is drinking anyway.

February 28, 1942
Victims

Fokko has been very busy lately. He came home later than usual today with a terrible story. Today, survivors arrived at the naval base from the destroyer *Kortenaar*, which had been hit by a Japanese torpedo during a naval battle in the Java Sea. It broke in half and sunk while survivors attempted to get hold of life rafts floating around. A British destroyer picked them up and took them to the naval shipyard in Soerabaja, where they were provided with clothes. They had watched the cruiser *de Ruyter* go down in flames, and the cruiser *Java* sink after a heavy explosion. Fokko saw the British cruiser *Exeter* being repaired immediately after it had reached Soerabaja, badly damaged. Around 6 p.m., the Marines were marching to music on the afterdeck, the custom at each departure. *Exeter* was leaving again. He came home, worrying....

I am thinking of Bob, as he stood before me only a month ago, healthy and handsome in the white uniform of a navy officer. How grateful I am that I was able to say goodbye. He was not happy at the prospect of going on that battleship, but he had been summoned and had to carry out his duty as a reserve officer. He spent his last hours on *de Ruyter* in a hellish battle, an uneven fight against a superior enemy. He died in the midst of fire and explosions, while the cruiser *de Ruyter*, our Flagship, disappeared into the deep waters of the Java Sea. How quickly the enemy is closing in on us. How incredibly terrible war is.

Figure 9 - Japanese soldiers
Imagebank WW2 - NIOD

They are here. The Japs came marching in today. I heard the sound of many motorcars, a heavy droning sound, along a wide avenue near our street. I ventured to look around the corner and saw the Japanese army, marching and driving. On both sides of the street many of the natives were waving small Japanese flags. I felt they were betraying us and hurried back home.

Yesterday, our next door neighbor, who lives in the large home on the corner, didn't come home from the office. He works in City Hall. He left in the morning, as usual, but didn't return in the afternoon. A telephone call notified his wife to take a small suitcase with some clothing and toiletries to the prison. The prison! She came to talk to me today, totally upset. Her husband, a high government official, had been imprisoned. She didn't know why.

Fokko has gone. I don't know anything about him. I don't even know where he is, whether he is still alive or whether we'll ever see each other again. You can understand how I feel. This is the worst thing that could happen to me, because as long as you have each other you can endure anything. I'll try to tell you everything that happened since March 1st, now exactly a week ago, also a Sunday.

Fokko had to work that day and wouldn't be back until Monday night. When Ronny and I said goodbye that morning at the gate I said, "See you tomorrow night." The funny thing was that we said goodbye twice, which had never happened before, and I thought, *how strange. I hope nothing happens to him. I'd always have to think about this.* We had our daily bombardments and around 11 our neighbor came over with a telephone message from Fokko. He'd called to ask if everything was all right. An hour later I was called to the phone (we didn't have one of our own) and Fokko asked me the address of Jos' wife's parents in Malang, where I was to go if we had to be evacuated. He said, "Just in case we don't see each other before you have to be evacuated, I need to know where I can find you."

That telephone call frightened me. I went home, only to be called over again an hour later, and there it was: he had been assigned to a group of men who had to evacuate to Tjilatjap, a harbor town on the south coast. That's all he knew. He asked me to pack a suitcase and didn't even know whether he would have time to pick it up himself.

"And what about me?" I asked.

"You are staying here," he said and he gave me an address where I would get money every month, part of his salary.

I went home to pack Fokko's suitcase. All kinds of horrifying thoughts went through my mind. In the afternoon I went to a phone booth to call him. He said he didn't know anything yet, but he was almost sure he'd have time to come by before he had to leave. "Say goodbye to Ron and little Paula." I got home just in time for the next alarm. That night Fokko called me again at the neighbor's and we had a good, long talk. He cheered me up again, but I didn't sleep much that night. Early the next morning, while I was sorting out some pictures for Fokko to take, I heard from one of the neighbors that the base would be destroyed around 9 a.m. When we heard the terrible explosions, tears started running down my face. You should have heard Ronny trying to cheer me up. Stroking my arm she said, "Please don't cry, Mam. Maybe Pappa will come home to pick up his suitcase."

When that didn't have any results, she said, "Maybe Pappa will stay with us for a little while longer."

"No, Pappa really has to leave."

"Do you love Pappa so much? Maybe then we'll get another Pappa," she finally said.

At noon the radio broadcast the news that the Japanese had invaded Java's north coast. A little later Fokko drove into the driveway for the last time. Of course he was depressed too. They had each received some money and a lifebelt (did that mean he would go overseas?), and the train would be leaving at 7 p.m. that night. We spent some time talking, while Fokko looked through the papers he wanted to take with him. Kokki kept the girls occupied, but we didn't feel like dinner that afternoon. At five Fokko and I left for the tram, which would take him to the train. It cut me through my soul when I heard him say, "Pappa has to leave now. Be good, girls."

He took them in his arms, hugged them and kissed them goodbye. They couldn't understand that it possibly meant goodbye for a long time. He had to leave them just like that. How terrible.

At the train station many people, including Marines, were all ready to leave. Fokko found his group right away. I stayed with him until 6, but then I had to go home to the girls. I turned around three times and saw Fokko above the crowd, waving, waving. After that, I lost sight of him. On the way out, the tram had been packed. Now, on the way back, there was no tram, but I got a ride to a place about fifteen minutes from home and walked the rest of the way. It was dark when I got home. Paula was already in bed. Ronny had started crying, and then Paula had started crying too, so they were very happy when I showed up. One of the neighbors from down the street, a nice lady whose husband had left on the same train, came over to talk to me for a while, a companion in distress. During the long, lonely night, thoughts about Fokko's unknown destiny and an uncertain future haunted me. I felt cut off from all my loved ones without hope of any communication whatsoever.

The next few days were terrible. Thinking of Fokko was almost unbearable. But I had promised him to fight my way through as best I could, and more adversity was in store for us. Yesterday, our *katjong* came to ask for his resignation. He wanted to go to the *dessa*. My heart sank. I gave him what I owed him, thinking, *Will the others leave too?* At the same time, however, I had a strong sense of strength, of being able to handle it all. Looking at your pictures, Mother and Father Kees, and at Fokko's, I thought, *I'm not going to give up! You will not have to be ashamed of my behavior!* And it was as if I heard you say, "Come on, Netty, we're here to support you!"

There was no bread that day but we had milk, so the girls had their usual breakfast. Baboe didn't show up, but thank goodness Kokki did. We were advised to stay indoors. The longer I am alone, the stronger I feel. Talking and listening to other women confuses me. I worked with Kokki, but this heat is extremely tiring. I heard there is one bakery in town that still distributes bread, if you get it yourself.

Early the next morning there was no milk outside. Usually the milkman delivers the milk in glass litre bottles, which I pay for once a week. I noticed a milkman across the street. When I called him, he said he would sell me some, but only for cash. I had him fill a large bottle, and was pleased that the children would at least have their breakfast. None of the servants showed up, so I had to get the bread, but my bike had a flat tire. Who would look after the girls? I asked one of the neighbors to babysit, and another to lend me her bike and in turn I would get bread for them. When I got to the bakery, they had just run out of bread, and waiting for a new delivery took an hour. All other stores were closed, but I was able to buy some supplies to fix my bike from a storeowner who had his door open. I went back to the bakery. Suddenly there was an air-raid warning! I shared a shelter in the back yard of the bakery with a few other women. When everything was quiet again, I was number one in line for bread, but was only allowed to buy two little loaves at a time. If I wanted more, I had to go outside and join the end of the long line again, which I did three times. Each time I took my loaves back to the bike in the back of the store. Then I went home in the sweltering heat.

We had some leftovers for dinner. Meat and eggs were no longer available. Without ice for the icebox we can't keep anything in this heat for more than a day. I boiled the milk once more, and stale bread is all right. I can toast that. Kokki had just made a large jar of peanut butter, so at least we had something. This evening, when I cut some grass for the rabbits, I heard the steady, droning sound of cars in the neighborhood: the entry of the Japanese into Soerabaja. We had capitulated. We'll hear more about it tomorrow, I guess. I am going to bed now. Ronny is sleeping next to me since Fokko left, a comfort to both of us. Where is Fokko? Will he come home soon? What will happen to all of us?

March 2, 1942
Tjilatjap
Fokko

Fokko clearly remembered saying goodbye to his little girls that afternoon before taking the tram to the train station together with Netty. Although a large crowd had gathered, he located his companions right away. It seemed only minutes until Netty had to go back home and they had to say goodbye for the last time. Saying goodbye was never difficult for him. At the moment itself he did not fully realize the importance of the separation. The impact didn't hit him until much later. He was quite cheerful, therefore, when he waved goodbye.

He had been ordered to take the train to Tjilatjap, on the south coast of Java. From there, they would leave on board a ship with an unknown destination. At times like this, Fokko felt as if he was *being* lived, as if he had become part of a herd of animals, participating in events, but only passively so. In spite of the chaotic situation caused by rumors that the Japanese had landed on the north shore of Java and were advancing rapidly, the train actually departed on time, rolling into the night. During the long ride through the interior of Java he repeatedly saw signs of "scorched earth" tactics—self-ignited fires to destroy important objects, like oil stocks—before the Japs arrived. It seemed strange that the war was already upon them, for direct violence was not yet present. The atmosphere in the train was not gloomy. They were crammed together, some of the men telling jokes. Later on they tried to get some sleep. After what seemed an endless night, daylight came. Around 10 o'clock they arrived in Tjilatjap. A day full of emotions followed.

They were assembled, a few hundred people, each with his own little suitcase, in a large open hangar close to the harbor. At first, mass confusion reigned. Officers aimlessly wandered around, pulling the badges and decorations off their uniforms in order not to be recognized in case they fell into the hands of the Japs. In the harbor, waiting for them, a ship called *Tawali* was to depart that evening. "Them," in this case, meant not only government officials of the naval base Morokrembangan, but all kinds of officers, petty officers and crewmembers of the Royal Dutch Navy as well, although the latter were embarking mostly on other ships. No one was pressured to go on board. They were allowed to go back if they wanted to. A number of *Indos* did so.

Against strict orders, some officers took their wives and children with them on board ship. As Fokko heard later, the total evacuation of Tjilatjap, not an easy assignment, was in the hands of Cas Vierhout, a reserve officer in the Royal Dutch Navy and a long-time friend of his. Like Fokko, he'd had to leave his wife and children, three little boys, behind at home in Soerabaja. Cas was a chief mate with the K.P.M., the *Koninklijke Pakketvaart Maatschappij*, which during wartime was integrated with the navy because the people of the K.P.M.

knew the waters of the Indonesian Archipelago like the back of their hands, even better than navy personnel. There had been no great display of courage, no heroic volunteers, at least not among the officers. During the hectic organization to get as many people as possible out of the harbor in time, Cas Vierhout himself stayed behind. He didn't want to leave Java, where his wife and kids would fall into the hands of the enemy. He was made prisoner of war a few days later. There was a real hero.

March 12, 1942
Life At Home

The days pass slowly. There is no mail delivery. The trains are not running. Each day at 3 p.m. the radio broadcasts a list of names of men who are safe in Bandoeng. I don't know whether Fokko is in Bandoeng or not. I don't eat or sleep very well since Fokko left. I do everything mechanically. The most important task of the day is to see that we get enough to eat for that day, and so far we've been lucky. In the afternoon I don't take a nap any more. I write, or read an English book, the dictionary next to me. The evenings, so cozy when Fokko was still here, together in our corner with the newspaper, tea and a cookie, are the most difficult for me now. The newspaper has been reduced to one page. I feel so lonely.

I've been out in the neighborhood several times on my bike trying to get ice and groceries, without result. There is no ice. Every house has an icebox with two doors. The upper part holds a large bar of ice, wrapped in a towel to delay the melting process. The lower part of this piece of furniture (it's brown and looks like a cupboard) is for storing perishables. It has four legs, resting on the raised center of little round trays filled with water, to bar the ever-present ants. Large icebars were being delivered daily, but not now. The stores are closed, empty, almost empty, or sold out. Eggs are 10 cents each, four times as much as they used to be. The Japanese have occupied all large buildings, and we have a new flag. I went home again and had a drink of lukewarm water. For a while we didn't even have water, but thank goodness that got fixed in a couple of days. The servants are afraid to work for us. The *katjong* and Kokki left. Baboe brought another Kokki and both of them work half-days now. Whether this Kokki is a good cook I can't tell; there isn't much left to cook. Oh, I've got a new *kebon* (gardener), who will come every day at 4 to clean up the yard, so that helps. They come and go, but I am grateful for any help I can get at this point.

Although we don't have air raids any more, we don't go out. I haven't seen any friends lately. Of course I know everyone in my street, and in case of trouble we can count on each other for help. But without Fokko here, and being so far away from all of you, I feel very much alone.

According to the rumors, a lot of men have been evacuated from Tjilatjap to Australia. Australia! Fokko on a whole different continent! That could mean that we won't see each other for years! The only advantages I can think of are that it isn't as hot there as it is here, and he probably has a job, which would have been difficult to find in occupied territory. Yet, he may be so far away from us that he might not see his daughters until they are much older. Oh well, I'd better not think about that. As long as we get together again, I'll be able to survive a few difficult years. It is questionable at this moment whether I can remain here, and whether I will receive any more money. Everything is up in the air.

Yesterday the girls and I went to see Aunt Rita. Her house is within walking distance. That is to say, you can walk there during the cooler part of the afternoon. We talked about the new situation. Her husband is still working and thinks he may not be replaced by a Japanese for the time being.

March 29, 1942
From One Day To The Next

Oh, to think that somewhere in Middelburg there is a house where I would be welcome with my two girls any time! I wish I could *walk* there! But no. That would mean I couldn't handle my own problems, and since this is the first time in my life that I have had real worries, I'd better deal with them. You see, when Fokko didn't pass the last physical exam necessary for renewal of his pilot's license, which was a tremendous disappointment for him, and when Ronny and Paula became so very ill, I still had Fokko and everything was different. Now I'm on my own and I have so many fears.

Last night I heard that the Japanese were searching all the homes and have already reached our street corner. I was told I'd better take the badges from Fokko's old uniforms and hide any money and valuables, because the search is very thorough and they are heavily armed. The road to the city has been closed off to Europeans. We are not allowed to leave our neighborhood, and privately owned cars are not permitted on the streets because of gasoline restrictions. The Japanese didn't get to our house this afternoon, but all those rumors and the thought of getting killed exhausted me so, that I just sat down and cried for a while.

Annie, Jos' wife, came to stay with us for a few days and brought a lot of vegetables and fruit, canned butter and oatmeal, all wonderful. The Japanese had occupied her house, stolen her bike and many other possessions, and she couldn't claim anything. Jopie Esser appeared unexpectedly. She and Henk were looking for a home to share. Since Henk isn't sure he will get his salary in the future, they have to cut down on their expenses. We discussed the possibility of them moving in with me. I had been thinking of taking in someone to share the rent. We agreed on sharing rent and utility bills, so they moved in with their suitcase on Saturday, March 28th.

We immediately started planning which items we could cut down on: electricity, and one servant. Jopie and I will share the household chores with her. I cancelled my subscription to the newspaper. We do all the cooking on charcoal because oil is no longer available. Since potatoes have become too expensive, we have rice and vegetables with some meat every day. We cook the vegetables together with the rice in one pan so we don't waste any vitamins. We always have fruit for dessert and eat bread for dinner when it is available. Last week I received half of Fokko's net salary with no guarantee about any future payments, but with the Essers sharing all my expenses we live quite inexpensively. All Dutch people are in the same boat. We are all trying to make our supplies last as long as possible.

Naturally, I gave Henk and Jopie the master bedroom. The girls and I share the back room. I sleep in Paula's bed and Paula sleeps in the playpen. I am grateful that we bought good-sized beds for the girls. It is a little narrow for me, and my toes hit the footboard, but it is adequate. I am grateful, too, that we still have our home. Many Dutch people have been thrown out of their homes, sometimes at one or two hours' notice. They had to leave behind all their possessions except for some clothes and things for their children. The Essers, for instance, have lost everything. The day after Fokko left for Tjilatjap by train, Jopie and Henk left their house in Waroe in their Ford, with a suitcase containing their valuables and some clothes. They drove all the way through Java to Tjilatjap, one full day and night, to try to get away on one of the ships, but they came too late. All the ships had left already, and they had to drive all the way back.

When they reached their home, it had been plundered. The Japanese had not yet arrived, but the natives had taken the opportunity to enrich themselves. The only things left when Henk came home were a pair of shoes, a hat, a few letters and pictures, a lemon squeezer, a table and a few chairs. When they had to leave at short notice, Jopie put all her jewelry (a lot and expensive) in an unobtrusive box in the suitcase. Henk, seeing the box, thought it was junk, took it out and left it behind. When he went back to look for it, it was gone. Even the light fixtures had been pulled out of the ceiling. Since no private cars are permitted on the streets any more they had to leave their car behind too. How sad. At least they still have each other for support.

It is so depressing not to know anything about Fokko's whereabouts and not to be able to get in touch. If only I knew how long it was going to last, I could count down. I have marked all the days of 1942 on the calendar. After that, there's a whole other year. I have the feeling our separation will be for two years. What a depressing thought. Every night I say, "Another day closer to the end of the war."

Life has come to a halt. All banks and post offices are closed. Food is available for purchase, as most stores have opened again, but that's all. All military men have been interned, Japanese money is being circulated, and we have to bow to the heavily armed Japanese soldiers we see in the streets. You are experiencing similar things in Holland, of course. I wish we could at least write to you!

March 3, 1942
Tjilatjap
Fokko

In the early afternoon, totally unexpectedly, Fokko bumped into Jos Vermeulen. It was the third time one of those infrequent, seemingly predestined encounters had happened. They first met in a train compartment in Holland at the end of August, 1935, on their way to Den Helder to begin their pilot's training. Sixteen out of six hundred men who had tried out for the rigorous pilot's training were selected. Within a few weeks, eight of those, the best, would emerge to complete the required two years' training. Two of them didn't make it, and after receiving their pilot's license, Jos, Fokko and three other pilots were sent to the Dutch East Indies. Fokko and Netty married soon after his training, and went to live in Soerabaja, on Java. Two years later Fokko had to stop flying for a while, not having passed his latest physical, while Jos stayed on. Jos married a nice girl named Annie, and then, since he and Fokko each had a different job in a different location, they lost contact. Throughout their lives, however, they were to meet; in different parts of the world, in different circumstances, always totally unexpected, like that day in Tjilatjap.

Fokko didn't know that Jos was in Tjilatjap with a seaplane of the navy, and Jos didn't know Fokko was going to be there to board a ship in the harbor. The first thing Jos said was, "Are you leaving on the *Tawali?*" which sounded like he would rather die! Through reconnaissance he knew several Japanese ships, among them submarines, were cruising south of Tjilatjap. Japanese reconnaissance planes could detect every movement of ships going in or out of the harbor. He strongly advised Fokko not to go. The previous day there was a Japanese air attack on Tjilatjap, which made the situation even more hazardous. In the harbor, Jos showed Fokko several Brewster Buffalo fighters in different stages of assembly. "The Brewster is an American fighter aircraft, the first monoplane fighter aircraft used by the US Navy," Jos explained. "We ordered them from the U.S.A. at the last moment and they arrived in Tjilatjap a few days ago, unassembled, shipped in crates. But it's too late. They can't be launched in time." A few days later the whole shipment was sunk. Because more air attacks were expected, Jos was to fly to Australia the following day.

Other seaplanes, waiting in secret places in lakes all over Java, would fly to Australia as well, and a number of women and children and other people would go along, against all orders. All seaplanes, as Fokko heard much later, were instructed to fly to Broome, a village on the northwest coast of Australia. Broome became well known in the air, as it was constantly mentioned in the instructions on the radio. The Japanese, who intercepted those signals, soon found out its location and directed several of their fighter planes and dive bombers to Broome. Along the coast near Broome, they discovered a number of our "sitting ducks," an easy target. Several pilots and officers, together with women and children as well as the commander of the naval base in Soerabaja, were killed there. Fokko heard all this much later from eyewitnesses. A number of them, who had left the seaplanes earlier in little rowboats, had made it to shore safely. Jos, who had left an hour or so later than the others, noticed from a great distance smoke bellowing in the proximity of Broome. He decided it couldn't be a bonfire of the natives, and flew in a wide curve around Broome to land farther down the coast. It saved his life, and the lives of his legal and illegal passengers.

April 12, 1942
My Daughters And Me

All of a sudden Paula can walk! I got Ronny's first pair of shoes out of the closet, the blue ones, but they were much too large. I guess Paula is a little smaller overall than Ronny at her age. I went to the shoe store, where I remembered having seen a pair of little white boots. They were Paula's size and I got them for 75 cents, but her instep was too high. She couldn't get into them! I cut off the tops, making sure there were two holes on each side left for the shoelaces. Then they fit, and we could go for a walk. This is the first big event Fokko can't experience with us. I wish he could see me walking down the street with a daughter on each hand. I'm so proud! They love to play with frogs. When Fokko was still with us he'd put one on the table occasionally. Just before he left, he gave one to Paula in her high chair. At dusk, when the frogs come out of the yard onto the patio looking for food, Ronny goes out hunting for the biggest ones. She likes to keep them in a box or a can, but I always give her boxes without lids so the frogs can get away again. We have moved all the sandbags from the dining room to the garage, moved the hiding table back against the wall, and put the dining room table back where it belongs. Will we have food on the table next month?

March 3, 1942
On Board The *Tawali*
Fokko

After Fokko and Jos parted, Fokko was vaguely aware he was walking up the gangplank with many others. Finally, the *Tawali* took off into the night, due south, destination unknown.

It was dark, with a drizzling rain. Visibility was poor. Among the people on board was a navy cook, who could bake delicious bread. Against strict orders, not always taken seriously in those days, a few women and children had been taken on board.

Had he been offered the choice, Fokko pondered, he would not have wanted Netty and the girls to come with him. There was too much risk involved. He estimated the number of people on board to be close to six hundred. For a freighter without passenger accommodations that was a lot. This large freighter, although its name suggested it, probably did not belong to the K.P.M. fleet. The ship was not at all equipped for a voyage with six hundred passengers. It had left Java a few days earlier but, after it had gone due south and arrived outside the danger zone, the Admiralty had ordered it back to Tjilatjap. The crew had not accepted the order with joy. *Quite understandable*, Fokko thought. Nevertheless, they had carried out the order without hesitation. That's how it goes in wartime. Sometimes a move like this is successful. Often it ends in disaster. Obviously, there had been enough time to buy the necessary provisions before the second departure, because there seemed to be plenty of food for all of them during their ten-day trip. The organization of the mass exodus had to take place as quickly as possible. War had been declared and the Japs were all around.

In constant danger of being attacked by Japanese submarines, surface vessels and airplanes, the *Tawali* went straight south for two days in a simple effort to get out of the danger zone as quickly as possible. The Japanese had plenty of reconnaissance planes able to direct their ships toward the *Tawali* as soon as they detected it. The rain and the darkness at their departure were in their favor. Visibility was practically nil. They observed total blackout and radio silence, meaning they were able to receive radio messages, but they did not transmit to avoid detection.

The second day, around noon, an air-raid warning alarmed all on board. How small Fokko felt, how lonely, in the middle of the ocean. There was no place to go, no place to hide. There was no airplane in sight, but it was possible they had been spotted, being such a large target. The uncertainty lasted. Toward the end of the afternoon a sloop was discovered, badly damaged but still afloat. Approximately twenty British sailors, some of them wounded, were manning it. Only one oar was left, or rather part of it, so that they could barely make any progress even if they had known in which direction to go. The *Tawali* did not slow down because of the danger of submarines, but managed to pick up all the Englishmen, whose small freighter had been attacked and sunk by a Japanese surface vessel that morning. Fokko thought, *what on earth were they doing in a small freighter in those waters in wartime?* There were only these few survivors, hanging on to the damaged sloop, which remained afloat, thank God. The Japs, who disappeared quickly, possibly heading for more important work, had left them behind.

Upon boarding in Tjilatjap, everyone had been asked to take one of two kinds of life jackets, one filled with cotton, the other with balsa wood. Fokko thought the balsa wood would be better, because it would float. He had second thoughts about that when they were told to use their life jackets as pillows at night while sleeping on the metal decks. Ten nights of sleeping on a metal deck with a pillow of balsa wood was not exactly comfortable.

The next morning the rumor went around that a torpedo had passed behind them during the night. Whether it was true, nobody knew. They did know they had passed a light that night, which might have been someone on a raft. The captain had not dared to slow down to pick him up, fearing it might be an ambush.

After two nights and two days due south, it started to get colder. The captain opened the sealed envelope containing his sailing orders and announced that they were sailing for Colombo, the capital of the island of Ceylon, a British Crown Colony. It was a disappointment. They had hoped they were going to Australia. The ship changed course to southwest for eight days, still trying to get as far away as possible from the Japanese danger zone. The days went by with many anxious moments, especially around dusk. The crow's nest was manned continually. If the "crow" noticed anything at all on the horizon, he passed the message on to the bridge. Not being able to detect at such a large distance whether it was friend or foe, the result each time was that all the ropes above deck moved and turned across the horizon, then stopped, indicating a drastic change of course away from the object. Everyone anxiously wondered all night whether the enemy would be gone the next morning. If it hadn't, it would probably be a Jap, who had noticed the change of course of the Dutch ship and was pursuing it. They changed course like this several times every day until a few days before they arrived in Colombo.

Toward nightfall of the tenth day, the Promised Land came into sight. They anchored in the roads just outside the harbor, to the dismay of everyone on board. It would have been quiet in the harbor, but outside a swell caused the ship to roll slowly. No matter how the passengers tried to make themselves comfortable that night on the metal decks, every move of the ship hurt them, and the heat was exhausting.

April 29, 1942
Hirohito's Birthday

Today we got the order to hang out the Japanese flag. Because I didn't want to run into trouble, I reluctantly decided to make one of some sort. I took an old white rag and sewed a red circle in the middle. The red material was from a dirty, tattered laundry bag that I didn't use any more because it had become too old. Attached to a stick and hung from the gate was a little flag made out of rags, my homage to the Emperor of Japan on his birthday.

Our cousin Ad, temporarily drafted in the Reserve Forces, has been interned. At first detained on an island with the Coastal Artillery after the capitulation, he was later transported to our area. In celebration of Hirohito's birthday, the newspaper announced that between 2 and 4 p.m. today visits to the internment camps would be permitted. Since different camps inside and outside of town were each holding thousands and thousands of prisoners, it was difficult to find out in which camp Ad was being held. Rumors held that the majority of the prisoners from that particular island were in a camp in town, but I still wasn't sure exactly where Ad was interned. I went to buy a few things to take with me, but because of the big day, all the stores were closed. Thank goodness for the street peddlers. They walk around in the neighborhood, carrying their merchandise in large baskets, hanging from a yoke on their shoulders. I bought ten large oranges, three packs of cigarettes, matches, Palmolive soap, some laundry detergent and two rolls of peppermint. I took all these gifts with me, together with a thermos of cold lemonade. In the mid-day heat I went to the camp in the high school building, surrounded by chicken wire. A few Japanese and native soldiers checked my bags at the entrance, and then I was allowed inside the fence. A couple of our captains sat in the burning sun at a table with lists, which they checked for me. They said they knew Ad Wisse from Batavia, but he wasn't in this camp. Other military men of different ranks also knew Ad, but didn't know which camp he was in. I felt sad that I couldn't give the men any of my gifts, but if I did, I wouldn't have enough left for Ad. All of them were hoping for a visitor, of course, but being all the way from Batavia, about twenty hours by train, they didn't have much of a chance.

All the way across town, past our house and along country roads I went, asking the way, following the stream of people on foot and a few *dogcars* (the only way of transportation other than bikes), in the direction of the other camp, Darmo. I passed a row of brand new little houses, all occupied by Japanese soldiers. Finally, I arrived at the gate, put down my bike close to one of the guards, hoping it would not get stolen, went to the entrance for bag inspection, and asked one of the officers for Ad Wisse. Before he could take me to the office, I saw Ad's face among the crowd. He'd been on the lookout! I told the officer I saw him and ran toward Ad at full speed. They probably thought he was my husband. At the entrance I had noticed a sign: *No hugging or kissing.* Even married couples could only shake hands.

The place looked like a beach. On a huge lawn people had put down blankets and made little shelters against the sun. Fathers with little children gathered around bags filled with goodies. I got a lump in my throat when I saw all those happy faces, so much joy. Ad and I walked back and forth for a while. We finally found a little spot where we could sit down, and Ad drank his lemonade. He looked good and said that he had been treated well, that the food was good and he shared a small room with five other officers. They slept on mats on the floor, but that was fine. The privates were sharing a large barn. Once in a while they were made to work outside the camp. Transported by trucks to different locations, they had to load or unload car tires or oilcans at the railroad tracks. The work was never too heavy.

A bell rang somewhere. Ad went to unpack the bags in his room. Then, waving several times, I left, feeling sad to leave him there all alone, but happy because it had been such a delightful afternoon for all those people. The following days the newspaper was filled with thank-you notes to the authorities from wives, mothers, children and fiancées of the interned men.

On the way back, five minutes from home and very thirsty, a young girl stopped me. Carrying a heavy pan, a toddler in her arms and a little boy by her side, she asked me the way to the Darmo camp. I pointed in the direction I had just come from and told her the visiting hour was over, whereupon she started crying bitterly. She told me they had to go to their father in the Darmo camp to tell him their mother was dying. She had gone to another camp for only fifteen minutes to visit her fiancée, but didn't know the way from there. I felt so sorry for her that I offered to ride along with them if we could find a *dogcar*. After a long time, we saw a *dogcar* and they got in.

All the women were home by now and the roads were deserted, when all of a sudden a Japanese soldier, chasing a couple of native women with a club, jumped in front of my bike yelling, "Sto, sto!" with a ferocious face. I got down, and he asked me in broken English something like, "Where do you want to go?" I looked him straight in the face and asked if he spoke English or German, but he didn't understand me and waved me on. The guard at the gate yelled at us and made it clear we had to stay back, when an officer on a bike appeared and asked what was going on. I thought I'd try again and called out to the officer, "Please Sir, do you speak English?"

"Yes," he replied.

"Sprechen Sie Deutsch?" I asked, thinking that maybe he'd speak the language of his allies better.

"Auch," he said.

I told him my story in German and he said we could go in. He accompanied us through the gate. I said very politely,

"Danke sehr, Herr Offizier," and he left. The children were so happy they could still get in to see their father!

I've often thought how wonderful it is that we had the opportunity as children to learn foreign languages. Not only because I like them so much, but because it's so practical. If you can get hold of an officer you can get a lot accomplished. They usually understand a little English or German, and are amazed that we speak three languages other than Dutch. The officers aren't that bad if you yourself are polite, and you can communicate somehow. The privates, however, start hitting people left and right, for instance when we don't bow deeply enough. I won't take that risk and always greet them politely. When I finally got home, tea was ready. It had been a very emotional day.

May 9, 1942
We Have To Be Registered

Two years ago tomorrow, the last day of freedom for you, preceded the German invasion, the camps. I think about you a lot. For us it has been a month full of memories too; May 14th, when we announced our engagement, and May 26th, our fifth wedding anniversary. When will we be together again? Every night I cross out the past day on the calendar. Each Saturday I cross out a whole week. I consider this to be a period we must struggle through until the war is over. I try not to think too much about how things used to be.

A large levy on the money I still owned came with the announcement that we had to be registered. Women had to pay Fl.80 and men Fl.150. If we didn't show up, we would not get an identity card and our life and possessions would not be protected. Registration took place in City Hall. I went and joined the long line of waiting women. Three hours later I reached the counter. They took my picture—I looked absolutely horrible, a real war victim—and they wrote down several things on a card that had a number on the top. From now on, I am that number. Below the number is my name, age, address, place of birth, marital status, children, my profession and that of my husband are listed. I lied about Fokko being a pilot in our Navy. You never know. I said he was a clerk. My thumbprint was put on the bottom of the card. I paid Fl.80 and contemplated how many days I could have lived with the girls for all that money. After they had stamped the card several times it was mine.

Jopie and I have been melting pork fat lately to use instead of butter on our bread. All butter is sold out. Canned, bad-tasting American margarine is available, but very expensive. Our 10-cent per person hot meal consists of rice and a vegetable and one ounce of meat per person. Jopie and I decided we couldn't very well cut down on that, but what else could we possibly cut down on?

March 15, 1942
Colombo
Fokko

The harbor of Colombo, a beautiful harbor, was now packed with ships on their way to Singapore or the Dutch East Indies, seeking temporary refuge in Colombo because of the Japanese advance. The advance of the Japanese had happened rapidly, a surprise to all. Dutch headquarters were established in Colombo under the command of an admiral with a few officers and petty officers who had flown over just before the Japanese invaded Java. A lot of discussions took place about what to do with all the military and civilian refugees. Navy personnel were scattered in all directions. Civilians were shipped to South Africa a few days later. They were the lucky ones, who literally celebrated the war, in every respect. All South African men were at war in North Africa against the Germans and Italians, so the Dutch men received a hearty welcome from the South African women. They got easy jobs and lived it up, and as far as they were concerned the war could go on. The *Indos*, who might have problems in South Africa because of their skin color, were sent to Madagascar, which wasn't too bad either.

A handful of people, including Fokko, considered indispensable in Colombo, were soon positioned on board the K.P.M. ship *Plancius*, moored in the harbor. It would remain there until the end of the war, and was used primarily as a place to lodge navy personnel and as a supply ship for Dutch, British and later for Italian submarines. Fokko was appointed manager of the supply unit, but at first there was nothing to do. Nothing at all.

Fokko found it fascinating to mingle with the crew members of the different ships that came into the harbor. The men from the submarines, in particular, told incredible stories. Submarine crew members as well as captains were usually around 25 years old. The submarine business during wartime was not for seniors. A typical crew would leave with a shipload of oranges to provide the necessary vitamins, because they wouldn't see daylight for three weeks. A British submarine came alongside the *Plancius* one day. It was listing to one side, heavily damaged. It had been forced to surface by Japanese depth charges. Normally that would be the moment to surrender. Not this ship, however. The crew had manned the cannon on deck as quickly as possible, and to the astonishment of the Japanese, their ship was subjected to heavy fire. They had no choice but to ram the submarine, but that had not been enough to sink it. The cannon kept on firing, and after a final torpedo attack, the Japanese ship sank.

After the surrender of Italy, its submarines joined the Allied Forces. Some of these came alongside from time to time. They performed cruises for the Allies, with an allied liaison officer always in command. The Italian crews were not as well trained for fighting a war as allied crews, but their ships were more modern, more maneuverable and a joy to watch, as far as that can be said of a fighting machine. Then there were the Dutch subs. They usually had a little rowboat tied to the top of the deck, with a hole in the bottom. On a mission approaching Java or Sumatra, they would surface at night. The rowboat would drain through the hole, after which they would close it with a cork. A native officer, serving in the Dutch Navy but dressed as a common native, would go ashore as a spy, carrying a transmitter. His assignment was to return to the sub on a designated night. However, a lot of them were captured and executed by the Japs. Such a mission was extremely dangerous. Everything was kept secret. The submarine would always leave the harbor of Colombo by night, observed only by the men on board the *Plancius.* At the start of the war Holland owned a number of modern submarines in the Dutch East Indies, as well as a few old ones in need of repairs. Those repairs were to be done in Boston, Massachusetts. However, in Boston they didn't see the need for time-consuming repairs because a new ship could be built in a relatively short period of time.

The story of one old sub became legendary. It was a very old ship, as was the median age of the crew. The commander had been told to take the wreck to the war zone in the Pacific north of Australia, where he was to await further instructions. Though committed to follow orders, the commander, prior to his departure, reported to the Commander in Charge at the Dutch Headquarters in Australia. "For your information, Sir, I cannot be responsible for taking a whole crew to war in a wreck like my submarine. Why, you can pierce its 'pressure-proof' skin with a pencil! I cannot possibly take the responsibility for so many lives."

The Chief Commander, seated behind an impressive desk in a very large room, then spoke the immortal words, "*You* don't have to take that responsibility, my son. I will take it."

March 1942
Colombo
Fokko

Before long, Fokko was put to work temporarily at the Dutch navy headquarters on shore. He went back and forth in a little boat. His quarters remained on board the *Plancius*, where he ate and slept and learned to play bridge. His work consisted of collecting and sorting all the telegrams that went out and came in. They had to be legible, put in order, and answered. It took two full weeks before one of his superiors came to the conclusion that in view of the kind of work Fokko was doing, it would be advisable to have him sworn to secrecy.

May 26, 1942
Our Fifth Wedding Anniversary

Our fifth anniversary has come and gone. Where could Fokko be? I remember those happy days after our engagement, coming home from City Hall quite unsuspecting; Mother opening the doors to the living room, and me finding myself in a flower garden. How wonderful that was! I still have all Fokko's letters. I read them almost every day, especially the ones written just before our wedding. He is such a dear, my Fokko. I miss him so. He used to send me a bouquet identical to my wedding bouquet every year, white carnations with asparagus greens. Do you know I still have my original wedding bouquet, all dried? I let out my wedding dress after Paula was born, you know, but today, coincidentally on my wedding day, I took it in again since I have lost weight. I know all this is only temporary. I must keep myself from dreaming about our reunion, because "man proposes but God disposes." Therefore, I won't propose. I keep counting the days, weeks and months, and crossing them off on the calendar. I hope we'll be together again this time next year.

April 5, 1942
Colombo
Fokko

Two weeks after Fokko started working at the Dutch navy headquarters, a navy colonel took over his job, and his work on board the *Plancius* began. All freighters destined for the Dutch East Indies tried to unload in Colombo. Everything considered useful to the Navy was transferred into the *Plancius'* holds, which were empty but for a load of rocks in the bottom hold serving as ballast for necessary stability. Two population groups inhabited Ceylon, a British Crown Colony at the time: Singalese and a minority of Tamils. Fokko had an assistant for his work on board the *Plancius* as well as a group of coolies, Tamils, under supervision of their foreman. When the Japanese advanced rapidly and invaded the whole Dutch East Indies, the British government, as a precaution, had evacuated all British women and children as quickly as possible. Only a limited number of women remained, needed in the army or navy for the war endeavor. A blackout order was issued for the whole city of Colombo, for the Japs were never far away.

One Saturday night Fokko struck up a conversation with a sailor sitting next to him in the movie theatre. They discovered that their paths had crossed before, under peculiar

76

circumstances. The sailor, afloat on a raft after a Japanese submarine had sunk his ship, had discovered in the dark of the night the contours of a large ship passing him by at a very short distance. He had been signaling with a light, to no avail. Fokko, on board the *Tawali* on the ocean south of Java, remembered that light in the total darkness and the feeling of helplessness at not being able to extend any help. Now, that man was sitting right next to him, alive! The sailor told Fokko that a smaller vessel had rescued him the following morning, a truly miraculous rescue.

The movie started, but was interrupted shortly thereafter by a summons for the crew of two heavy cruisers stationed in the harbor, *Cornwall* and *Dorchester*, to report to duty immediately. Much later when he came home to the *Plancius*, Fokko noticed in the dark of the night the silhouettes of both cruisers gliding out of the harbor in complete silence. They had been were summoned because the Japs were in the neighborhood.

The next morning, Sunday, sitting on the afterdeck shortly after breakfast, someone pointed at a number of small aircraft flying low over Colombo and said, "The British certainly built up a good amount of fighter planes lately." Fokko quickly counted about fifty of them. Fifty! The largest number of British fighters Fokko had seen around Colombo was six. *They can't be British*, he thought. *They must be Japs. No air raid warning yet.* He yelled, "Japs!" and ran toward the centre-castle of the ship, where he would be less vulnerable. The others had noticed the danger too. The third mate leaped up and ducked next to Fokko, together with a number of Chinese with little prayer mills. All hell broke loose when the Japanese dive-bombers started to drop bombs all over the harbor. Finally, the air raid warning sounded. Subsequently, the whole air defense system of the harbor and on board the ships added to the pandemonium.

The *Plancius*, moored to a buoy together with a British destroyer, got a near miss near the bow, which caused it to jump three feet into the air. The destroyer, however, received a direct hit and caught on fire. In the midst of all the bombing, the *Plancius* crew was ordered to cut the hawsers and get away from the burning destroyer. When the ordeal was over, they assessed the damage: the *Plancius* had none. There was some damage on shore, but the only direct hit involved the destroyer, which, loaded with fuel, kept burning for a month. To send out the two cruisers, with limited air defense of their own was a big mistake. That same Sunday morning the Japs discovered them not far from Colombo and destroyed them within fifteen minutes. Both crews, consisting of two thousand men on each ship, perished. Had they remained in the harbor with the stronger air defense, they probably would have remained unharmed.

During a walk along the beach that afternoon, Fokko and one of his colleagues discovered only one downed Japanese fighter, contrary to the rumor that claimed there were eighteen of them. The Japs did not return. They had ventured far enough from home with their aircraft carriers, which they also needed against the Americans in the Pacific. Some other night, a few days later, when Fokko and his friend were in the cinema again (there was hardly any other place to go for entertainment), one more air raid warning proved to be a false alarm.

June 14, 1942
Adjustment Of Our Radio

Life goes on. They officially announced in the newspaper we won't be getting any more money. How long can we go on living like this? A little while ago an order was issued that we had to take our radios to a certain building to have them "adjusted." We are not allowed to listen to America or England and now they are going to technically enforce that order. I am very fond of our radio; Fokko ordered it from New York and mounted it into a shell he made himself. I hope I can keep it until he is back home with us. Since it is very large, we wrapped it in a sheet. Two coolies carried it to the building, suspended from a pole resting on their shoulders, while I rode my bike next to them. Five days later the newspaper announced that my number was up for radio pickup, so I went back with Ronny on my bike. Suddenly, a Japanese soldier drove straight into us on the wrong side of the street. He hit and completely bent my rear wheel. Luckily, we were all right. I was furious, but I hurried away with Ronny by my side. We had to wait for the radio for five hours. Then we walked all the way home with the two coolies, the radio and the crooked bike. It was very hot. What a day! The radio now has a seal around one of the dials so we can't receive short wave any more. We got a small strip of wood with some red letters on it and a number, which we have to nail to our front door. I keep thinking about the Israelites, who had to mark their front doors with blood for the Passover. Now all we can do is wait for the next thing to happen.

Since the radio has been sealed we don't get any news about the war, yet I heard something that has given me hope. I tried very softly, because it is strictly forbidden, to find a station on the radio with a news broadcast. I heard, although I could not understand everything the announcer was saying because he was speaking so fast, that there are battles going on in the Solomon Islands! America is starting to hit back! It sounded like music in my ears.

Coupon books are issued to people who have run out of money. They can get a meal of rice and a vegetable at one of the eating houses the authorities opened. We can still supply our own food. I think I will have enough for the girls and myself for about six months if I don't have to pay rent. The Essers only have a month's worth of money left. Our landlord is very nice. I've paid him through to the middle of May, but I'm going to ask him if we can pay the rest when the war is over. We have to save every penny for food. We can't touch our savings. The banks are closed. Thank goodness I got some money out of our savings account before Fokko left. The whole situation is very depressing and it feels so empty without Fokko that I can only imagine how apathetic a woman must become when she really loses her husband. It will be so exciting to get the first message from him after the war if everything is all right. So much can happen to him, though. It's a terrible time.

November 1942
Colombo
Fokko

The days turned into weeks, the weeks into months. Fokko tried not to think too much about home, Netty and his little girls. What good would it do? He had heard nothing from them for almost a year. All communications with Java were broken after the Japs invaded the island. His cabin was his home now. It would be home until the war was over. He had grown a black beard, to his own surprise. He remembered how light blond his hair used to be when he was a boy, almost white, and now he had this black beard. Netty would laugh when she saw it, he thought. Or maybe she wouldn't recognize him....

Then it happened. While he was on the top deck supervising the loading of a shipment of supplies one morning, Fokko bent over the edge of the open hatch to call down to the foreman two decks lower. Behind him a platform with barrels of paint, dangling from the extended arm of the electric crane, swung toward the opening on deck to be lowered into a lower hold. A stack of crates blocking the crane operator's view prevented him from seeing Fokko, bent over the open hatch. The platform hit Fokko in the lower part of his back and he fell twenty feet down into the open hold. By reflex, he extended his arms in front of his face. Both his wrists snapped when they hit the two half-inch wide iron ledges on either side of the narrow catwalk between two of the holds. He hit the ledge with the left side of his forehead. His body flipped to the right of the ten-inch high ledge and landed on the catwalk. Then there was nothing. Had he been swept a few inches more toward the left, he would have fallen another twenty feet and his body would have been crushed on the rocks stored in the bottom hold of the *Plancius* for ballast and stability.

Upon arriving at the hospital, Fokko regained consciousness. He didn't feel any pain. He didn't remember what had happened. However, he could answer all the questions the hospital personnel were asking him in English. He answered in English as well, spelling his name without making any mistakes. His brain was working properly. He asked them a lot of questions too. "What's wrong with my arms? I cannot move them. What happened?" He didn't understand the state he was in. Just before he dozed off again after they administered an injection of morphine, he heard the surgeon say, "You have broken three legs and four arms!" This was such an incredible revelation that he would always remember it. The surgeons did an excellent job. He was brought to the hospital, his body limp, and his head black and bloody. They thought he had broken his neck. A cross lesion would have paralyzed him from the neck down, but the doctors thought he had a chance of survival. It was a very small chance, but enough to justify their utmost efforts. Fokko was in shock. A high temperature kept him on the brink of death.

He slowly regained consciousness again a few days later. With it came agonizing, never-ending pain, only now and then diminished for a few hours by a morphine injection. To endure such excruciating pain for a long time exhausted him. All he wanted was peace and rest. To die did not seem a problem. In fact, it would end all his problems. His life? He couldn't remember anything any more. He didn't care any more. The pain was so intense; it so totally overpowered all of his senses that he wanted to die. He desperately wanted to die, so there would be peace and no more pain. Again he lost consciousness.

July 8, 1942
A Visit With Ad In The Hospital

Two nurses visited us last week and told us that cousin Ad was in the hospital. Since visitor's day had been announced for today, Ad had told them he would love fried chicken, fried potatoes and applesauce, and a lot of canned meat for his sandwiches. I was worried about Ad at first, but they assured me he was recovering nicely. I filled my bags with about ten cans of meat, coffee and sugar, peanuts, a few packs of cigarettes, matches, soap, toothpaste and detergent. I wasn't sure I could fry a chicken properly, so I asked the neighbor's Kokki to do it for me. I fried some potatoes and made rhubarb sauce, since apples are out of season. Finally, I was ready to go. I loaded up my bicycle and left for the hospital. I had to fill out a form: who I was, and whom I wanted to visit. They searched my bags and me before I could go in. I followed the signs *To the Prisoner's Ward* (poor wretches) and found out I was in the wrong place. Ad Wisse was in the contaminated section. I went straight back and had to stand in line with a few other women to find out whether we were allowed to visit those patients.

Finally, we were admitted and I saw Ad in the distance coming toward me with slow, shuffling steps. When he came closer his looks frightened me. He had dark, hollow eyes in a narrow face, skinny arms and wrists, and legs so thin that it looked like they could give way at any moment. I felt so sorry for him. He told me that there was an epidemic of dysentery in the camp, and at one point he was one of the three worst cases. When there were three vacancies in the hospital, he was admitted and he was overjoyed. Imagine being overjoyed when you go to the hospital. "I have a good doctor," he said. "At first they put me on a strict diet, but now I may eat normally again." His eyes shone when he saw the fried chicken and all the other things I had brought for him. "I hope I can stay in the hospital at least two more weeks, and perhaps I won't have to go back to the camp at all. The food is worse than before. We got rice three times a day and only one scoop. I am sick and tired of that camp."

I sadly said goodbye when time was up. I didn't think the war would be over in two weeks, and I couldn't bear the thought that they would send him back to the camp with insufficient food. He wouldn't be strong enough yet! I hope his wife can come to visit him from Batavia. It is an eighteen-hour trip by train. If he was my husband and I didn't have children to take care of, I would travel eighteen *days* to be with him!

September 4, 1942
Sharing a Home Isn't Easy!

It has been a while since I have written. I have been ill for a few weeks. I couldn't stay in bed, however much I wanted to, because I couldn't let Jopie do all the work. That was at the same time that the radio had to be turned in, and I had to do that myself. I thought of you, Mother. So you often you kept going with some aspirin. I followed your example, but I was sure glad when it was time to go to bed at night!

It isn't easy to have people in your house constantly. Henk is especially difficult. He doesn't venture outside any more. He gets very nervous from long periods of idleness and gets into arguments with me constantly about some noises the children make. That makes it very difficult for me. I am trying very hard to keep the children quiet all day. Henk is drawing in his bedroom and I am terrified of his outbursts of anger. It's horrible. In the afternoon the children take their naps, and after we have had some tea I usually take them to the park so they can run and yell. When we get home they get their dinner and go to bed. The children's room is our sanctuary. Paula especially loves to go to bed, and after they sit on their potty for a while, cozily playing with some dolls, it is kissing time, and they go to all the pictures for a goodnight kiss. After that, I leave them and Ronny teaches her sister a song. That is, she sings the words and lets Paula say the last word of every line, just like I did with her when she was little. That's how they fall asleep.

One morning I was awakened by Henk at my open window, "Netty, we have an air raid warning!" The sirens were going when suddenly an airplane came low over our house with a terrifying sound. I jumped out of bed, snatched Paula out of her cot, pulled Ronny into my other arm and ran with them to the hiding table with a pounding heart. The situation is now reversed. When I started this diary, our people were having air raid protection exercises against possible Japanese attacks. Now the Japs have exercises against possible attacks from the Allies. We had four days of alarms. They took us completely by surprise, because we don't read newspapers any more. The only radio station we can receive broadcasts in rapid *Bahasa Indonesia* (the Indonesian language).

One afternoon I heard Ronny talking with a tearful voice. When I peeked around the corner I saw both girls sitting in a chair. Ronny had our photo album in her lap and said, "Pappa, why aren't you coming back now? Oh dear, dear Pappa, we are all *so* sad. Please come home soon," over and over. Paula sat quietly in another chair, her thumb in her mouth, rubbing her head with her foot. A few minutes later, Ronny was really crying, tears rolling down her cheeks. I almost cried too, but this time it was my turn to comfort her. How very grateful I will be if Fokko really does come home. How many women are waiting in vain? We haven't heard anything at all from him since he left six months ago. Six months! At least we have struggled through that time and survived, but how much longer? No one knows.

In July I received a tax bill for about Fl.200. It is a war tax, which I can't pay. No one can pay. People say the Japs will come and confiscate our possessions. I just don't know what I can do about it, and what I'll do if we totally run out of money. How long will this go on? Some people have started little businesses. My neighbor is selling smoked fish. A lot of people are selling soap, and Henk is thinking of starting a shoe repair business. I'll tell you more about that in my next entry.

September 12, 1942
Esser's Shoemaker's Shop

Four days ago, after a discussion with the neighbor who is selling smoked fish, Henk decided to start his shoe repair business. It is booming already. The Essers had worried for months because their money was running out, when the neighbor suggested they start making soap. There is some kind of straw that you have to burn and then use the ashes to make soapwater. Soap and detergent have become very expensive lately. Thank goodness we had bought twenty-five bars while they were still relatively inexpensive. "How can I sell soapwater door to door? Where will I get the bottles? I'd rather mend shoes," said Henk, and went to another neighbor to ask him where he could get some tools. When he came back, he was carrying a shoe-last, a hammer, nails and two sheets of shoe leather. It was a miracle, and we all saw God's hand in it. *When bale is highest, boot is nighest.* When I picked up my bike from the bike shop, I went to ask a few people for work and returned with three pairs of shoes and the promise they would spread the word. Henk sat down on an empty oilcan in a corner of their bedroom and went to work immediately. Jopie does the administration and delivers to the homes in the neighborhood, and I make deliveries on my bike to more distant places in the afternoons. We get our shoes repaired free of charge, and we all have fun. In three days Henk repaired twelve pairs of shoes. He keeps prices low and does a good job, although he sweats profusely while he works. He learned this skill as a nine year old right after the First World War, when his father made him mend his own shoes. He won't make a lot of money, but very likely just enough to cover their food expenses, which is a load off their minds.

October 30, 1942
Tax Worries And More

"We often suffer most from the suffering we fear, which never materializes," I remember saying to Jopie a few weeks ago, when I was worrying about things that didn't turn out to be as bad as I had feared. But a few days later I caught myself worrying about the same things again, so I still haven't taken this quote to heart. My two fears are taxes and the internment of Dutch women and children. Both will bring more worries in the future. These days we live a day at a time; each day we can live in a normal way in our own home is one gained.

September 20th was the deadline for paying our taxes. I went to City Hall to find out what I could do. I was wondering whether I would have to address a Japanese? Would he speak Malay? The employee at the window was a native, doing his usual work. I understood that as many people as possible will have to stay in their jobs for the time being, so everything will continue to function. That means that most Dutch men will be able to continue in their jobs. I'll talk more about that later. I had to fill out several forms about my income, number of children, etc. I will also have to write a letter to the Tax Office here in Soerabaja in February, to request deductions. For now, I decided I would pay monthly installments of Fl.2.50. No one could advise me about that. I had mixed feelings when I got home. Early in October everyone got a warning shoved under the door. By October 10th, the taxes had to be paid in full or else!

During that same time we heard rumors about Batavia, eighteen to twenty hours by train from here. Women and children were locked in "protective camps" in designated areas of town. Apparently, a lot of looting was going on and burglaries were taking place on a daily basis so the women and children had to be protected. To me it meant internment, being allowed to take only a few belongings, and sleeping with other people in the same room. Oh, there are hundreds of questions that pop up in my mind, but there haven't been any announcements like that in Soerabaja, so I really shouldn't worry so much.

As far as internment is concerned, a lot of men, like Aunt Rita's husband, are still free, because they are indispensable at their place of work. They have to wear a white band around one arm, about four inches wide, with a red circle in the center. Aunt Rita's husband told us the Japs have taken over management of the business, but experts like her husband are consultants. The Japanese managers are citizens who moved here from Japan.

The whole city received an extension from the Tax Office until the end of this year. Thus the month of October has passed, and this Sunday it will be November. A whole year has gone by since I started this diary, a terrible year, never to forget.

The Second Year

November 1, 1942
Jan's 21st Birthday

Happy Birthday, dear Jan. This is a very special day. I wonder if you have a boyfriend yet. We are completely cut off from all news sources and live by rumors constantly going around. At first we believed what was being said, but we have found out that most things turn out differently. We'll just have to wait and see. During the last few weeks with all the family birthdays, I've been thinking of the ones we celebrated together. I have lost track of the time difference between you and us. The Japanese have a different calendar and time than we have in the Dutch East Indies. We now live in the Japanese year of 2602 (their era beginning 660 years before Christ), and we had to put the clock one and a half hours ahead to Tokyo time. Nevertheless, my thoughts have been with you all day. I hope you will have enough food and fuel to last through the upcoming winter. I couldn't bear the thought that something would happen to any one of you.

November 12, 1942
I'm Living Alone Again!

I have peace and quiet! What a wonderful relief to have my house to myself again. On November 4th, after a final thunderous scene, the Essers left. The situation had worsened because of Henk's constant outbursts. I readily admit, and therefore have put up with so much for seven long months, that life for a man without his usual work, hiding inside someone else's house, afraid of internment and having lost all his possessions, is extremely difficult. He had terrible temper tantrums. He was very sorry about them afterwards, but they kept recurring so frequently, and for no particular reason, that it was very hard on me. All day long I felt those two ears and eyes coming from the bedroom. He heard everything. Jopie pleaded with me to put up with him. I learned to control myself and constantly hushed the children. I distracted them when I felt an outburst was imminent.

On Tuesday the 4th Paula woke up crying. She was covered with an itching rash and couldn't be quieted down, although I walked around with her in my arms, even taking her outside. All of a sudden Henk bellowed, "Could I please request silence?"

An hour later I went to their window and said, "I can't get Paula to stop crying. She has a rash, and if you can't stand it, why don't you go and sit outside on the patio?"

"Hah!" he replied sarcastically. "She shut up right away when she heard my voice, didn't she?"

"Who wouldn't, at the sound of a voice like yours!?"

He got dressed and went outside, but he remained furious. The meals were trials, and I retired early with the girls. Jopie suggested they'd move out. She went to the Salvation Army Military Home to inquire about a place to stay. They could have moved out right then, but decided to wait two more days in order to finish the shoe repairs for the neighborhood. The next day I came home with the children and didn't notice Henk, who was sitting in a corner on the patio. Ronny, however, who always runs ahead, saw him and shouted happily, "Hi Uncle!"

"Go away! Shut up! I'm not your uncle!" he snarled.

I swallowed, and told Ronny quietly, "Come here, Darling!"

"I wasn't talking to you!"

"No, but I'm not calling you darling either!"

Then he came running toward me like an angry bull. I thought he might hit us in his anger, so I called out loudly, "Mr. Hubbema!"

Mr. Hubbema is our neighbor. Henk yelled, "Get inside, you! Inside!"

"No! This is my house, and I will go where I please, and right now I'm getting out with the children because I'm scared to death of you!" That was our goodbye, and I went to the neighbors. Jopie came home, and I watched them leave. An hour later she returned to get their clothes and said she would come back the next morning to pick up their suitcase. "Never do business with a friend," the saying goes. I can add to that: "Never *live* with a friend either." It was a relief to see them go. It was such an indescribably wonderful feeling. We don't have to pay rent any more (our dear landlord gave us an extension until after the war). I only have to pay for electricity Fl.3.35, water Fl.2.36, Baboe Fl.7.50, and our food. We used to share all that, but we are eating better now. I think we ate too scantily and looked like ghosts. Since we don't know what the future will bring and we could all use a little extra weight, I am now using the best quality ingredients. We are eating potatoes again, which is much nicer than rice every day, and not much more expensive. We use butter on our bread, because my ration lasts twice as long since I don't have to share it with the Essers, and I can fry some things again. Oh, the freedom! I can have other children over to play. I don't have to work, and I can do my sewing again. Baboe cleans the rooms and does the laundry every other day, since we have less to launder now, so we are saving soap too.

You know, I am doing the cooking. It's so funny; I can cook without a cookbook now; of course not as well as Mother, not by far. I have never tasted better food than Mother's. Do you remember that whenever I had cooked something, and nobody said anything about it right away, I would say it was delicious? I say that here sometimes to the children. I'll say, "Yum, these meatballs are really delicious!" and then I snicker out loud because I remember praising myself way back when, at home.

I had to get used to the loneliness at night. I'm grateful that we are under the same roof with the neighbors. The houses are built side-by-side, two under one roof. Our bedrooms and living rooms are wall-to-wall. When they talk loudly we can hear them. We should plan some kind of signal, a knock on the wall or something, in case of an emergency. Rain is pouring down at the moment, with thunder and lightning in the distance. It makes it extra cozy inside, and I am thinking longingly of the good times we used to have, Fokko and I. He's been gone almost nine months; where could he be?

A few days ago something happened that indicates a change in the relationship between the natives and us. I was about to take the girls for our little afternoon walk when I heard the latch of the garden gate. I saw a native approaching, and recognized him to be Tamin, Baboe*'s* husband. We met him occasionally during our stroll in the neighborhood, where he would bicycle slowly. I always greeted him and let the girls wave at him. Now he was coming up to the house. Somehow I didn't like it, and I stepped forward to meet him halfway. "Hi, Tamin. Can I help you?" He took a bottle of cologne out of his pocket and made a move to give it to me. The thought flashed through my mind, *Reject it properly. Be careful not to hurt his pride!* I didn't take it and said, "That's very kind of you, Tamin, but my husband gave me a bottle just before he left, so I still have enough, but why don't you give it to Baboe Sima? She deserves it. She always works so hard." Thank heavens he understood and went away. I still don't like it. Something like that would never have happened before the war. It was simply unthinkable. There always was a certain distance between master and servant, but now, our army defeated, men in camps, women alone, the Dutch no longer seem the masters.

November 20, 1942
The Camps

Well, I'd better stop dreaming about having Fokko home again. I don't think we will have the privilege of staying in our own house. It would be nothing less than a miracle if that happened. Everywhere in Batavia, Semarang, Malang and many smaller cities, all Dutch women have to live in special camps. Persistent rumors are that preparations have started here in Soerabaja too. They also say that the situation is not as dangerous here as in other cities, so that they will postpone internment of Europeans in Soerabaja as long as possible. I hear bits and pieces of information here and there and try to draw my own conclusions. It confuses me.

Anyway, what I heard about those camps was that a large section of town is surrounded with barbed wire, and each house has to be shared by several families, three to four people to a room. I hope I won't have to share a room with anyone else but my two girls. I also heard that those who still have some money might take care of their own food and share the rent. Apparently, we can't take any servants with us, but we may take as much furniture and as many personal belongings as we can store in the assigned room. The rest we can sell to the Japanese government. Several Dutch and native government officials are still doing their regular jobs, but gradually most positions are being taken over by Japanese citizens who moved here. There seems to be a curfew in those camps. People can probably only get in and out up to a certain time. They are called "protective camps" because the relationship between the natives and the Europeans is so bad in Batavia that these camps have been set up by the churches to protect women and children. After all, most of the women are alone now, just a handful among all the natives. It seems a safe solution. Such a camp will contain a very large section of town, including stores and the *pasar* (open-air market), so we will still have relative freedom. On the other hand, when we're fenced in, we will be locked up! That is a scary thought.

A few days ago we received news that we will have to turn in our radios. We have to take them to the police station in our neighborhood. I'm very sorry about that. I would have loved to keep our radio until Fokko comes home, but everyone has to turn them in, so I will too when the time comes. So far, I've been very lucky to still be in my own home with all my own things. So far.

Little Paula's second birthday yesterday was a great success. After I got dressed and had breakfast, I picked flowers and "shook the coffee." That is a special treat these days. First I brewed fresh coffee, and then added sugar. I shook it in a glass jar with a lid for a long time until it was foamy, then poured a little in each cup, to which I added hot milk. Voilà! Delicious coffee-with-cream for the special occasion. The ladies down the street came with their children for coffee and cake, which I had made in my little *pan-bakaran*. I missed Fokko terribly all day. I'm sure he was thinking of us too. I have taught both girls a bedtime prayer, the same one we learned when we were little, and I added, "and please keep our Oma's and Opa's in Holland safe and bring back our Pappa soon. Amen."

December 5th, 1942
St. Nicholas' Eve

This is probably the strangest fifth of December I've ever had. All my relatives are on one continent, my husband on another, and I am on the third, with large oceans in between. It's sad and scary when I realize those enormous distances. I remember the evenings at home, every fifth of December, with the last minute rush of wrapping a gift, or even writing a whole poem. Mother, you always made our birthdays, Christmas, Easter and St. Nicholas day so special that I remember them in great detail. The sounds of the doorbell, Mina doing the dishes, Willy arranging the gifts in the basket, Mother upstairs doing last minute things, and Father Kees sitting quietly in his chair with the newspaper, pipe or cigar, waiting for the things to come. Then tea, and "shall we start?" and the many surprises and jokes. Oh, what a wonderful evening it always was! And then, I remember the fun evenings of last year, when Fokko played St. Nicholas so beautifully, and the year before, when I was "it" and couldn't stop laughing.

We have air raid protection exercises again. This afternoon, after the children had set their shoes full of grass for St. Nicholas' horse, I put all the gifts out in the living room, where they could find them after their nap. I had just gotten into bed myself when the alarm started. Ronny woke up and immediately said, "Oh, Mamma, there's the alarm! Now St. Nicholas can't come!"

I said he might have come already, and she ran to the living room and danced for joy when she saw the colorful display on the windowsill. This afternoon we saw St. Nicholas and *Black Piet* in the neighborhood. We shook hands with *Black Piet* and waved at St. Nicholas, who moved a little too quickly for such an old man. Both girls were very excited. Later that night Ronny asked, "Mamma, does *Black Piet* have charcoal on his tummy too, when he takes off his pants?"

I split my sides with laughter, my face in my pillow.

December 28, 1942
Ronny's Fourth Birthday

On the morning of Ronny's fourth birthday, when I was decorating the cakes, she asked if she could go across the street to see her friend, Rink. I pointed out that he and his mother would be here for her birthday party a little later, but she said she wanted to give him a piece of candy, so I let her go. A few minutes later she came back jubilantly with a box of blocks. She left again to show them to her other neighbor, from where she returned with two red hair ribbons and a little red mouth organ. "Now I'm going to ask Liesje and then Aunt Henny," she said.

"Ask what? You haven't asked for anything have you?"

"Sure," she said. "I'm asking everyone if they have a present for me. It is my birthday, isn't it?" I told her she couldn't do that. They would all come over for her party in a little while, so she had to stay home. Inwardly I laughed. That was Ron all over, collecting presents door to door. Apparently it worked well!

New Year's Eve, 1942
Thoughts

One year ago I sat in this same spot at the same time. The children are asleep. It is raining softly, just like last year. Fokko is separated from us by at least one ocean. I'm glad this is not last year. I wouldn't want to re-live one single minute of it. I am not in the mood to think about the things that happened this year. On the contrary, I'm excited and happy about the fact that this terrible year, which has brought nothing but misery, is almost over. Let the clock turn! Every hour is one less to go! I crossed out the last day of 1942 and grit my teeth with devilish joy. I have looked forward to this day since March! On the back of the sheet I marked 365 new days, 52 new weeks and 12 new months. Ron, knowing that Pappa will return in the New Year, and that it begins tomorrow, wanted to cross out the first day tonight, but we won't cheat. Will you stay up until midnight, because you are confident, too, that 1943 will have a happy ending?

Fokko is probably a free man in a free country, but I doubt he will stay up tonight. In 1937, our first year together, we sat in the patio in front of our room in Hotel Embong Woengoe. I had bought a few *oliebollen* (oil-dumplings), a special treat on New Year's Eve. We could not imagine a New Year's Eve without our traditional Dutch *oliebollen*. The next year I was in the hospital after Ronny's birth. I was in Batoe in the mountains with her after her serious illness, in 1939, and Fokko came over for the holidays. New Year's 1940 there were a lot of fireworks up and down the street, but we didn't stay up, because I was still tired six weeks after the birth of little Paula. Fokko had to work in 1941, and I wrote to you that night after the occupation.

Fokko is far, far away now, and I'm writing to you again. For 1943, we'll celebrate together, children in bed, with a long letter from you in liberated Holland. Oh, how happy we will be! We'll be able to send you pictures again. We haven't taken any since Paula was ten months old, because the photographers don't have film or paper any more, but that is the least of my worries. We'll catch up on that later. It is 9:30 p.m. A friend from across the street came to visit for a little while, and now I'm going to bed. A few more thoughts of you and Fokko, and then I'll go with courage on into the New Year.

January 7, 1943
Worries

One week of the New Year has passed. It wasn't a very happy one. Ronny has such a bad cough that I asked the doctor to come. She had been coughing off and on for a few weeks, but now it was so bad she hardly slept anymore, and neither did I.

She also has a fever. The doctor gave her an expensive cough medicine, and he said that if it doesn't help within a day or two, she might have whooping cough. We have other worries too. We received a notice that all Dutch women have to register for admission to a section of town especially for them and their little children. A high bamboo wall, covered with barbed wire, surrounds that particular section of town. It has one gate through which people can go in and out. *Indos* do not have to participate in the registration process. If a woman can prove that one of her parents or grandparents is a full-blooded native, she may remain outside the camp. I discussed our registration with Loekie Vierhout, who already lives in that area with her three sons. She invited me to move in with them. I can move into the garage, but first the car has to be moved out, and she needs permission from the Japanese authorities. Loekie's house has two bedrooms taxed by the authorities for two people per room, so she would occupy her bedroom with Casper, the older son. The two younger ones would get the other. The garage is a room in itself with a tiled floor, a ceiling, a window, a door and the double doors. It is just large enough for the three of us. I like the idea. It will give me some privacy, since the garage is separated from the main house.

I hope that we can keep one servant. Loekie isn't very strong, and although I thought I could do a lot of work, I got scared yesterday when I got palpitations after taking her on the back of my bike to get registered. Back home, I had to clean and do the cooking, because Baboe didn't show up. I didn't quite know what to do, so I just sat down and rested for a while. Then I put all the dirty dishes in a large bucket in the shower until the next day and went to bed. Even though I have two hands to work with and the desire, the heat, or maybe the long stay in the tropics, can play tricks on me. It makes it difficult to do all the work around the house.

It seems likely that we'll have to move by January 15. I sold old clothes, cans, bottles and old magazines, which gave me a nice sum of money and less junk to take with me. The people who buy such things are women from the island of Madoera, who walk the streets early in the morning and buy everything we want to get rid of. They used to buy only bottles and cans, but now they can be seen with their baskets on their heads full of shoes, drapes, clothes, dishes and the likes. They announce themselves by uttering a loud cry. I dread the thought of moving, but that time is approaching, slowly but surely. At first, I lay awake at night, thinking it can't possibly happen to me. Then I thought, *what if it really happens? How can I keep our house to move back into after the war?* I consider it a temporary move, and try to see the positive sides of it: the relative privacy I will have; the more economical way we will live by sharing expenses to stretch our money a little longer. I remember Mother or Father Kees saying, "Always look at people who have less than you do." At least we are still alive. So on we go.

January 27-28, 1943
It's Our Birthday Again!

I would have preferred to just forget my 33rd birthday, just let it pass like any other day. It is a funny feeling to lie in bed at night and think about all of you. To imagine that you are saying to each other, "Tomorrow is Netty's birthday. Where will she be? Still in her own home?" To imagine that Fokko is thinking about me too, the night before and on the day itself, all the time. Then, one day later, I remember our dear Wim's birthday. Happy birthday, Wim. I have thought a lot about you. We "little ones" are approaching middle age slowly but surely.

Remember, you and I were always "the little ones" and Willy and Piet "the oldest."

My birthday was also the last day that I was on my own in my own home. When I went outside that morning, a delivery boy from a flower shop came into the gate with a beautiful bouquet of pink roses. For a moment it was as if Fokko had sent them, as he used to do on my birthday, but that was impossible of course. They were from Jopie and Henk Esser. I was astonished. Apparently, they wanted to make up, so I decided I would go and thank them in person later. The day went by quietly. Several friends came for coffee in the morning and for tea in the afternoon, with lovely surprises: candy, three yards of blue and white gingham material for a dress, and a lot more flowers. I made the usual two cream cakes again, a success as always.

I haven't told you yet that I've been asking friends and neighbors if they knew a family who could live in my house during the time that I had to stay in the protection camp. I found a family looking for a place to live, Mr. and Mrs. D. They came to discuss the situation with me and we agreed they would move in as soon as possible with their son Frank. On the 28th, early in the morning, their furniture came. They had to move out of their own house in the area that was designated for the women's camp, because Mr. D, the husband, was still at home. Since the master bedroom was available because I sleep with the children again, they moved in before I moved out. I couldn't believe all the junk they brought. It was incredible! They had borrowed furniture everywhere, so they had more than one of many things. You should see all the suitcases, baskets, crates, refrigerators, furnaces and bicycles. I almost broke my neck everywhere I went.

I moved my wardrobe into our bedroom, so we have less room there too. However, they brought two Baboes, so each day some of the mess gets cleaned up. Remember when I wrote you that all white people who are still here have started a trade to earn a little extra money? One is smoking fish or bacon, another is selling soap, and Henk Esser repairs shoes. Well, Mr. D makes *borstplaat* (a kind of fudge) and cakes in my kitchen. They are nice people, and their son Frank, nine years old, is a cute boy.

After my experience with the Essers, I decided to stay on my own, because I have a different daily schedule than the D family. I started having breakfast with the children in the back room and cooking my lunches on my little charcoal stove outside. At night, after the children have had their meal, I have dinner with the family, and we sit and talk for a while afterwards in the living room before I turn in to sleep soundly. We have a man in the house again. Mr. D is a robust man, and they brought a nice dog, a good watchdog too. I have decided that I will never be without a dog of my own after the war.

Since I will have to leave most of my furniture behind when I move into the camp, I started planning what to do with it. I found a solution when I heard that another family in my neighborhood needed dining room furniture. They picked it up and handed me a receipt, so I could get it back in the future. It was strange to see my own furniture in someone else's house, which is located just around the corner. Yet it is good to separate from my belongings gradually, to have other people move in. I have enjoyed everything, including my freedom, for the past three months. Now the time has come to part. With the dining room empty, the D's moved their furniture from the garage inside, and it looks different already. Another neighbor needed our nice green living room set, because she didn't have any furniture, so the moving committee, all Dutchmen, moved it for her free of charge. If she has to go into a camp, she will take it with her. All we can hope for is that we'll see it back sometime. We have to give up so much these days. On that day even my living room was furnished differently, and it didn't feel like our home any more.

Two weeks had gone by with the new situation when I was awakened one morning at daybreak by men's voices outside. Nervous discussions went on for a while. When I looked through my door, I saw three native men leave, while one stayed behind and waited. Then I heard Mr. D throwing up, again and again. I donned my robe and went to ask what was going on. They had come to get Mr. D. He probably had to go to jail. His suitcase had been ready for months, packed with underwear, soap, towels, medications, and so on. Most women did this because they knew they would be too nervous at the time their husbands might have to go. Mr. D got dressed, and then discussed briefly with his wife the *borstplaat* production. Apparently, she is going to continue the business, poor soul, and didn't know the exact recipe. A quick cup of coffee, and there he went with the man in a *betjak* (bicycle-taxi).

I don't know which is worse, to be without your husband from the beginning, as I am, hoping he is still alive in another part of the world, or to have a year together under these circumstances and have to say goodbye like this because the Japs take him to jail. Rumors of razzias have been going around. A lot of men are being picked up just like this, having done nothing to deserve it, and put in jail. It is a nerve-wracking time for the families that still have a man in their midst. Mrs. D told me, in tears, that she had heard about a camp in the far eastern part of Java, an unhealthy area, where some men were taken after having been in jail for a few weeks. Pour Mrs. D. Will she ever know where they took him? It was a depressing day. I thought about that poor man all day long. At night we were without a man again. At least we had the dog as our protector.

Waiting for Loekie's garage to become available while Mrs. D started looking for someone she could share our house with, I had a piece of good luck. Awnings were stolen all over the place. They were making clothes and bags out of them, and were willing to pay a good price for them. I kept mine, still in good condition, in the garage after it was almost stolen. I offered it to passing peddlers for Fl. 25, but that didn't work. After a few days of trying, I finally sold it to one of them for Fl.15. Isn't that wonderful? It was about time something good happened to me.

One thing I made myself do before I moved. I went to the dentist. I think taking good care of your teeth is very important, yet I hadn't gone for eighteen months. I had to force myself to make an appointment. I had eight cavities, as you can imagine after such a long time, but the dentist had me come back every day for a week, and so I'm all set, just before the move.

March 1, 1943
We Are Moving Into The Camp

Loekie's car has been confiscated. Her garage was ready for us to move in. A few days before the move, I started packing. We still have cases and crates from Holland, which we always kept in the garage, and I filled them with the small oil stove, tools and so on. I sanded them smooth, cleaned and oiled them so they would stay in good condition for an indefinite time. I'm so glad we have those crates, because we can't get them here. Sunday, the day before the move, I was so busy packing all day and concentrating on selecting the things I wanted to take that it was easy to suppress the sad feeling that we were about to leave our home. At dusk, I went to say goodbye to all our friends up and down the street. Then I collapsed in bed. Although I was very tired, sleep wouldn't come, and for a while I had a very hard time thinking about how far apart everyone is now: you, we, and Fokko. Will we be together again sometime, the way it used to be?

The morning of March 1st had just started and we barely had breakfast when eight movers appeared. For a little while I was confused. There were still last-minute things to pack, and everything was extremely hectic, but it went fast. They brought a large truck and made two trips. The first time I went with them and back. Then I paid Baboe, who was not allowed to go with us. She said she wanted to return when the war was over, when Fokko would be home. I said goodbye, took my bike, walked out of the gate and down the lane behind the truck. I could have cried bitter tears about everything.

The children thought it quite a sensation, of course. Ronny and two boys from down the street sat on the back of the truck and had the time of their lives! Paula would rather sit on the back of my bike, and that is how we drove the two miles to Moesistreet, through the barbed wire, through the gate and into the camp. I thought, *If only you could see me now*. But again there was no time to worry. It took a few frantic days to get everything organized in my garage.

I thought it would be warm there with only one window, an opening without bars, so that the shutters had to be closed. But it wasn't warm at all—on the contrary. My bed stands against the large exit door. A lot of cracks in the door and four little windows covered with chicken wire allow for ample ventilation, so I sleep under my blanket. In spite of that, Paula and I caught bad colds. This part of town is totally different. It's always windy. We had to get used to that. I hung a set of our woolen curtains against those doors, and now it's much better. We are using the desk for both a table and a chest of drawers. I brought my own little chair with a blue pillow, our three beds, the wardrobe with the full-length mirror, the nightstand, and the blue curtain from the children's room for the window. It really looks cozy.

I put the light fixture from the children's room on the ceiling. The embroidered wall hanging, which used to hang behind the dressing table, hangs on the wall behind the desk. The Seven Dwarfs, which Fokko made, hang around it, and the Pinocchio coat hanger hangs to the A birthday calendar and my little cuckoo clock are on the right. The pictures of you and Fokko are on the opposite wall. At home the children used to have a tiny nightlight, which I turned off when I went to sleep. I borrowed an extension cord from Mrs. D, so that we can have a small table lamp on the desk. When I want to read or write at night I screw in a stronger bulb and sit cozily in my own little corner.

Anyway, when a native official from City Hall came the next day to ask whether I had moved in with everything, I could truthfully tell him that Mrs. Herman had indeed moved to 44 Moesistreet.

March 13, 1943
The Camp Is Closed

The first twelve days went well, which made me very happy. I had a Baboe for Fl.6.50 per month and cooked my own meals. Loekie has been eating with a family down the street for a year and will continue. She cooks rice and beans with some vegetables and bouillon every day for her sons, but I think that is too one-sided. I can't serve the same meal every day. I need some variety. I like the idea of living here until the end of the war, because we don't have to pay for water, electricity or rent. That way, I can stretch what little money we have left. I gave myself a pat on the back for this wise decision. Our own home wasn't what it used to be anyway, with other people and other furniture in it.

On the thirteenth, Loekie and I got ready to go downtown to exchange a pair of Loekie's shoes, because they were a little too narrow. A neighborhood boy came running in to tell us that the camp gate was closed and no one could get in or out. Imagine the shock. We couldn't get out. The rumor goes that after tomorrow we will not be allowed to have servants any more. We couldn't believe it. We know, of course, that had been the case in Malang since Christmas, but Malang is in the mountains. Here it is so much warmer. It is common knowledge that Soerabaja is located in the hottest part of the island. Surely they will let us keep one servant. But no, this rumor appeared to be true too.

We were allowed to buy bread and milk from the natives through the barbed wire. When I got there the bakers had left, the milkmen were selling milk only to their old customers, and my own milkman wasn't there. Thank God, a day later milk sales were allowed within the camp. One of our neighbors with grown boys helps us tremendously by sending the boys to get milk and bread for us. They have to stand in line for hours. Loekie and I are really stuck here with the whole house to clean and five small children. Casper is five; Ronny and Robbie are four; Eric and Paula are two years old. Those first few days were very confusing, because, since the camp had been closed so unexpectedly, most of the women still had to do or buy things outside. Every day there are many women standing by the barbed wire, talking to people on the outside, exchanging packages or even laundry, which some women had their Baboes do outside the camp. At our house we had work, work and more work. We had to do the laundry and the ironing, and then mop all the floors. Floors are tiled here, and we have to keep them clean, because this is a tropical country with a lot of vermin.

Many people sleep on mats in order to save on laundry. Two of Loekie's boys are still wetting their beds every night, and often during their afternoon naps too, so they sleep on mats, which she put on top of their mattresses instead of sheets. I had a great idea. I cut a few of those twin sheets, of which I have five, into two parts as sheets for the girls. They are a bit short on the top and bottom, but I can still tuck them in at the sides. How wonderful that they don't wet their beds any more. We have cut down on the ironing too. We only iron the clothes. Underwear, sheets and towels get folded straight from the clothesline. We were exhausted those first few days. Working tires us much more than in Holland. We went to bed right after dinner.

Figure 10 - The Pasar

After a few days, things were more organized. The open-air market, the *pasar*, was opened again. I took it upon myself to buy the groceries, because Loekie absolutely hates it. I went to the *pasar* with all five children, but was greatly disappointed. Everything was very expensive and sold out immediately, so you have to go at daybreak in order to get anything at all. Later, prices were controlled and the number of salesmen increased, and now there is plenty of everything for sale, even if you go later in the day. They have a separate room for the meat sales, screened against the flies, in a brand new building. Two doctors have their daily consultation hour in a clinic. We have church services on Sunday; there is a kindergarten and organized sports for older children in the afternoon. In a central kitchen you can get inexpensive meals. So it isn't all that bad, but all contact with the outside world was broken when they issued the prohibition against talking to people on the outside. We are captives. However, I'm saying again, it isn't too bad, if it will remain as it is now.

We got used to the workload somewhat, and it makes us very hungry. At first, I tried the food from the central kitchen: a lot of rice with a little meat and boiled vegetables, 5 cents per portion. They didn't have enough variety to my liking. I decided to wait until it becomes mandatory to get food from the central kitchen. For now, this is our solution: I eat a hot lunch for Fl.5 a month with Klaartje, the same lady down the street who also cooks for Loekie and a lot of other people. Her meals are delicious. Loekie and I cook a wholesome noon meal for the five children, with a variety of fresh fruits and vegetables, so they are doing well. Paula is even gaining some weight. It feels wonderful that we can give sufficient nutrients to the children despite the situation—another reason I'm very grateful.

P.S. It is great that we live close to the *pasar* and the clinic. There is also a large general store right down the street.

March 27, 1943
Robbers

The days go by. We are constantly busy. At night we sleep deeply after all our hard work. Since there is more than one family in every house, we lack the room to put the stroller and bike inside at night. At first, I put them in the bathroom, but when the camp was closed, and "protected" by barbed wire all around, I thought, *How wonderful that we don't have to be afraid of robbers any more.* I left my bike outside at night, in the back of the house next to the bathroom. The back yard is separated from the street by a wire-covered door with a strong lock, so theft was the last thing on my mind. Friday night at 1:30 a.m., Ronny woke up and asked for some water. While we were chatting, I heard a noise in the back that sounded like a wooden door slamming. I put Ronny back in bed, told her to be quiet, and climbed on a chair to look through the screen at the top of my window. The night was very dark, but I did see the outlines of my bike and Loekie's laundry on the line. Since I didn't hear anything any more, I went back to bed and instantly fell asleep again. The next morning we discovered that my bike and all the laundry were gone, as well as our irons and some pots and pans. We found my iron skillet and a new mop on top of the high wall. Obviously the thieves had climbed the wall to get access to our yard. We were thankful they had left the tubs and the stroller. I went to the police to report it, but we didn't hear a thing about it any more, of course. The police, natives under Japanese command, don't do anything for us any more. Now we take the tubs, the stroller and the wooden ladder inside every night. Loekie doesn't leave her laundry out any more, which I never did, and I double-check the locks on the doors like I used to. I am upset about the loss of my bike, as you can imagine. It served me for almost four years. I lent it out often. I guess in this district I can do without it, because we live close to everything. So on we go.

I got a sore throat one day with a high fever. An older neighbor advised me to call the doctor. I didn't want to do that at first. When I started feeling worse, however, I called him. He found an abscess on each side of my throat. He gave me medication, told me to stay in bed for at least three days and to take it easy after that. How depressing. What about all the work? Some of our neighbors came over to help. When I got up too soon, it came back again and I took several weeks to get back to normal. Ugh.

All homes are being searched for radios and homing pigeons, just like on Brouwerstreet. One day, before I got ill, some Japanese came to search for radios while I was sewing. I saw them enter the house across the street and had heard them next door earlier, so I was expecting them at my front door any minute. It took so long that I went outside to look. My neighbor said that they skipped my house. I thanked God on my knees, because the radio is the one thing that I want to keep for Fokko, and I still have it. When I moved into the camp I was allowed to take it with me. We were allowed one radio per house. Loekie's radio was confiscated in November. Now they are collecting all of the radios!

I was sick and in bed when they came again, a Japanese officer and a young native. They searched everything, but didn't see the radio on top of which I had put all my medicine bottles, and I didn't say anything. But there it was: One of them said, "*Ada siempen radio?*" which meant, "Is there still a radio kept somewhere?"

The words cut through my heart because I had to answer "Yes." I have the responsibility for the children, and I don't have the guts to lie. I know how severe the punishments are. People are being decapitated, especially for hiding radios. Besides, they have all been registered, so they can be traced. I have always complied with all the rules. You can imagine how I felt when that native said, "The police will pick it up later."

I could have cried, but I bit my lip. It is a good thing that during the day I have no time to worry about such things because of the workload, and at night I sleep like a log from fatigue. I would have worried myself to death about this on Brouwerstreet. In the afternoon, barely awake while the girls weren't dressed yet, two police officers came in and dragged their loot away, bumping it and carrying it upside down. I remembered how I had treated it like a baby when I registered it. I didn't pay attention to the children, just watched our radio disappear, sticking halfway out of a delivery truck. When I got back into our room, the children were gone. Then one closet door opened slightly and Ronny's little head peeked around the corner. "Have they left, Mam?" The door opened wider and there they were, both sitting inside.

"Why did you get into the closet?"

"Those men weren't supposed to see us naked, were they?"

They must have jumped into the closet with their bare behinds, quick as lightning. I would have loved to see that! I had turned my back for only a minute to open the front door for the men. In spite of everything I had to laugh about those little ones.

April 1943
Colombo
Fokko

Four months went by. Very slowly Fokko recovered. His memory came back, except for the last ten minutes before the accident. He heard what had happened from eyewitnesses. In the hospital they had shaved off his beard. One of the nurses told him that he looked like Jesus Christ when he was brought in, his face with the black beard so mangled and bloody. The Naval Chaplain and a Naval Minister, who each in their own way wanted to save his soul, visited Fokko regularly. The Chaplain gave him a little blue book entitled, *Prayers for the Sailor*. It didn't help that Fokko told him he wasn't a sailor; the man had nothing else. The Minister, however, while trying to save Fokko's soul, was less worried about his own. He repeatedly urged Fokko to introduce him to a particular nurse, so that he could ask her out on a date. His slogan was, "I am not a Chaplain." He did not mention that he was married and had a number of kids at home. The war was considered a good excuse.

One day, when Fokko was a walking patient, Jos Vermeulen stood before him. Some time after his flight from Java to Australia (avoiding Broome, where so many were killed), Jos heard rumors that several ships had been bombed and sunk while trying to escape from Java. He assumed that Fokko was among the casualties. He had felt intense sorrow for Netty. However, in time of war you don't have much time to ponder sorrowful happenings. You have to try to survive. He was sent on duty to Ceylon. Upon his arrival they informed him, to his great surprise, that Fokko was still alive. He hurried to the hospital to see him. There they were, facing each other once again, in the hospital room in Colombo. During the days that followed, they took short walks together, sharing their experiences, full of wonder that fate had brought them together once more.

Upon his discharge from the hospital, Fokko stayed for a few weeks in Nuwara Eliya, a vacation resort at 6,000 feet elevation. Lodging was inexpensive and the climate wonderful. One morning there was even a thin layer of frost on the lawn. *It is a long time ago I saw frost*, Fokko thought. Before going back to work, he was invited to stay on a rubber and tea plantation, deep in the interior of Ceylon, owned by the parents of one of the British volunteer nurses. There, in the remote comfort of a real home and the loving care of the nice, elderly couple, seemingly far away from the perils of war, Fokko regained his strength, and with it his confidence in life and hope of a better future. A large scar across his forehead would remind him of the accident for the rest of his life.

Figure 11 - Tea Plantation

April 16, 1943
Ronny Goes To Kindergarten

I have to tell you something wonderful and very important. When your first child goes to kindergarten for the first time it is a milestone in your life. On April 16, I took Ron and Robbie, both now over four years old, to school. I pay Fl.1 per month, and she will be going every other day. At first Ron wasn't happy about going to school. She kept saying that she wanted me to stay with her. When she sat down on the little chair we had been asked to bring, I said, "Well, goodbye, Ron."

She said with a quivering voice, "Goodbye, Mamma."

I felt a lump in my throat and thought it best to leave quickly. I can cry about everything these days; it's really strange. Peeking through the window, I saw that she swallowed, rubbed her fists in her eyes and gained control of herself. When I came back two hours later to pick her up, I saw her singing in class with an expression of "I know this song" on her face. She was totally absorbed. Back home she wanted something to drink and a banana and asked, "Mam, may I take off my shoes?" Then came the stories of everything they had done that Friday. The following Monday was her second school day. When I stopped to look through the school window on my way home from the *pasar*, I saw her sitting in her chair after her blocks were collected. Then they did exercises. Oh, how I wish I could go and watch her for a whole morning, but it is impossible. We simply don't have time for that. On Monday she had made a little envelope with a letter inside. The teacher told them they could write a letter to their daddy. Ronny had drawn straight lines on one side "to Pappa" and on the other "to Oma and Opa." Isn't it thoughtful of her to think about you? Each day she brings home something different, which we hang on the wall. That makes her very proud.

April 25, 1943
Easter

The day before Easter a deluge, probably one of the last rainstorms of this season, flooded the back yard. When we were drinking our tea, Loekie remembered we still had to get milk, fruits and vegetables from the *pasar*. I draped Fokko's beloved raincoat across my shoulders like a cape, down to my heels, took an umbrella and left. I hadn't gotten very far when a totally flooded street blocked my way. I took off my shoes to save them from being ruined, and continued on bare feet. The water came up to my ankles. I thought, *this is something I have to write home about, that I'm going shopping on my bare feet.* Then I remembered the poem, "She was bareheaded and barefoot and was wearing old clothes." That is true of me now, because my dress is old. My whole wardrobe is old. I first got the milk, then went to the *pasar*. The merchants started laughing when they saw me. I first put down my shoes, then got out my wallet. They had fun, and so did I. In the meantime, it had stopped raining. When I was on my way home more people came out. The *slokans* (cement gutters on either side of the street and about two feet below street level) had become six-foot wide streams in which the native boys were playing.

At night I usually read the children a story. This time it was about the Easter Bunny, of course. One of the neighbor boys wanted to paint eggs, so we gave him ten eggs that morning. There are no Easter things for sale these days, but at the pasar I saw some cute baskets, which Klaartje, the lady who cooks for us, filled for the children. Early on Easter morning Loekie went to get the eggs. We put the nicest ones on the table next to each plate and hid the others, so the children could go on their egg hunt.

We heard that all Dutch women who had stayed outside the camp until now would move in within two days: registration was completed. The camp won't be enlarged, so the homes will get fuller. Maybe we'll have to take in another family. I'm glad I moved when I still had the choice of where to go. I'm glad Easter is over. I was a little down, homesick and longing for you and for Fokko in spite of the joyous Easter message of the Resurrection. But on we go!

May 26, 1943
Sixth Wedding Anniversary

Last year I was hoping that today we would celebrate our anniversary together, but there is not a chance, and I'm not saying that we'll be together again for our seventh, because I'm not sure about that at all. It's awful. It was a bad, disorderly day from the start. When I awoke and got out of bed I got my period before I could do anything else. That caused some delay, and I was late in the first place. It was room-cleaning day but I also had to go to the *pasar*, so I left my room untidy. At the breakfast table Ronny spilled her water and got into a fight with

Casper. I finally left for the *pasar* with the stroller, the shopping basket and the broken wheelbarrow, hoping to get it fixed somewhere. I didn't take the children because there is a diphtheria epidemic in camp, and we are advised to keep children away from other people.

Something else bothered me incredibly. On Saturday I read on the bulletin board of the District Office that everyone who owned a car or other motor vehicle had to register it on Monday. My heart broke when I read it. The motorcycle. It's hidden so well here in our *goedang*, that I had the secret hope I would be able to keep it. This is the first war I am going through. I'm learning that war and sacrifice are inseparable. It is so difficult. I am especially attached to the motorcycle and the radio, because Fokko worked hard to save up for them, and he loved them so. Now I will have to give them up. The reason we have to register them is so they can come and take them away. The Japs are taking all valuable things away from us: stoves, refrigerators, furniture, everything. Oh, Fokko, Fokko, when I read that! I will grow old and grey before my time from all this misery. I was furious with myself for having read that bulletin board. If I hadn't read it, I wouldn't have known. However, the news spread quickly, so that excuse would not really have worked. I worried about it. Should I risk keeping it? They still have to come for the stove and some furniture, and if they look in the *goedang* I'll have had it. They torture and decapitate people just for hiding radios and other items. What would my little girls do without me? On the other hand, Fokko, your motorcycle! I asked a few people for advice. They all advised me against hiding it. "You will lose everything in the long run anyway."

On Monday night, at 7 p.m., I went to the District Office. They were closed. Tuesday I brooded, and at night I thought, relieved, *Well, I will certainly not go on my anniversary day.*

This morning, however, after going to the *pasar,* I thought, *now I must go. Oh, no, first I have to get milk.* On the way back I argued with myself. *Should I do it or not?* I turned my stroller into the driveway and walked behind it like a puppet, still undecided. If they search the *goedang* I'll be lost. I had to do it. When I finally came to the window they said, "You are too late, you had to come on Monday." The list had already been sent to the P.I.D., *Politieke Inlichtingen Dienst,* or Political Information Service. The P.I.D. has been here for a long time as part of the police force, reporting directly to the High Court of Justice in Batavia. Now under Japanese command, it is in charge of all interrogations and checking whether Japanese orders are being followed.

The P.I.D. office in Soerabaja is a scary place where people sit for hours to be interrogated. It's probably better that I've registered it. I have to think about the children, and I realize we'll be poor after the war anyway. How naive of me to think that I would be able to welcome Fokko back in our own home with everything in it! No, Jeannette, you should be very grateful if you can welcome him back at all, never mind where and how. This is war! If I get Fokko back, I will thank God on my knees and start over.

Loekie tried to get flowers for my anniversary but she couldn't get any. After we cleaned the rooms, there was so much to do I forgot my laundry and didn't have time to tidy my room. A friend invited us for coffee to celebrate her birthday. We went there for a while, but afterwards we had to hurry. These days we really can't go out during the day nor have visitors over ourselves, because everything goes wrong. We are in a rush, the children won't go to sleep in the afternoon, and we won't get any rest. That's how evening came today.

Sometimes I break out in a cold sweat when I think of the things you are going through: food shortage, fuel shortage, cold winters. Are you surviving? It is good that our days are so full. We live like animals. We eat, work and sleep, nothing more. Life has no highlights any more, only anxieties, fears, worries, insecurities and burglaries. No pleasant thoughts on my anniversary. My children are asleep behind my back in their beds. The mosquitoes are stinging me everywhere, from my toes to my bare back. It is bedtime. I don't dare have more visions of an anniversary with Fokko's flowers, your letters, tea with a cookie and Fokko sitting by my side. It seems impossible, too good to be true and definitely too good to be true on May 26, 1944. I am convinced of that now, however sad it may be. We haven't heard any news at all about the situation in Europe. Hopefully, you will be liberated before next winter. Won't that be wonderful? And now, dear people, even May 26, 1943 is a thing of the past, thank God.

May 30, 1943
Our Children

It is Sunday night. Tomorrow will be the last day of May, thank God. The children are asleep. They are growing, slowly but surely. When I looked at some pictures of our vacation five months before Fokko left, I thought how much Fokko would find them changed. They are much taller and wiser already.

It has been three weeks since the diphtheria epidemic started. The schools are still closed, and all children must get booster shots. We went to the clinic with all five children, expecting to stand in a long line again, which I detest although I should be used to it by now. Even though masses of people entered the clinic, a lot of nurses administered the shots, so it only took fifteen minutes before it was our turn. I had five peppermints with me, and as soon as the needle went into their arms, I popped a mint into their mouths. On June 7th they will get their second shot, and two weeks after that, the last one. Children who already have diphtheria are taken to the hospital immediately, and only the mothers may go with them for a little while, outside of the camp, and visit twice a week. After ten days those patients have to leave the hospital again. Since they are still contagious, they are isolated in a special home while their treatment is continued.

A new word has been created: *camp sores.* Every day the clinic is full of people with the most persistent sores. We've always had to be very careful because of vermin in the tropics, but with so many people living together in a relatively small area and using possibly contaminated water, the situation has worsened. When you fall or even get a little scratch, it gets infected and grows into a monstrous sore. A while ago, for instance, Paula bit Ronny on her arm, the little monkey, and that festered for several weeks in spite of my good care. Then, Ron got a little splinter in her heel, which we took out with a needle, and it became a sore the size of a nickel. When it had almost healed, she played in the yard for a few minutes without her bandage, and it started festering again.

I don't know whether I told you that I shaved Paula's head. Remember she was always twisting her hair around her fingers so that she got bald spots on top of her head? Well, I had treated that with the juice of the *lida boeaja,* the aloe plant, and her hair was growing back. Then she started twisting on the back of her head! Several people advised me to shave it all off, but I couldn't bring myself to do it until I decided about six weeks ago to go ahead. Paula loved it. I keep treating her head with the aloe juice, and her hair has since grown back into a nice stubble. She reminds me of Wim with her short hair, but she has a pair of eyes that can sometimes look so naughty, like a little clown.

I have almost run out of money. I know we can get financial support, but I don't like that idea at all. Nevertheless, I took the first step today and went to see the lady who is an intermediary for the Japanese. She wrote down my name and address and promised me she would look into it. At home I discussed it with my fellow inmates. They all advised me against it. The thought made them as uncomfortable as it made me. We would be categorized in a certain group and be dependent on the Japs. We might be separated from the others, transported to another camp, or whatever. At lunch Klaartje said, "From now on you won't have to pay for your meals." That was very generous of her, and I accepted on the condition that I'd pay her back as soon as I can. I have been thinking about my furniture outside the camp. Maybe Aunt Rita, who still has her freedom, can sell it for me. I will try to get in touch with her. This afternoon I hurried back to the lady in charge of financial support to tell her I had received money from a friend and to please take my name off the list of applicants.

The thought of being without money while Fokko must assume I'm getting seventy-five percent of his salary every month made me sad. When the girls saw tears in my eyes, I pretended I was crying because I had a hole in my nightie and no money to buy a new one. They both became anxious. Ronny said, "Please don't cry, Mam. You have to sew it," and Paula in her baby language said, "Not cry, Mam, not cry. When my Pappa come home I ask if you can have a penny, nice penny." Paula doesn't know what to do when I pretend I'm crying. Ronny is more in control. Paula still can't say the "r" and the "l" so she talks very comically. I enjoy it and don't correct her. She will learn to talk properly soon enough. Always occupied with the thought of Pappa, she sometimes saves her peppermint for him and puts it by his picture. Or, like last week, she wanted to save her banana until Pappa comes home. "Well," I said. "It will surely be ripe by then." Paula can easily share things, but Ronny protects her possessions. Maybe that will change with age. I am very strict with them whenever I hear them say bad words. They hear them on the street, of course. I won't have any part of it, and have to yell at them sometimes. That's when I think, *I wish Fokko was here to help me raise these kids.* The months go by, and the children are growing up. I know that they will be at least five and three years old, and I thirty-four before Fokko is back. Isn't that terrible?

June 17, 1943
There Are Days And "Days"

Sometimes I catch myself singing while I work. I think, *As if everything is so wonderful*, yet I am happy enough to sing and can hear women in neighboring houses singing too. I think this very busy life is a blessing for all of us. Each day our work is laid out for us, each piece fitting into the next, and before we know it, it's afternoon and we are hungry. After lunch our midday nap is very welcome and necessary, and then we begin again, around 3:30 p.m., after a cup of tea.

There are also days that I am hard on myself, worrying about Fokko and you. I become so fed up with everything, the endless waiting, that I don't know what to do. I experience a great need for Fokko's letters after a week goes by and I haven't had time to re-read them. How happy I am that I've saved all of those sweet letters he wrote to me when we were still engaged. I sit down in my garage and it is as if Fokko is talking to me. So intimate, so private are those letters that they really give me a boost. If I didn't have those letters I would truly be miserable.

I often think that I would be happier if I could sit out the war with my own children alone in a little cottage on the moor, because the rumors and stories from other women make me nervous. For instance, "The Japs are coming to get the sewing machines" (not true) or "They are coming to search the house" (they aren't). One time, neighbors scared me by saying that the Japanese were collecting mirrored wardrobes. We were only allowed one wardrobe, so I had "loaned" my linen dresser to a total stranger, a man, through the moving committee, hoping to get it back after the war. It was quite a hassle, for it was full of linens and books, for which I had to make space. Our mirrored wardrobe was quite expensive at the time. Its mirror is beautiful. One afternoon I unscrewed it and put it against the wall between the children's beds, covered it with a cloth, and put some picture frames on top of it, all to mislead the man. In the closet door gaped the empty wood panel where the mirror had been, but I would say that it broke when we moved. For weeks the mirror stood this way to my great annoyance, because I have no other mirror. I had to lift the cloth and go down on my knees to comb my hair every day. It was a pain in the neck! When I heard from someone that the man had not taken her mirror wardrobe, I decided to put the mirror back where it belonged. Now, thank goodness, the wardrobe looks beautiful again and I can comb my hair standing up.

We experienced things like this a hundred times, all nerve-racking. First it was our money. Put it here, then there, no, there! Then came the motorcycle, the radio, the furniture, everything. I have used up almost all my savings, so that is easy; I don't have to hide that. The bike is gone, the radio is gone, and the motorcycle will follow. If only we had known all this ahead of time! We had no experience with a war, you know. Now about our visit from the Japanese official who goes from home to home to see what can be taken away. One afternoon a neighbor boy warned us that he was four houses away. Nice to know, of course, so I could be prepared, but it made me nervous anyway. I should not be afraid he would take anything away from me any more. I only have one bed for each of us; one wardrobe, one chair and one desk. But two days ago I heard from others (you go stark raving mad from all the things you hear) that they wanted the sewing machines. New fright. You can't be sure of anything these days. Everything is uncertain, and I don't need much to throw me off balance.

Well, concerning my old faithful sewing machine: I can't possibly do without it. I make new clothes from old for the children. I do the alterations, mending, everything on that machine. So I was in anxious suspense. Then he appeared, a little man in a tropics helmet and large round glasses, followed by two native men. I was braiding Ronny's hair and kept doing it when they arrived, so I had something to do. He wrote down the stove in the kitchen. It will be picked up soon. We'll have to do the cooking on charcoal from now on. Then he asked me, "How many people?"

"Three."

"One wardrobe, one chair, one table and one machine," he said, and then went to look in the *goedang*. He lifted everything, saw the motorcycle and asked three times if I had registered it. You see, it was good that I did, because I would have been in big trouble if I hadn't. The *Kenpetai*, the Japanese Military Police Force, is feared by all for their cruel punishments. He only took Loekie's bookcase, not her wooden chairs and coffee table. I think those were too plain.

Now it is bedtime. Rain is drizzling down, very unusual for the middle of June. Through the blanket of clouds, I can see a full moon. I never looked at the moon so much in my life. I cheer when I see the first little sliver. I can count with it, and know that another month has gone by. It is the only thing we wish for: that time may go by quickly.

July 4, 1943
The Camp Gets Fuller

First I have to say "happy birthday" to my sister Willy on her 37th birthday, because tomorrow is July 5th. So, Will, have a happy day. I hope you all will be liberated soon. I think of Mother's usual treat on your birthday: strawberry pastry, delicious. I also remember your favorite flowers on that day: dark peach gladioli and large blue thistles, a beautiful combination. I'm sure you are still happy with your job in the pharmacy, and I hope your colleagues and the pharmacist will celebrate your birthday as well.

Last week we heard from the district leader that a lady with a two year old child will be added to our house. Sunday afternoon the moving van appeared, and the new woman, Betsy, moved into the front bedroom. Loekie has two of her own boys with her now. Betsy has her own child and one of Loekie's sons with her, and I am staying where I am. I'm so happy about this, for I have so much privacy in my garage. The first few days were disorderly, but now a week has gone by. Betsy, only twenty-three years old, is quite nice. We get along well. In the meantime, all the people from Brouwerstreet have been moved into the camp. We don't see each other often because nobody has time. There will be at least another thousand women admitted to our camp.

In most homes the dining room is still empty. We just heard we were to get another lady with her child, but we asked if we could please get someone without children, because we have six under the age of five already. Sometimes we are quite bewildered. We have simplified our evening meal by preparing sandwiches to eat outside with our hands, like a picnic. I had to get used to it because I like a well-set table, but it saves us from doing seven dishes, forks and knives, and the children love it.

Recently, all the dogs in the district were picked up. A while ago they announced that all dogs had to be disposed of, but a lot of women couldn't bring themselves to do it and kept them. Then they came door to door with a lasso, put them in a *dogcar* and took them away to be killed. I'll bet they do it just to hurt the women. Why else would they? Dogs don't do any harm, and they protect us from the many burglars.

July 22, 1943
Bombardments Again

The night of the 21st of July, dead tired, I went to bed early and I would have slept like a log if Paula hadn't coughed so much. All night she kept coughing and calling for water. At 3:30 a.m. I gave her some more water and was just beginning to worry about her when I heard a sound in the distance. I thought it was a train, but it became stronger and turned out to be one or more airplanes. When I thought a plane was right over our heads, I heard a heavy boom. Everything shook and the door rattled. I sat up straight in bed, scared to death.

We have had air raid exercises since July 16th. We were told that the alarm could go off at any time, and we had to go indoors and stay there. So when I heard this plane flying so low, I thought it was one of the Japanese exercise planes. Then came another boom and immediately afterwards a hellish noise of defense gunfire. The artillery must be close by, because it sounded like cannon shots. I jumped out of bed, talked with Paula to reassure her, and looked through the little window in the door. A searchlight shot into the sky, and more heavy booms followed. I thought, *that's for real*. I quickly got Paula out of bed, and then the sirens went off. I put Paula under Ronny's bed, woke up Ronny, who was sleeping like a log, pushed her under her bed as well and crawled in with them.

Outside it sounded like all hell had broken loose. It was a real bombardment. Scary.

Behind my garage I heard two women talking. "Exercise," said the one.

"No," the other one said decidedly. "These are our men." The way she said it gave me goosebumps. In a surge of joy, I said to the children, "There is Uncle Jos with his airplane. Now Pappa will be home soon."

Somebody knocked on my door and there were Loekie and Betsy. Loekie said, "What do you think?"

"I think it's real," I said, and then we saw a series of orange lightballs fly up into the sky, like fireworks. That was strange. It looked like an exercise after all. Then it started all over again with renewed intensity, and we decided to put all the children in the bathroom. We stayed at the door, not knowing what to think of it. Just when we put the children back into bed it started up again. In the direction of the harbor we saw a red glow against the night sky that got dimmer, then flared up. The next morning several people called us stupid for thinking that it had been a real attack. They had stood and watched. Other "heroines" just stayed in bed during the whole ordeal "because it was an exercise of course." Much later we heard it was the very first bombardment of Soerabaja, on July 22, 1943, at about 2:30 a.m. For a few days we lived in a different frame of mind. The fact that such a night, however scary, means a glimpse of hope for us proves that we desperately need such hope.

We have an underground shelter in the back yard, which we cleaned out the next day and put into use a day later during an alarm in the afternoon. Ronny called out loudly in between the sounds of the sirens, "Mamma, I will never again bite my nails or suck my thumb because Pappa will be back soon." She is still doing those things, in spite of my efforts to break her habits, but now she has a good incentive to stop. I'll have to take advantage of that!

August 1, 1943
Time Goes On

Thank God, the eighth month has begun; the end of the year is approaching. Time can't go fast enough. The bombers have not come back, so that hope has been taken away. A few days ago a Japanese man accompanied by three officers came to look at Fokko's motorcycle. It will be taken away, and I won't get anything for it. To think how hard Fokko had to work to buy it, and how he took care of it! These things are "war pills" that we have to swallow. They can be quite bitter.

The children distract me in more than one way. Sometimes I roar with laughter because of the way they do something or say something, but there are also days that I can't bear anything they do. Those are the days that I get a war pill to swallow, when the Japanese come to take something away or frighten me terribly in one way or another, so I worry myself sick. At those times I want the children to leave me alone, but then it seems that not a minute goes by without them calling me for one thing or another.

School has started again, and this week I had reason to be very proud. Ron's teacher told me that Ronny was so smart; she wanted to put her in the class with older children if it was all right with me. Now Ron goes to school every day from 11 a.m. to 1 p.m. She liked it from the start and came home with a lot of stories, and it made me feel very proud of her, as you can imagine.

At night I am doing a lot of sewing. The children are growing. Ronny has hardly any dresses left, and I need to make some things for myself. We have another woman in the house now, without children. Her name is Anneke. She is a nurse, and I think she will be put to work in the little hospital we now have here in camp. She is very good with the children. I used to read to them at night, and now she sings with them and tells stories. As a nurse she is permitted to go outside the camp. Yesterday I asked her to investigate what had happened to our furniture. Our green living room set, which I loaned to someone before I went into the camp, has been moved three times. The upholstery is torn, and she told me that it is not worth anything as it is, but I could get about Fl.60 for it if it was reupholstered. What should I do? I'll tell you more about the furniture some other time.

September 10, 1943
I Have Amoebae Dysentery

August and September are terrible months. That says it all. All the children have been coughing non-stop and had diarrhea and worms. Ronny had a swollen ear and cheek, which looked like the mumps, and I finally had the doctor come. Then Loekie got terrible cramps and diarrhea and I was soon to follow. A diet didn't help, and when I went to the doctor he told me I had amoebae dysentery, for which he prescribed some kind of powders, a strict diet and bed rest. Well, total rest is out of the question in a situation like ours, but the other two women are working extra hard so Loekie and I can sleep in for an hour or so every morning. Amoebae dysentery is a tropical disease that is very hard to get rid of. It really scared me when I heard the diagnosis. I am glad, however, that the children don't have it. I'd rather be sick myself and have the children well than the other way around. So on we go.

One Saturday morning we heard that seventy-three women would be admitted to the camp that day. Nobody knew who they were or where they came from. I was sitting in front of the clinic with the children when they came by: a truck full of white-garbed nuns, with Japanese police officers in the back, guarding them as if they were criminals. Behind it came another bus full. They hadn't received any warning and were taken away from Mass or their work. All the women in the district waved a welcome to them. As they were dropped off in front of the schoolhouse, the district leaders, Dutch women, quickly went around asking if anyone could take in a nun for a few nights. We signed up for one and got Sister Magdalena.

The doctor gave Loekie a permit to try to get household help so we could get more rest, and we found someone who, we heard, was a former barmaid. Cousin Ad Wisse would say, "The company is quite heterogeneous, a nun and a barmaid." Well, if rest is necessary for our recovery, we don't mind what company we are in. The bad news is they have run out of the proper medication for our disease. I hope I will be cured of it after the war.

As I told you, after months and months I finally heard that our living room set was so filthy nobody wanted it. I'll never loan any of my furniture out again. I had to decide whether to have it reupholstered and sold. Who would buy furniture these days? I sent a card to my outside contact, Aunt Rita, in a last attempt, asking her to sell it for me if she couldn't find a place to store it. Communication with people outside the camp is forbidden except by postcards in Indonesian, which take weeks from one street to the next. I didn't hear anything for a while, until a woman came to bring me Fl. 70, smuggled into the camp "for the furniture." I'm sorry it had to be sold, of course, but it is not a bad deal when you consider we used it for about four years and had already turned the upholstery over once. I am delighted with this windfall. I paid Klaartje for the meals she gave me and we can hang on for a little while longer. I don't know if I can keep our bedroom furniture. Rumors are that eventually we'll be transported to a larger camp with only one suitcase of belongings. I hope that is not true. I just can't see it happen with two little children. My heart tightens with fear when I think of it.

I am writing fast. There is so much to tell and time goes by so quickly. My pen is galloping across the paper. Can you see it? I am very glad the year will come to an end soon: only three and a half more months. On to 1944.

September 19, 1943
Cholera

We are almost better, Loekie and I, each of us with different medication, which the doctor tried after running out of the proper kind. Finally, a so-called camp nurse's aid came to help us with our chores. She is not allowed to do the laundry and the ironing, and when asked if she could go to the *pasar*, she said she didn't have to do that either. She is not much help at all, but we'll use her for two weeks. By then Loekie and I should be back to normal. Isn't it strange that in six years I didn't need the doctor once and now I've needed him three times within six months? It must be the hard work in this climate and all the worries that made me lose my resistance to infections.

This week they announced that everyone had to be vaccinated against cholera. Loekie and I didn't know whether that included the two of us, as we had been ill, so we sent the children with the others. They all were as excited as if they were going to a party, Ron and Paula each with their straw purse with peppermints to hand out. I learned long ago that when I put something into their mouths just when they start to cry, they won't, because they have to close their mouths. I heard Ron had been very brave again. She had just looked at the doctor with her big eyes. Then came Paula. As she had watched me do, just when Paula began to cry, Ron popped a peppermint into her mouth and Paula was quiet. After asking the doctor, Loekie and I went the next day. Thankfully none of us had bad reactions from the shots.

And so we live on. I have been in this camp for almost seven months now. A bamboo fence topped with barbed wire marks the end of every street. The longer it lasts, the more I get the feeling of being locked up. Yet we have little reason for complaints. Isn't it marvelous that there are so many well-schooled women among our Dutch group? We have doctors, nurses, dentists, teachers, sports leaders, pharmacists, garden specialists, laboratory personnel, secretaries, and all our own people. Oh, I'm so proud of them. Wouldn't you think that would impress the Japs as well?

October 3, 1943
Dark Clouds Are Gathering

Here is a big birthday kiss, Mother, since it was your birthday two days ago. I have been thinking about you all day. Are you free? Are you still all together? The children kissed your picture and when I was doing the laundry, I heard them singing. They had taken your picture out into the yard, "planted" flowers in little piles of sand in front of it, and with a lot of friends gathered around they all sang "Happy Birthday" under Ronny's guidance. When they saw me they asked for a candy for the happy occasion. How sad that I can't even write to you. Let's hope I will be able to next year. These are depressing days.

The whole camp was shaken about ten days ago by the news that all people who received financial support had to leave. They will be leaving by train. An adult is allowed to take one trunk and two suitcases, children under eleven, one suitcase, and children under four, a small one. That means we will have to part with everything else we have. You can imagine how upset I was. Tomorrow the third group is leaving. They are not allowed to talk about their destination or to stick their heads out of the train windows. The morning of the first group's departure we were at home, but when the second group left I was on my way to the *pasar*. I stood there and cried. For hours all seven hundred women and little children had to wait in the hot sun before they were taken in trucks to the station. Rumors are that we'll all have to go like that. Of course people talk a lot, but we are preparing ourselves slowly to be ready when it happens. We have to make sure to take good, sturdy clothing. I have altered one of Fokko's khaki flight suits to fit me. I am fixing up my old boat hat, which I plan to wear when I have to stand in line in the hot sun. I am going through my trunks in the *goedang* to sort out what I would like to take that isn't too large. What a job! The suitcases are underneath other heavy trunks, and all are full of cockroaches. How is it possible that in Brouwerstreet I was hoping to have all our things together for Fokko's homecoming? Not a chance!

After more than two thousand women left the camp, all the women who had been able to remain outside were told on short notice that they had to move in. So Aunt Rita, my last faithful outside contact, is here too. I went to the gate for a little while to see if I would see her arrive, but it was so hot and so much work was waiting at home, I couldn't stay. We haven't had any bread for a few days. We had to go and get it, but sometimes it was sold out. One day I gave half of my bread to a friend, and she returned with a can of oatmeal. What a treat. I haven't been able to buy oatmeal for a long time. I am saving it, however, to take with us in case of emergency.

I have disengaged myself from all my possessions. I have learned a lot this past year. On Brouwerstreet I couldn't let go of anything. It would have been more sensible to sell everything at that time, but that is Monday morning football coaching. The doctor was here again. The children have the flu. Ron had a fever and a bad cough, and Paula threw up six times in one night. I was dead tired for a few days and my back felt broken. I still tire easily since my disease. There isn't one night that I don't have to get up several times to get water for one of the children. Oh, how I am longing for a day of total rest, with all of you, in a free country, in Holland, in Middelburg, at home. Home, how wonderful that sounds! Carefree, peaceful, cozy. How much longer?

October 1943
Colombo
Fokko

Months passed. In his time off, Fokko played tennis and went swimming in the British swimming pool, not open to colored people. He often walked along the Galle Face Green in the cool evenings, when the restaurants on wheels came out and were parked for the night to serve all of those strolling along. Galle Face Green already existed in the 17th century, when the Dutch were in command. The Wolvendaal Church dates back to that era, as well as many Dutch names in Sinhalese families. Fokko grew accustomed to the various styles of architecture of many of Colombo's buildings, for example the Islamic influence in the city skyline, of which the Devatagaha Mosque near Town Hall was a beautiful example.

Figure 12 - The Devatagaha Mosque

Stacks of sandbags were piled up in every building in the city as protection against possible bombardments. Once he went to the zoo, a few kilometers south of Colombo's city limits. Occasionally he and a friend took a day trip to Kandy, 116 kilometers from Colombo, nestled in the foothills of the hill country surrounding a lovely, rectangular, tree-lined lake. Kandy, the last capital of the Sinhalese Kings, is the repository of traditional Ceylonese culture. The Sacred Tooth Relic of the Buddha, symbol of sovereignty over the island and Buddhism's most sacred treasure, is preserved there in the temple, the Dalada Maligawa.

Every August Kandy was the venue of the annual Esala Perehera, a colorful torch-lit pageant of elephants, dancers and custodians of the temple, in honor of the Buddha's relic. Many maimed beggars were always present in the streets around the temple.

Figure 13 - Kandy and the Sacred Tooth Relic

Fokko thought about the future. He had a paying job, since the Dutch Navy still officially employed him, and although they withheld part of his salary for later, to be paid out when the war was over, he was able to save a nice sum of money. He bought many books, including children's books, all imported from England. The abundance of gems for sale in Colombo, laboriously mined deep in the interior of Ceylon, caught his attention. He admired their beauty and, with careful selection and bargaining, he bought precious stones, as often and as many as his budget allowed. He saved them folded in a layer of cotton in an unobtrusive yellow *State Express* cigarette tin.

Cigarettes, together with many other supplies, were imported from England. Supplies to Ceylon, a crown colony, took a long detour around the world, a world at war. Many supply ships, destroyed along the way, never reached their destination. He bought yards of cotton and silk, and two beautiful Persian rugs, which he frequently laid out on deck in the sunshine, to keep them from getting damp. He also bought several metal trunks in which to store his treasures. Later he added a number of sturdy American airplane-parts crates.

Figure 14 - Player's Cigarette Tin

Fokko learned to think and even dream in English. He enjoyed drinking Ceylon's delicious tea, and learned about the start of tea growing in Ceylon back in 1867, when a Scotsman, James Taylor, had planted tea seedlings near Kandy on some twenty acres of forestland that originally had been cleared for a coffee plantation. Since then, Ceylon has become one of the world's largest tea exporters. Still living on board the *Plancius*, he had a cabin to himself, a stroke of luck, because most were double cabins. A little yellow canary kept him company. When it sang, which was most of the day, it could be heard all over the ship. It loved the small pieces of lettuce Fokko fed him, and taking care of the little creature made his cabin feel a little like home. Home—the thought of it made him wonder whether he would ever be back there again. It was no use crying about the possible fate of Netty and the children. He tried to focus instead on things he could laugh about, like the bug incident.

One day he and a colleague, Ian, went to Kandy, headquarters of Lord Mountbatten. The next morning Ian appeared at breakfast red-eyed and exhausted. His bed had been crawling with bed bugs, and he had not slept a wink but had been chasing the bugs all night. Fokko had experienced no problems and had slept like a log. The mystery was solved much later. One day when Ian was doing some paperwork at Fokko's desk on board, he showed Fokko the back of his thighs: they were covered with itchy swellings. Bug bites! There were bugs in his chair, he told Fokko, who had a hard time believing him, because they had never bothered him. However, he was convinced when Ian banged his chair hard on the floor a couple of times. Bugs fell out by the hundreds. The whole seat was one large nest of live bugs. Fokko laughed and considered himself lucky: the bugs apparently didn't like his blood!

As the immediate Japanese threat lessened, life in Colombo resumed its regular pace. More troops arrived, male as well as female. Soon the British organized concerts by playing records at the Y.M.C.A. in a room with a stage and a large loudspeaker. In those days stereo was not yet known. They played classical music once a week in the afternoon, free of charge, and Fokko went there as often as he could take the time. Usually he was the only Dutchman among all the British. A sergeant telegraph operator on board the *Plancius* wanted to do something similar. He gathered a handful of listeners, including Fokko. They put together a symphony orchestra, the brass section of which was initially the responsibility of the police. However, during one performance, the brass section was so terribly off key, the conductor dismissed them and continued without brass.

At one time they got permission to send a letter to relatives in the Dutch East Indies. Those letters were first sent to London, where they were deposited in a small dark room with only one door. Once in a while someone would open the door to grab a bundle of cards and letters without looking. These were first censored and then mailed on to the Japs. Fokko, who had just sent his first and only letter to Netty, wondered whether she would ever get it. Strict orders were given not to describe one's location, not even with a single word, and to omit words of affection, love and tenderness. Sometimes a little news trickled in about the situation in the Indies through spies who were able to transmit messages by radio.

October 10, 1943
Father Bach In Camp! I Love It!

Did you know that we have a concert once in a while on Sunday nights? Isn't this a model camp? On previous occasions I could not attend because of illness or something else, but last night, although I would have rather crawled into bed at 9, two of my campmates persuaded me to go with them. A loudspeaker was set up in front of a building, out in the open, and the audience sat on the lawn, in chairs or on benches, pillows or mats. We had brought the children's chairs and Mrs. G a small folding chair. We found a place opposite the loudspeaker and waited.

Gradually more and more people came sauntering in. Half a moon was sailing across the sky, or at least it seemed that way with all the clouds around. At 9:30 p.m. a lady announced the record program: first, *Symphonia* by Bach, by some symphony orchestra. Everyone became silent. How I enjoyed it. It is a beautiful piece; I know it well. I'm a Bach fan, like my father, who always played Bach pieces on the church organ. I closed my eyes and forgot I was fenced in by barbed wire, forgot the war and the rut of everyday life. I saw all of you around me and just let the music float through me.

Next was the *Kreuzer Sonata* by Beethoven, then a ten-minute intermission, and after that came Beethoven's *Fifth Symphony*. I enjoyed it tremendously and am going again next time. It is good for us to still be interested in something like this, and again I am proud of our Dutch women, who are taking the initiative to give these concerts and do not let themselves be pushed down. When it was over it was odd to watch the group take up their mats and walk. Behind us walked a row of five women who carried four chairs between them and covered the whole width of the street. We were carrying our chairs on our arms like baskets. At first we all walked in the same direction, then spread out over the various side streets. We were very hungry when we got home, but there was nothing to eat except some bananas that weren't ripe yet. That was indeed a harsh reality. There wasn't anything else for us to do but go to bed.

The Third Year

November 1, 1943
Jan's Birthday

Actually, I'm dead tired, but I just have to get in touch with you today. Let me first congratulate my little sister. Happy birthday, dear Jan, and a big kiss on each cheek. How I would love to be with you, if only for a moment. When I left, you were sweet sixteen, and now you're twenty-two already. What does your life look like? It has already been three years since the Germans occupied Holland. I hope you were able to stay in your house. You must be suffering from the measures they take. We are a minority here. Therefore, we were put into camps. I'm awfully tired. Paula is still seriously ill and very restless during the night, so I don't get much sleep.

I'm glad, Mother, that you won't get to read all this now, because you'd worry a great deal about us. I am writing down all my feelings, and I'm aware it's often depressing. However, you can skip some pages if you'd like. For me it's a relief to write about all my misery. It really helps as sort of an exhaust valve. I haven't even been able to read Fokko's letters lately— his letters from the years we were engaged, such a happy time. I can't describe the comfort and support they always give me, which I desperately need. As you know, we were far apart. I was in Middelburg and Fokko in Den Helder, but we had a wonderful correspondence. Now we are even farther apart. I hear nothing from him. I don't know where he is.

In this camp we feel alone and totally helpless. I ask God every night to keep you safe, to bring Fokko back safely, and to give me the patience to wait until the war is all over, but it is so difficult to be patient for so long. It seems this everyday rut will last forever. The music we heard the other day suddenly made me realize that there is something else besides this dreadful life. By worrying about so many things I have almost become a machine.

I will be so relieved when Paula will be better and we know what was wrong with her, so I can sleep the whole night through again and be rested to do my daily workload. I'll tell you what happened. Before Ron got the flu in October, Paula had scratched at a rash on her chin, which became badly infected and spread across her whole face. The doctor gave me some powder to treat it, and it slowly disappeared. In the meantime it spread to Ronny's face, which became covered with campsores. She was still in bed with this condition when she got the flu. The doctor prescribed a cough medicine with codeine. When I told him Paula had a fever too, he prescribed the same syrup for Paula. However, Ron was better in four days, but Paula continued to have a high fever. Ten days later, when the doctor finally came again, he said it might be malaria. He himself or the nurse would come to give her a blood test. No one came, so I went to the clinic to remind him. When they finally took a blood sample, the needle had probably not been sterilized. Paula's little finger tip got infected and turned into a big blister. Two weeks later she was still ill, with two campsores on her knee. Ron bumped her toe, which became infected to the point that the nail came off. All this at the same time!

At night, Paula has to have a drink of water and go on the potty at least once an hour. It is so sad that a sweet little thing like her has to suffer one disease after another. I give her all my love and care, but I can't give her the normal life of a two year old. One night she was delirious. She was restless, and she laughed strangely, singing a little, then screaming at the top of her voice, "Mamma!" I was afraid she was going to die. I left the light on and stayed awake until morning, when she became a little quieter. Then to start a hectic new day in this heat with no improvement in sight, neither with my child nor with the whole situation really made me desperate. Loekie's boys also suffer from aches and pains, campsores, and diarrhea, and everything is contagious. On top of all this I started to have problems with my tummy again, and had a very sore throat for a few days in a row, so you can imagine my feelings.

November 7, 1943
Are We Leaving Or Aren't We?

After the first three transports of women had left, the whole camp was thrown into a commotion by the announcement from the district office that all those who had entered the camp between October 1st and 12th, had to prepare themselves for departure and had to register the next day to get a number. A day later the luggage would be picked up, then the people themselves. Terror loomed everywhere, and we were convinced now we'd all be going. Everyone started sewing in a frenzy, the noise of sewing machines going everywhere. I needed to fix a lot of things too, but with Paula so ill I hadn't had time for a single stitch. Loekie and a friend of hers bought nice yellow leather backpacks for Fl.12.50 each and gave me one as a present; wasn't that nice of them? From the heavy brown linen bag Fokko used to store his raincoat, I made a little bag for Ronny to carry clothes, some soap and a bite to eat. We also bought a straw hat each at the market. Nobody knew anything, but everyone was getting ready.

After the first group left, the next one had to register and leave: those who had entered the camp between October 12th and 26th. Among them was Aunt Rita. One night she came to see me, dead tired. She had heart problems. She loaned me Fl.100, which I will pay back after the war. She also asked if I would pick up a case of her husband's books from her room after she leaves and keep them for him. She offered anything else I might like that she couldn't take with her, including her bike. That was nice, of course, but I felt so sorry for her. She wasn't really well enough to travel. I offered to help carry her luggage the next morning. It was still dark when I went to her house, and she, her daughter and I walked to the square. I carried her heavy backpack and pushed her heavily loaded bike. I was relieved when we got there. What do you say at a moment like that? "Till we meet again?" We didn't have the words. I couldn't wait until they left, because Paula was still ill. I went by Aunt Rita's room where I found quite a few things I could use: a lot of food, a good umbrella, soap, a bucket, games for the girls, a few books, lamps, two bedsheets, and three pairs of shoes that fit me perfectly.

Oh dear, Aunt Rita's bike, which I enjoyed so much, had to be handed in at the gate yesterday. I only had it for a very short time. There was no other way. Only doctors, nurses and other working women were allowed to keep their bikes. Again we had to stand in the sun for hours to turn them in. Before this, some boys ruined whatever tires they could, so the Japs would have to fix them, but what's the use? I am so glad we live close to the *pasar* and the clinic. I borrowed a little pushcart for going to the *pasar* from someone who left, because one wheel of mine is broken. We are still here, and the district has quieted down for the time being.

November 21, 1943
Little Paula Is Three Years Old

If I think about the afternoon when Fokko left, and my misgivings that our separation might last two years, and the scary feeling when I realized that by then Paula would be three and Ronny five, I could cry. Now Paula is three, and a month from now Ronny will be five, and Fokko isn't back yet, not by far. It is enough to make me want to bang my head against a brick wall.

Well, Paula's fever didn't go down as much and as fast as I had hoped, and Ronny got diarrhea and came down with a fever again. I became so depressed. It felt as if it would never stop. They have been ill since August! One Sunday morning, when they were still ill and had those camp sores, and I was hardly getting any sleep, it all became too much for me. I had both sitting in hot soda water for their sores, crying of course. Paula spilled on my bed; Ronny dropped an eggcup, which broke. I had so much work ahead of me and was so tired, that suddenly I started crying. I cried and cried for a long time. Then I took a shower, washed my hair and felt like a different person with a bit more courage to continue. Once in a while you have to have a good cry.

Finally they could both go outside again. When we awoke on the morning of Paula's birthday, she knew it was her great day: she was three years old now! There are no real toys for sale, neither in the store nor in the *pasar*, but I had bought a little wooden cart—a dreary brown color because there was no paint. Ronny gave Paula a crudely made wooden elephant on wheels. At breakfast, all the children and adults together sang "Happy Birthday" for her. Paula was very happy and kept on singing to herself: "Happy birthday to you." The day went by quietly. I thought about Fokko a lot, and about you.

We have air raid warnings again. One night around ten o'clock the sirens started, followed by low-flying airplanes and an enormous boom, and immediately the defense artillery started cracking. We hadn't heard that in a long time. Both children were still ill. What could I do? I heard the others go into the shelter. When it started raining and the explosions got louder, I wrapped the girls in blankets and took them into the shelter. It lasted for hours, poor kids. That shelter is so small and they were feverish. The following night nothing happened, but the night thereafter it started again. Rain poured down in sheets. I hesitated again. It is so scary when you don't have any cover, and those booms are so loud. The shelter leaked, so after a while we went back to our room. I decided to stay in bed when it happens again. Besides, we have strict orders to stay inside. We aren't even allowed to go into the yard during an attack.

From now on we will be able to get bread only on weekends, and just a small ration. Milk will be rationed even more, except for baby milk. I get about a pint a day to make pudding for the girls' dessert. However, we are able to buy powdered milk for our coffee. I am gaining an hour each morning by getting up an hour earlier. At night however, I am dead tired and go to bed at 7:30, otherwise, I couldn't keep it up. One advantage—we don't have to be bright and cheerful at night for our husbands. We could never pull that off! Now we go to bed tired and as early as we want to.

December 29, 1943
Ronny Turns Five

When I look back at what I wrote you last year on this day, I realize I could repeat it exactly this year. We just live from one day to the next, on and on, and it's enough to make us lose all hope, all courage. Ronny is five, Paula three, just what I anticipated with so much fear the day Fokko left. I am sorry I can't stay the same age either. This January, I will be thirty-four. I have that from you, Father Kees, the fear of growing old. Thank God the children look great. Paula has gained some weight after her illness, and Ronny looks better too.

Long before her actual birthday, Ronny couldn't stop talking about it and invited every child in the neighborhood. That's just like Ron, always very enthusiastic. Of course she also asked for the Christmas tree, which we keep in the *goedang*. Loekie has her ornaments handy, so we promised the children they could trim the tree the Thursday before Christmas. We adults don't feel like celebrating, but for the children's sake we do as much as we can. On Christmas Eve each of the children got a candle next to his plate, and we lit the candles on the tree after dinner. For this occasion I opened the bottle of milk I got from Aunt Rita in August. It is sterilized milk, which can keep for months, and it was a very special treat for the adults to have coffee, and for the children to have cocoa with real milk. I don't get extra milk anymore for Paula, so we only use powdered milk these days, which has become very expensive. Ronny had a memorable birthday. I am glad she was happy. I'm also thankful that it will be another year until her next birthday, because I'm not in a position to spend so much money often. My wallet is flattening again. It scared me when I counted the money I have left. I spent almost Fl.40 this month and I really can't afford that. We'd be broke within four months. Everything has become so terribly expensive that money just runs through my fingers, and you know how thrifty I can be. I am so grateful that Aunt Rita gave me some money before she left. Other people are down to their last savings too, and many are getting their meals from the low-cost central kitchen.

New Year's Eve, 1943
Thoughts

It is now 8:15 p.m. Old East Indies time, which is 10:15 Japanese time. On other nights I would be getting ready to go to bed. This year I am not sitting on the same cozy sofa as the previous two years, but in the dining room and happy to be alone. We were invited to spend the evening with Klaartje, who cooks our lunches. Betty, Mrs. G, the nurse, and Liesbeth went. Loekie went to bed early. Liesbeth is the young woman who came to live with us when Sister Magdalena left to share a house with other nuns. I didn't feel like going out. I had a headache this morning, and would have liked to stay in bed all day. After a day's work, when the children are in bed, I often still have mending to do. Everything gets so old and threadbare that it tears easily. The daily laundering of thin material makes frequent repairs necessary, so clothes will become a problem if this war lasts much longer. Sometimes I wear one of Fokko's shirts in the morning. We still "dress" in the afternoon. I wear his pajamas at night, which gives me a nice feeling. I laughed with the girls about "me being Pappa." I sure look charming at night.

Another reason I stayed home is that I want to write to you all tonight, so I'm very happy to be alone. The fact that I didn't feel well, and the incredible heat and humidity at this time of year because of the monsoon, contributed to a lot of sad feelings today. Often thoughts of you or Fokko or New Year's Eve crossed my mind. This is the fourth year I cannot write directly to you, and the beginning of my third year without Fokko. There is no way of knowing where we'll be this time next year. Often I have said to the children, "Next time Pappa will be home." But the holidays go by and Pappa does not come home. All these beautiful years are passing by while I'm still so young. I'm afraid I'm going to lose all courage. I don't cross off the days on my home- made calendar any more, but I do think every night, "Thank God, another day has gone by." I just cannot worry about the whole year ahead of us, so I won't. I'd better look back to the other "Me," always singing songs about sunshine and happiness—"On the Sunny Side of the Street,"

"Happy Days are Here Again" and "There's a Rainbow 'Round my Shoulder"—the other "Me" with never a headache and seldom ill. Yet, I have many reasons to feel grateful, and I really do. Both my little girls look healthy again and are well fed, so I'm delighted.

I have learned that you can bear any burden as long as you are healthy. At the beginning of this month I had diarrhea and stomach aches for a week. I was very tired, weak, and depressed, because I thought I had amoebae dysentery again, but some tests proved it wasn't. After three days of taking yet another kind of medication, I felt well again, but I can't get my weight over 107 lbs. I'm sure that when I'm happy again and can get milk, butter, cheese and good bread, all that will change. I am pleased that I got some money and many good things from Aunt Rita when she left the camp. You see, there are a lot of things to be happy about, and when I look back I am actually happier than I used to be.

Last but not least, I am happy that tomorrow morning, I will be able to say it is 1944, and will count the months. Each month is one closer to peace. The war is going on and we know nothing. We are completely without any news from the outside world. I wonder what the natives know about it. The last time I was in town, I remember hearing a loud broadcast, voices in the native language, and music coming from the top of the tower at the beginning of the main street, Toendjoengan. I'm sure the Japs will tell them only what they want them to know.

During the past few months, things have been made more difficult for us. Even bacon fat is not available any more after we had to give up butter, then milk. We get bread only three days a week, which we eat for dinner. The slices are very small and thin. Ron and I eat three slices each, Paula two. Sometimes I spread peanut butter on them or mashed banana. It is enough for the children, but leaves me still hungry sometimes. For breakfast we have boiled rice with a little milk powder, a scrambled egg and some brown sugar. We haven't seen cheese or chocolate in weeks. Oh, how I will enjoy a slice of good brown bread with butter and cheese when this war is over! But I will not think about that any longer. I will go to bed now, truly hoping that the New Year will finally bring us peace. But I am not as convinced as I was last New Year's Eve. How hopeful I was then! Now all I do is wait. Yet I am glad that 1943 lies behind me.

I forgot to tell you that at the end of December the Japanese took all gas stoves away from us, which makes our lives more difficult and more expensive. We take turns lighting the fire in the morning, each of us for a week. Five days out of my seven, it took me more than half an hour. At home I had done it often and had no problems, but then we still had newspapers for kindling, and now we don't have any paper at all. I have to light it with petroleum, a candle (to save matches) and a fuse, and the charcoal doesn't burn easily. It was hard. I can't stand all the smoke. When it is lit, it is a constant worry to keep the fire going. Sometimes you have to sit there, fanning, when it has almost gone out.

January 17, 1944
Contagious Disease, Diphtheria

The sign attached to our front door reads *Contagious Disease, DIPHTHERIA*. Our Ronny has been taken to a hospital outside the camp. These are miserable days. It is foremost in my mind. It controls all my thoughts, and everything else has been moved to the background.

One morning I got up with a sore throat and started gargling with Dettol, a disinfectant mouthwash, for lack of something stronger. The next day it was worse. I put a scarf around my neck, kept my mouth closed and tried not to breathe when I lit the fire in the morning. The third day I felt so bad that I decided to go to the doctor at 11. It was one o'clock before it was my turn. We always have to sit and wait for hours. The doctor seemed alarmed after she saw my throat, and asked if I had any children. I told her I had two of my own and four others in the same house. She shook her head and said she was very worried because of a new dyphteria epidemic in camp. The district nurse would come by the next day, Saturday, to take a sample from each of our throats. We would not be notified if it were negative; otherwise, the ambulance would come. Ron had a sore throat and a fever, but by Sunday night it was gone, and she played outside again. My throat got worse. Even the medication the doctor had given me didn't help. Sunday night I woke up around two o'clock because I couldn't swallow, and I panicked. I switched on the light and looked in the mirror. Only one side of my throat was still open; the other was completely swollen and closed. It felt as if I was suffocating. I couldn't go back to sleep.

The next morning I was unable to go to the *pasar*, but I sent Ron to school, and then went straight to the clinic. After waiting for an hour a native doctor arrived, entered the building, and I heard him ask for the "Diphtheria Book" so he could add the new cases. He then said, "These are positive" and "Ronny Herman." I stiffened in my chair. I realized that they had just received the results of the tests, and they concerned us. I decided to ask the first person who came by for more information. After a while, the district nurse came in from outside, asking for me. Then I knew for certain it had to be one of us. It was a strange moment, just like the time when I took Fokko to the train and we turned the corner and saw the station in front of us. It was the inevitable. You keep walking, with leaden feet, purely mechanically, automatically. That's how I walked up to the desk. "Who is it?"

"It's Ronny. They will be coming to pick her up from home later." These moments I will never forget my whole life long.

"Would you please fill out this form?"

There was Mrs. G with a sobbing little Ronny. "Mamma, I don't have to go to the hospital, do I? I don't have to go alone. I'm not sick. I don't have to go, do I? You are coming with me, aren't you, Mam?" Big tears rolled down her cheeks. I couldn't talk, but I knew that I had to control my own feelings and help her get familiar with the idea that she had to go alone. That was hard, so incredibly hard. I couldn't concentrate enough to fill out the form, asking our names, birthdates, religion, etc. They had to prompt me. "Residence of the father?"

"Unknown."

"Friends or relatives of the patient outside the camp?"

Luckily, I remembered the name of a very nice native woman who lived on Brouwerstreet. She always liked Ronny very much and Ronny knows her well. We were also lucky that she had just sent us her change of address last November.

Then we went home. I was half-crying but continued to reassure Ronny. "You have been in a hospital twice before. Remember, Ron? And you didn't mind it at all. The nurses there are very nice. They'll read to you and play with you, I'm sure."

"Yes, but I was just going to fold something in school."

Poor thing. Big tears kept rolling down while she showed me a piece of pink paper in her hand. "There are so many Japanese there, Mamma. I don't want to go in the ambulance."

"Of course there are no Japanese in the hospital you're going to, and do you know what is so special? It is the same hospital where Mamma got you when you were a tiny little baby, and you'll get to see it again now that you are a big girl."

At home there were upset faces and tearful eyes, and in the middle of the garage, leaning against my bed, an alone-in-the-world little Paula. "Paula, why are you crying?"

"Aunt Loekie says I can't go over there." She was considered contagious and was sent to the garage where she just stood, lost, crying pitifully. I swallowed hard. I couldn't hug her, afraid I would pass on my throat infection, but drying her tears, I said, "Mamma is here now. I'll stay with you." That reassured her. Turning again to Ronny, I said, "Do you remember Aunt Simone, Ron, who always had so much chocolate in the refrigerator? Well, she is so nice, I bet she'll bring you a chocolate bar when she comes to visit you." Slowly the tears stopped. "And do you realize that you will drive all around town, and we have to stay here? You can look through the window. Maybe you will see our house. If you do, will you look at the *mangga* trees?" Her face brightened. "And you are not really ill, are you? You have no sore throat and no fever. Well, then, I bet you'll come back in a few days. Or maybe Mamma will come too, and then we'll put our beds next to one another. Won't that be cozy?" She was almost reconciled with the idea. In the meantime I had such an abnormally sore throat, that we all thought I would soon follow. Whenever my voice failed me, I said, "Mamma has such a sore throat that it makes me cry."

"Oh, please don't talk any more, Mam," said Ron. She had to take a suitcase with some old clothes, because sometimes things get lost in the hospital. It wasn't a difficult choice. Actually, almost everything she has is old. I quickly marked everything "R.H." in red. I know what a comfort it is when you have some candy in your pocket, but I had nothing in the house as a treat for Ronny. I asked Loekie if she had anything. Loekie burst out in tears, but she did give us some toffees. During this time Mrs. G, who understands things like this so well, came with some peppermints, and Ronny began to laugh. In one of her pockets she put the toffees, in the other the peppermints (but she took one of each for starters), and on top of those her handkerchief, wet with tears.

I had no idea what time the ambulance would come, but we expected it to be about four. I bathed Ronny and started serving dinner. I had Ron where I wanted her. She was happy that she could go outside the camp. She yelled at the boys, "I am going to the hospital, and I can look out of the window and see the whole town, and I'm going to get chocolate from a nice lady!"

I quickly interrupted Casper, who started saying that going to the hospital was nothing to be happy about. Then I heard, "There it is," and immediately saw the large, closed ambulance backing up into the driveway. Horrible. Four men jumped out and came toward the garage. Four dark-skinned native men to pick up one little child. I wanted to feed her more of her dinner, but the nurse who came along said we couldn't let the men wait. I asked her whether she was going with Ronny, but she wasn't allowed outside the camp. "She is going alone."

"Mam, will you ask that man if I can look out the window?"

In Indonesian I asked the *mantri* (head nurse), dressed in white, and he immediately laughed and was very friendly, although he had looked so threatening a minute ago.

"Will you ask him what I'll have to eat when I'm in the hospital, Mam?"

"The doctor will tell you that," said the nurse. "Are you ready?"

I quickly dressed Ron and put her clothes in the suitcase, but in my rush I forgot to pack her comb and her toothbrush. I felt sorry about that later, because she has long hair and brushes her teeth faithfully every day.

When I looked outside, I saw that a curious crowd had gathered. I couldn't stand it. It felt like a funeral. I asked Mrs. G to go outside and ask the people to leave. Almost all did. How terrible that people are so tactless, so totally insensitive. I gave Ron a handshake. I couldn't even hug or kiss her because she was contagious, but kept talking, talking, my mouth in a frozen smile, with a strange, high voice, though not tearful. Inwardly, I cried. The doors opened and my little girl got inside as bravely as if she were going to a party, all alone. One of the men jumped in with her, and the others hung onto the side or sat in the front. "Look, Ron, there is the window, can you look out?"

If she stood on the seat she could barely reach it. "I'll come visit you soon," I said (a lie).

"Yes, Mam, please come soon. 'Bye, Paula".

Paula waved, and so did I. Then she was gone. Oh, it is so hard. This is the third time she is going to the hospital. This time we are prisoners and aren't even allowed to go along. We will hear nothing until she comes home. These are days I will never forget. She is not ill, but a germ-carrier, so she has to be isolated until she is not contagious any more.

Now I have Paula to take care of. I am so happy that she, at least, is well. When she woke up that afternoon, the first thing she asked was, "Is Ronne in the hospital?" She sat up straight and peered through the mosquito net of Ronny's bed, which was empty. "Will Ronne ever come back?" She talks about Ron constantly. This afternoon she said, "When I have to go in the ambulance, will Mamma cry for me too?" I told her that she didn't have to go in the ambulance, but if so, yes, then I would cry for her, too. That night the doctor came because I was still struggling with my closed throat. The nights were especially miserable. I woke up every hour since I couldn't swallow and had a dry mouth.

Tuesday morning the sign *Contagious Disease, DIPHTHERIA* was posted on our door. We all had a second throat test. Nobody will be allowed outside the gate for ten days. A neighbor boy does the marketing, and our meals are delivered to the gate. We were all anxious to hear whether any of us are infected too. Tonight the doctor came and said everyone had tested negative. So it was only Ronny. Why, we'll never know. I had to disinfect all her clothes and all our mosquito nets. Mrs. G took care of that for me; she is priceless. I scrubbed Ron's bed with Lysol, and then put everything in the sun. I still have to stay indoors for one more day. My sore throat is gradually hurting less. We have all our things in the garage: plates, forks, knives, separate dishpan, and soap.

My thoughts are with Ronny constantly, especially during nights while I lie awake. It was like when Fokko left. At night, when everything is quiet and you can do nothing else, it hits you. I broke out in a cold sweat when I thought of what could happen if we get a bombardment. The hospital is all the way across town. What if she got some kind of disease, or what if she didn't get enough to eat? I had to fill out a form whether I could pay for her care. Actually, I can't spare Fl.30, but sitting in the waiting room back then, I heard someone say that if you couldn't pay, the patient would have to lie on a mat. So I can pay. We'll worry about the future later.

I must say that Loekie is very nice. She said that we would share whatever we have and find a solution together. Mrs. G came and said that if I had to go to the hospital, she would help me with the payments. There is another older lady who more than once has said to me, "My child, if you ever need money, come and see me." They are all so nice to me. Everybody is helping me with the work too. One lady who had just come out of the hospital told me that the doctor and nurses are very nice, so I shouldn't worry.

I am grateful the Japanese do provide treatment for our patients, even though they don't allow us any contact with them. It has been raining all night. I hope the nurse has dressed Ron in her warm pajamas. She always loved going to bed when it rained. I am counting the days. The doctor said yesterday that I am much better, but when I look in the mirror my image scares me so. I wonder how I looked on the day that Ronny left. What if Fokko saw me now, lean as a rake, lines in my face from all this heartache? Paula prays every night "that Ronne may get better soon." I hope Ronny prays too. Maybe that will help her feel better.

February, 1944
China Bay
Fokko

One day Fokko heard he was transferred to China Bay near Trincomalee, situated in the far northeastern part of Ceylon. Long rows of barracks marked the large air base close to China Bay. The British had been there for a while, and the Dutch moved there a little later. The Dutch flyers were getting their own separate squadron of *Liberators*: large, four-engined bombers. Fokko asked himself what in the world he had to do with that. One Marine reserve officer, Johnson, found out that on board the *Plancius* was a Navy man, Fokko Herman, who used to fly with the M.L.D., and therefore knew a lot about planes. So Fokko was summoned to China Bay. To his delight he met a lot of people there whom he knew: flyers, airplane builders, and Jos Vermeulen, who had been stationed in China Bay for a while, flying a Liberator landplane. It was another one of their seemingly coincidental encounters. Their line of work was different, yet in China Bay they had some things in common. They spent a lot of time together in the months to come.

Fokko was put to work in a hurry. Close to the airport, hidden among the trees, an enormous rectangular tent was

156

erected. It looked like a very large, long hangar. Stored inside were a large number of small and large crates. Inside the crates Fokko found multiples of all parts of Liberator bombers you could think of, including self-closing wing tanks. One huge crate contained a full-scale office, with a chair and desk and all papers necessary for administration of parts for a whole squadron of Liberators, including a list of the contents of each numbered case. It was a complete unit for a squadron in action. They asked Fokko to familiarize himself quickly with this American setup. A couple of Tamils would help him with the heavy work, but he had to perform some heavy-duty jobs himself, which made him strong as a bear.

Figure 15 - The B-24 Liberator Fokko serviced

February 18, 1944
Ronny's Homecoming

While Ron was in the hospital, a lot of things happened. First we had an anxious day because of a house search by armed Japanese soldiers. Then there was a transport of women and children from a large section of the camp to an unknown destination. First they evacuated all the outer sections of the camp. Our district is in the middle. We expected to follow soon, so we sewed until late in the night to get at least the machine sewing done of any strong material we had. We could finish it all by hand later. We expected to be put in a large hangar, so decent nightwear was a first requirement. For that reason we cut up sheets. From one of my large unused sheets, I made pajamas for the girls and myself. Trimmed with colored ribbons, they looked quite nice.

You can imagine my anxiety after the first group left, and the second one three days later. I anticipated we would be sent in a few days, but Ronny wasn't home yet. The fear of leaving without her was unbearable, and I had some terrible days. Some people depressed me even more by saying that germ-carriers usually need six to seven weeks to get rid of germs. That was all I needed to hear. The next morning I went to several strangers, who also had children "outside," to ask them how long they had stayed away. Some came home after fifteen days, so I felt a little more hopeful.

It was Ronny's sixteenth day away, close to noon, when a girl from down the street came running in. "Ronny is coming home!"

I ran outside: "Where is she?"

"In a *dogcar*."

The *dogcar* appeared with two children, one of them Ronny. I ran toward them, and lifted her out of the *dogcar*, "Hello, Ron!

Oh, Ron!" She said, "Hello, Mam," put her arms around my neck as if she were never going to let go again, pushed her head against my shoulder and cried softly. After her many experiences, to be back in mother's arms was too much for her, and for me. She looked pale and thin, her hair loose and straight, as she squeezed her two red ribbons and a bunch of flowers in her hand. "These flowers I picked for you, Mam." She had picked them in the garden of the hospital just before she left, then the nurse put both children in the *dogcar* and sent them back to camp.

I said, "Oh, Ron! I'm so happy; I'm going to squeeze some oranges for you!"

She didn't say much, but asked me if I would please cut the nails of her fingers and toes. A lot of neighbors gathered around, but this time I didn't care. I was just happy, so happy. I made her bed and tucked her in. She still wasn't her old self yet, and she talked strangely. That straight, set face without any expression in her eyes wasn't our Ron yet. But I was so grateful that before we had to leave camp, I still had some time to feed her well. Paula kept saying, "Ronne, Ronne, Ronne, this is Ronne." At dinner Ron was very hungry, and during the following days she seemed famished. She said she had been given only two meals a day, rice with vegetables and ground beef for lunch, and rice with a piece of egg at night. Anyway, within a week she had regained her weight, and after two days talked more normally and was laughing again, and her eyes looked brighter. I took her to the doctor for a checkup. She gave Ron a bottle of codliver oil, free of charge. Isn't that nice? I haven't received the hospital bill yet, and I hope they'll forget about it.

Bit by bit we heard the stories about the hospital and the nurses. There was one good nurse and one bad one. "The days in the hospital are starting really early," she said, meaning that they start bathing the patients in the early hours. She still wakes up early in the morning, gets up, goes outside and brooms the patio for me. (It is my job to broom and mop the patio every morning). She then comes inside and says, "I broomed for you, Mam."

We are still here and I have changed our mattresses. We are allowed to take one narrow, thin mattress each. I happened to have one of Fokko's, sewed two pads from the playpen together for Paula, and made Ronny's mattress smaller. Nobody knows whether we'll have to go or stay, but we keep on sewing and working every night on our wardrobes. I bought shoes for the girls, one size too large. I don't think we can buy anything where we are going, because the women had to hand in all their leftover money before their departure. The whole camp is in a commotion. I had to pay Fl.3.50 for those shoes, even though they are made of paper with rubber soles. If they get wet once, they'll have had it.

I didn't celebrate my birthday this year, even though my fellow inmates gave me presents: soap, a handkerchief, material for clothes for the children, and a calendar. When Ronny came home I baked a cake, as I had promised. Do you know that we get wrinkles from all the fears we have? Almost two months of 1944 have gone by. Will I see Fokko back before I'm old and grey?

April 1944
China Bay
Fokko

Trincomalee, a small village, had a movie theatre, a wooden barrack with a tin roof and sand on the floor. It was always very hot inside and filled with a cloud of dust. Although the temperature inside was almost unbearable and the men had to wear their long-sleeved khaki shirts because of the mosquitoes, they liked going there, because there was hardly any other entertainment around. It was relatively far from China Bay, but trucks went back and forth to the village regularly, so the men hitched rides when they wanted to. Someone played classical records in a small theatre in China Bay. He would first explain the nature of the music, to make it more easily understood and more enjoyable. Fokko often attended those evenings, and again he was usually the only Dutchman present. They lived, two to a room, in wooden barracks around the bay. Fishing was great, especially at night, and could be done from the shore. Although it was wartime, the men were given Saturday afternoons and Sundays off.

Johan, one of Fokko's colleagues, purchased a canoe. It was actually a large hollow tree trunk, which they used during the weekends to go fishing for parrotfish and small sharks. It could also be used for sailing. One afternoon Fokko went sailing with the owner. Given the rudder to try, Fokko made a wrong move and their boat took water. In an effort to undo the mistake, he threw the boat into the wind, which would normally have worked, but in this case it resulted in a total standstill. Because of the water in the boat, it rocked and filled up. Nearby was the large French battleship, *Richelieu.* The captain, assuming that the two men were in danger (which was only partially true because of all the sharks in the bay), quickly lowered a large motorsloop and sent it to their rescue. That was a nice gesture, but in his zeal the mate put the brakes on too late and rammed the canoe midship, and it almost broke in half. After tying on, Fokko and his friend, holding on to the canoe, were towed to shallow water. That was the end of their sailing trip.

Days, weeks and months went by. Swimming, fishing and preparing the catch for dinner became part of Fokko's daily work. China Bay would not be his final destination, however.

The squadron he was with was to move to a base in the Indian Ocean.

The Death Camps

Commentary

When we were put on a transport, one of the few things that Mamma packed in her suitcase was her diary. During the years that followed in the next camp, paper and pencils were forbidden. Therefore, she could not write down her experiences and feelings anymore, but they were etched in her memory for the rest of her life. The second part of this story relates Mamma's memoirs. Some memories brought tears to her eyes and a lump in her throat when she told them to me, even now, so many years later. Time has not been able to erase all of the suffering she endured.

The Transport

The blow still came unexpectedly. One day, shortly after I had written the last entry in my diary on February 18, 1944, the Japanese, through the district leader, told us that we were to leave on a transport in two days. Many streets were deserted, as many women and children had already been transported out of the city. Still we had hoped, against our better judgment, we would be able to remain where we were. It was not to be. We were allowed one suitcase of limited size, and whatever else we could carry. With the exception of a few very dear mementos, it was important to take things that would last, such as a pair of sturdy shoes for each of us, practical clothes, and a couple of strong sheets that I could use for different purposes. They also told us, that bunch of liars, that we were allowed to fill one footlocker with items we wanted to keep, which they would store for us until the war was over. Everyone packed and left their most valuable possessions in footlockers, but never saw any of them after the war. Some women buried silver in their back yards, but they were easily discovered with metal detectors and never returned.

It was not easy to pack just one suitcase. I constantly had to put things aside because they didn't fit in any more. When I finally finished, shortly before our departure, they announced that the suitcases had to be one size smaller. It caused more panic on top of all the commotion. Where could we all get a smaller suitcase at such short notice? Miracle of miracles: I managed to borrow one, and then had to start sorting and packing all over again.

When we were married in 1937, we were handed a large Bible during the church ceremony. On the first page it had our names, wedding date and name of the town: Middelburg. We took it with us to our new homeland, and now I had to leave it behind. I could only take the little Bible, a present from Mother and Father Kees, with their names in it. The large one simply didn't fit in the small suitcase. I leafed through it one last time and it was as if I felt the presence of my little grandmother, telling me, "Do as I do, my child, read one page a day." I packed it in the large trunk, which they would keep for us until the war was over. I worked until the wee hours, selecting and repacking. Even the small backpacks of the girls were vital. They each had to carry some of their own things, little as they were. We had to leave so much behind.

Over the last couple of weeks I had re-read Fokko's letters one by one, and then destroyed them. That saddened me deeply. Because I didn't know what was going to happen to us, I thought it better to do away with them. And so, the next day, we left 44 Moesistreet. We had to assemble on a field early in the afternoon during the hottest part of the tropical day. We were allowed to sit on the ground, but there was no shade anywhere. Although we each had a large straw hat and something to drink, the wait, especially for the little ones, was not easy. Hour after hour went by. It became 4 o'clock, then 5 o'clock. We were still waiting. It was almost dark by the time a number of trucks appeared, supervised by armed Japanese soldiers. We climbed in. They drove us to the railroad station, where we boarded a waiting train. We each had a seat on the train, but it was hot and crowded, while armed native and Japanese soldiers stood or sat in the aisles. We were well guarded!

Twilight in the tropics is short, and soon it grew dark. Mosquitoes were buzzing around us. By the time it was 8 o'clock, the children were tired and thirsty. I had brought sandwiches and water. I was glad I had brought Paula's potty for the children, because the bathroom on the train was very dirty. Stars appeared in the sky. Later, I saw the moon. The mosquitoes buzzed as we just sat there, not moving. The children fell asleep, sitting up. I took Ronny on my lap for a while, so little Paula, three years old, could lie down. The moon climbed higher. It became midnight. Would this last all night? Finally, around 1 a.m., we heard rattling and puffing in the quiet train station, a sign that something was about to happen. The train pulled out of the station. We traveled all night and part of the next day before the train came to a stop. According to some of the women, we had arrived in Semarang, a city on the north shore of Java. Was it the end of our journey? What was to become of us?

Semarang
Camp Halmahera: First Impressions

Japanese soldiers ordered us out of the station and made us climb into waiting trucks; quite a hassle for those tired women and little children, all carrying their own luggage. When the trucks were loaded, we departed. We drove along country roads for hours. People whispered the camp must be a long way from the city. At last we saw in the distance a bamboo fence, called a *gedèk*, with a large open gate the full width of the road. When we got closer, the first thing visible inside the fence was a furious Jap, armed with a club, hitting nuns from the street. The nuns had probably noticed the approaching trucks, as did the other women and children in the background, and wanted to come to our aid. Having journeyed for more than 24 hours, tired and exhausted, we felt like crying.

Figure 16 - Kamp Makasar
Imagebank WW2 - NIOD

They shouted at us to get off the trucks and stand in line to be registered. A couple of Japs and a woman, apparently the camp leader, took our names and numbers. Waiting in line, I unexpectedly saw a familiar face. It was Jopie Esser, who had lived with us for a while in Soerabaja when she and her husband had lost all their possessions. How happy I was to see her! She took the girls with her for a drink of water and brought me some too. After registration, she took us to the little house we were assigned. It consisted of two small rooms already occupied, with a narrow corridor, slightly wider close to the front door, about 8 x 8 feet. That hallway was our domain. Everyone entering or leaving the house had to pass by us. Our three small mattresses just fit next to each other on the floor, with a little space left for the suitcase. That was it.

We were just in time for lunch. A boy came by, ringing a bell and calling, "Block five, get your food."

One of the women in our house explained to me how it worked, and walked with me to the kitchen. Two women, standing in the street, one behind a drum full of rice, the other behind another drum full of some kind of soup, dished out one flat scoop of rice per person and one ladle of watery soup with a few vegetables. I had brought my two pans, got our rations, and returned to my hungry girls. They ate as if it was the most delicious treat they'd ever had. The evening meal consisted of a ladle of starch, sago boiled in water, without sugar. Sago, the product of the sago palm, derived from its marrow, consists of little round beads, which are translucent when you boil them. It is a tasteless starch, like cornstarch. I just swallowed it. It was better than nothing. Ronny made an effort with a wry face, but Paula kept her lips tightly pressed together after the first spoonful. Not being a porridge lover in the first place, she wouldn't eat this starch, but she had to. There was nothing else.

This would be our daily breakfast and dinner for a long time to come. With a lot of tears her first portion of starch went down.

We were so tired that we all went to bed early. I laid down with five-year old Ronny on my right side and three-year old Paula on my left. We huddled together and went to sleep with the sound of raindrops clattering on the roof. In the middle of the night Ronny woke me up. "Mamma, my bed is all wet." I felt water trickling down the wall. I covered the wet spot with a towel, moved the three mattresses even closer together and changed places with Ronny. We fell asleep again immediately, but the next morning we were in for another surprise. Next to me the towel and the wet mattress were crawling with *rajaps*, (termites), white ants that eat wood and cloth. I quickly took everything out into the sun. Monsoon rains had caused the gutter to overflow. Luckily we were approaching the change in seasons, so it didn't always rain every night.

The women in our house were very different from one another. The one who had explained the kitchen procedures to me the previous day was a sturdy, helpful, no-nonsense type of woman called *Tante Marie* (Aunt Marie), a name that suited her perfectly. She always wore a large apron with two pockets. Her husband was in the navy. The other woman, Mrs. H, looked like an elderly lady: gaunt, with greyish hair and glasses. She didn't look at all like the mother of thirteen-year old Yvette, yet she was. We didn't see Yvette very often, because her mother treated her like a precious, fragile doll and kept her in bed a lot, telling us she was a very weak child. Yvette had a real bed. Halmahera was their first camp, and they had taken some furniture with them, like I did in Soerabaja. Mrs. H and Yvette occupied the larger of the two rooms, and Tante Marie, who had no children, lived in the second room. Since there were no other rooms in the little house, the three of us were put in the 8 x 8 hallway. I made a curtain out of one of my sheets for some privacy. That made it a little dark in our domain, since the only light came through a window in the front door.

Like the other women, I had brought a bar of soap, a scarce commodity during the war. I washed our sweaty traveling clothes as Baboe had always done it. I wet the garments, rubbed them with the soap and rinsed them. I did not beat the clothes on a stone, the common way of washing clothes by the natives, so they would not wear out that quickly. When the children and I walked to the kitchen twice that day with our pans for the two starch meals, and one meal of rice with soup, we saw some of our surroundings. The lights went off at 9 p.m. Our first complete day in camp was over.

Camp Halmahera: A Description

The camp, a district on the outskirts of Semarang, better than a *kampong* but nothing like a European district, consisted of a few streets, village squares and a large field. The houses were brick, very primitive, each with a corridor and a couple of small rooms. A squatting toilet and a *mandikamer* (a do-it-yourself dip-bucket shower) sat outside, behind the house. The cooking was done outside as well, on an *anglo*, (a clay barbeque) with *arang* (charcoal). Now, however, there was no *anglo*, no *arang,* and nothing to cook.

The central kitchen consisted of a few stokeholes in a row for burning wood, brought into the camp on a regular basis. Over the fires hung large iron drums in which the starch, the rice and the "soup" were cooked. A supply of vegetables was brought into the camp daily. Sometimes there was enough, and sometimes there wasn't. Tante Marie, one of the women in the vegetable shift, a group of mostly single or older women, sometimes brought home a treat, like a carrot, for Yvette. Seated behind a long table the women cleaned and cut the

169

vegetables, and often a carrot or another piece of a vegetable disappeared into their apron pockets.

Figure 17 - The Camp Kitchen (taken after the war)
Imagebank WW2 - NIOD

The soup was made with inferior quality meat. At first it consisted of cattle parts such as heads, including eyes and ears. Later on, when no beef or pork was available, they used dog meat. However, "the kitchen" always gave you a choice: dog soup or meatless soup. I always chose the latter. It didn't really deserve the name vegetable soup, because it had very few vegetables, but at least it was a meal. When the wood was wet and the women could not get the fires going, there simply was no meal. A request for dry wood was usually refused. This happened on New Year's Eve, 1944. Ronny cried. She was so hungry. We were all hungry. I told her a beautiful story to hush her to sleep, so she wouldn't feel her empty stomach anymore. Little Paula didn't seem to mind so much.

The Red Cross sent packages with food and medications to the camps, but they never reached us. When Ronny came down with dysentery, the only advice we got was, "Don't give her anything to eat until it is over." She cried big tears, and I just couldn't let her starve, so I gave her the rice. Eating has become so incredibly important. Our ration of rice was so small, yet we sometimes tried to save one little bite. We would pour some water over it to make it expand: a treat for later in the day. We very seldom succeeded however, our stomachs growling even right after a meal.

Our camp leader, Mrs. S., a lawyer, communicated with the Japanese on a daily basis and represented us when there were problems. She had her office on the square together with the office of the Japanese Camp Commander, Takahashi. The head physician of the so-called hospital, assisted by nurses, and a female doctor with a few nurses to assist her, had their offices in the hospital. The hospital consisted of a few adjoining houses with small rooms, in which the beds stood right next to each other for lack of space. Close to the hospital the towering bamboo fence marked the edge of the camp. Orders were to stay at least three feet away from it. Once, when Ronny came within that range while picking some wildflowers for me, a soldier stuck a bayonet through the fence, barely missing her. It scared us both to death.

As was to be expected, our conditions deteriorated quickly because of malnutrition. The little ones weakened even more quickly when they were struck by measles. Paula started with a high temperature, lying on her thin mattress like a sick little puppy. The doctor's diagnosis was measles, and I knew that Ronny would get it too. Had this happened at home, I could have given them fruit juices and other care, but there was nothing, not even milk: only the starch, the rice with soup, and water. They recovered in due time, but I had nothing to help them regain their strength. We had only been in this camp for a short time, but it had already weakened the girls considerably. How long could we go on? The horrible measles did bring us a blessing though: we got a bunkbed. Through the district leader and the doctor, I got one of the few bunkbeds that were available, so the girls didn't have to lie on the floor anymore. How happy I was!

A sign of my own deterioration was that I stopped having my monthly periods. It was a blessing under these circumstances, because they did not supply us with any soap. When our bar was finished, we had only salt to do our laundry. The days went by, one after another, with one main concern: how to stay healthy. It was exactly the opposite of what the Japs had in mind: to weaken us as soon as possible, to withhold medication in case of illness, and to undermine our morale.

We Are Put To Work

A lot of reorganizations took place in the camp. As more groups of women and children came in from different locations, more moves took place. One day I was ordered to move to another house. Since it couldn't be much worse than where we were, we cheerfully said goodbye to the two women and Yvette. Our new domain was a house where the front room was occupied by a mother with several children, among them a girl of seventeen. I cannot remember much about our stay there, except for a few things.

The first event I remember was that a group of Japs came into the camp, looking for seventeen year old girls to work as prostitutes for Japanese soldiers. The mothers of these girls were desperate. I was grateful that my girls were only three and five! The mother in my house didn't waste any time. She put her daughter to bed and made her drink a concoction of herbs. The girl developed a hacking cough and looked flushed. When the Japs came to look at her, the worried mother indicated to them that they shouldn't come close because her daughter had a contagious disease. Since their goal was "the more dead the better," the Japs didn't treat diseases anymore, so they quickly left the room and the girl was safe. Later on, we heard that a few young women who had been prostitutes before the war had volunteered to save innocent girls from being raped.

The second event I remember was that on one particular day we were called to assemble on the field, where a Jap screamed loudly (they were always screaming) that from that day on we would be considered prisoners of war. Whatever the difference was, it didn't sound too promising. All we could do was wait and see.

We had a roll call every morning at 7:30 a.m., and one at night. We had to stand in front of our homes until the block leader arrived with a Jap, who screamed three commands. The first was, *Kiwotsuke*, which sounded like *djoeskit* and meant you had to stand at attention. The second, *Keirei*, meant you had to make a 90-degree bow, and at *Naore*, which sounded like *nore*, you had to stand up straight again. Then we had to count in Japanese and bow again when the Jap moved on.

After roll call and the mandatory morning exercises on the large field (more later about that), we got our starch breakfast Then we each got a shovel and had to follow a Jap (bayonet on his rifle) to a plot of farmland that had to be plowed for planting. This was hard work for us women, especially in the heat of the tropics. But the guard, sometimes more than one, watched us closely and screamed loudly at anyone who dared take a break to rest. The children were home alone, of course, but there were always women who were too old or too sick for labor in the field, who kept an eye on them.

Figure 18 - Keirei, Bowing for the Japanese
Imagebank WW2 - NIOD

For a short period the children gathered on the ground under a large *Waringin* tree (Banyan), and one of the nuns read to them. The nuns also taught Ronny and the older children cross-stitching on small pieces of material with remnants of yarn. It was a nice way to keep them occupied. It didn't last long. Reading, writing and any other kind of education, however insignificant, were forbidden. The girls were always overjoyed when I came home from work, and so was I.

Figure 19 - 5-year-old Ronny's Cross Stitch

After days of shoveling, the clods of soil, hard as rocks, had to be pulverized, with only our hands as tools. We kneeled or sat sideways trying to break the clods by hitting them against each other, and rubbing the pieces until our fingers bled. We worked as slowly as possible. I remember I was clodding in the shade of a banana tree one Sunday morning. The long leaves over my head were moving in a little breeze, making the sound of sails rustling in the wind. For a moment, eyes closed, I imagined I was sitting in a sailboat on the water in a free world. A little later, working again, I saw a diamond in a nearby patch of grass. It sparkled in all colors of the rainbow as I moved my head. Then I saw more of them, dew drops in the morning sun. Beautiful. I had never noticed them before.

On our way back to camp we always passed an area where the Japs had sown tomatoes. The plants were already starting to bear fruit, and I saw one woman in our group pick a small red tomato and quickly put it in her pocket. The guard caught her, called her names, and hit her with his rifle as hard as he could until she fell. Then he kicked her a few times with his heavy boots, made her give the tomato back and sent her home with us. It was horrifying, yet we knew we could not lift a finger in protest, solely for our own preservation, which was proven to be true later on in one of the other camps. Dejectedly, we walked back to camp.

Hygiene

We hadn't lived long in the second house when a notice came that we had to move again, and many others with us. The reason wasn't clear, but for me this would prove to be the best place of the three, although we only had our bunkbed with one foot of space at one end and two feet at the other. That's where we put the suitcase. Our spot was in the back of a narrow room, about 13 x 8, which already contained two other bunkbeds, one in front of the room's only window.

Figure 20 - Block 6, House 12, our last house in Halmahera
Gift from the late Els van Vliet

Our roommates—Mrs.V, a lawyer's wife, and her three daughters, eight, ten and twelve years old—were nice, pleasant company. Ours was a dark area, but we were outside most of the time anyway. The houses were full to overflowing, with more women and children arriving daily. Our dwelling, actually meant for one family with a couple of children, housed a total of forty people. Because of the overcrowding, our squatting toilet soon became too full and threatened to overflow. That happened to most of the toilets in camp. Shortly thereafter, two rows of squatting toilets were built in the camp along the bamboo fence. They, too, soon threatened to overflow. It became apparent something had to be done.

As usual, when a difficult, nasty, or lengthy job had to be done, the Japs selected a Sunday to tell us. We had to empty the toilets within two days. First, a spot had to be found for disposal of the stinking filth of the many dysentery patients. Instead of going to work in the field, we had to dig a large, deep hole, about 9 x 9 x 9 feet. It was so deep, in fact, that in the end we had to climb down a ladder to continue, and full buckets of dirt were pulled up with a rope. It was torture in the heat, but with so many women, we finished the job in one long day. Then we were to dump the contents of the toilets into the hole. How? That was our problem. The block leaders thought of something: a can that used to contain three pounds of margarine, attached to a stick, could be used as a dipper. Taking turns, we dipped the can into the filth to fill a three-gallon oilcan. The natives used these types of oilcans for many purposes, like carrying water. A piece of wire was stuck through two holes on opposite sides of the can so it could be carried from a pole. I tied a handkerchief over my nose when it was my turn. Together with another woman, one of my young roommates, I had to carry the full can to the hole and empty it. We stuck the bamboo pole through the wire of the full oilcan and lifted it. We had to walk quite a distance to the hole in the ground. The can was heavy and swung back and forth when we walked. Suddenly...crack -

boom! The pole broke and the can bumped on the ground, its contents splashing all around. Both of us leapt to the side and couldn't stop laughing! Luckily, there was no Jap in sight. We cleaned up the filthy mess with water and brooms. There was no soap for us to take a nice bath afterwards.

Figure 21 - Squatting toilets
Imagebank WW2 - NIOD

In another part of the camp an order was issued to tear out an old privet hedge with thick roots. The women had to remove the whole thing, roots and all, without tools, in one day. How they did it I don't know, but we were all becoming very resourceful, and they managed somehow. Later on, in the same area, the shoulder of the road had to be dug up so vegetables could be planted, to be watered with urine, collected from the potties. It was a haven for flies. Not surprisingly, the number of sick people grew rapidly.

The Japs tried to hurt us in ways other than malnutrition, such as unexpectedly making terrifying announcements. One day they issued the command that all twelve-year old boys had to leave the camp. Nobody knew where they would be taken. It was a heartbreaking farewell for both mothers and boys. We all felt enormous empathy for them. They were still so young. Correspondence was impossible. The little boys left with their suitcases; the grieving mothers didn't know whether they would ever see them again.

Once I was asked to come to the Jap's office, and he handed me a typewritten letter, which I had to read standing in front of his desk while he kept watching me. It was a letter from Fokko. For a moment I was on cloud nine. Although I realized it had been heavily censored, the tone wasn't the same I was used to in Fokko's sweet letters. I found no loving words. I didn't know what to think of it. But hearing from him that day meant he was alive. What a blessing! After the war, Fokko showed me the original of the letter as he had written it.

Figure 22 - Kamp Tjideng, Batavia
Imagebank WW2 - NIOD

From Day To Day,
Walking Guard And Searching Houses

Days and weeks went by. We hardly knew the day of the week and were kept ignorant about the course of the war being fought in and around the Pacific. No newspapers, no radio messages, no news at all got through to us. We were completely cut off from the outside world.

Each night I thought, *another day has gone by. Thank God, another day closer to the end of the war. We must already be in the second half, which always goes faster than the first half.* Thoughts like these gave me a little hope. I knew that the Americans were on their way to defeat the Japanese, step by step. Hadn't I heard with my own ears on our forbidden radio in

May of 1942, with a pounding heart, that the Japanese had been defeated during the battle in the Coral Sea? Port Moresby, the Solomon Islands—hearing those names still gives me a joyous feeling. Listening to the radio became too dangerous after that. Spies were everywhere and people who did listen and were caught were decapitated. Therefore, I didn't learn about the capture of Midway by Admiral Nimitz with the American Pacific Navy in June of 1942. Neither did I know that this defeat meant the turning point for the Japanese in their seemingly unstoppable advance, during which one country after another was occupied. Our misery lasted three more years after Midway.

At the most unexpected moments, the Japs would call us to assemble, to listen to some punitive measure, which often affected the whole camp, because somebody had done something wrong. It might be no food. That really hurt, because it included the children. None of us looked well. We had grown thin, and our resistance was low. Every time the little ones had a cold, were coughing or had diarrhea, I held my breath. I couldn't give them any restorative food because there was none. The best times for us were during the rainy season, when long, heavy, tropical rainshowers clattered on the roof and enveloped our little house in sheets of water. We were safe then. No Jap would walk around in the rain announcing some disastrous measure.

One lucky day we all received a little sugar and coffee. To watch those faces at the delight of a teaspoonful of sugar! It didn't mean that we women could make ourselves a cup of coffee, because we didn't have any hot water. Only the women in the kitchen and a few others who had befriended them could put a kettle or a little saucepan on the stove next to the drums. There really wasn't much room, so we couldn't use this method. We had become very inventive, however, and before long the recipe of a real treat spread throughout the camp: *klop klop*. We put a teaspoon of sugar in a cup, added some coffee and a little water, and whipped it with a teaspoon for fifteen minutes to half an hour, until it became fluffy. An unknown delicacy, it was short-lived, because we had received such a small ration. A similar distribution was done one more time.

In the fall of 1944 we received a ration of flour and some yeast, so we could knead dough, put it in a tin and take it to the kitchen. The fires were lit for this specific purpose. All cans were done at the same time. This was an important event, and even though it hadn't risen very well, we were eating bread. There was nothing to put on it, of course, but it was a feast, a wonderful replacement for the sago porridge. Our flour didn't last long and no other distributions followed, but from December on everyone received a small loaf, baked by the kitchen, on her birthday. Ronny got hers on her sixth birthday, December 26, 1944, and to her it was just as delicious as the most wonderful birthday cake with candles. I got one for my birthday in January 1945. Those were the highlights of our meager existence.

At 8 a.m. we had daily mandatory exercises on the field. We were not exactly in the best physical condition, and they were excruciatingly painful for many elderly women and nuns. Trying not to participate was useless; the Japs walked in between the rows, always ready to deal blows with their clubs or rifle butts. First a Jap, and later a young girl on a raised platform, showed us how to do the exercises. We always had to count out loud in Japanese, which sounded like: *it - ni - san - si - go - rok - sid - hat.* At the same time, we had to sing a song, sounding like:

Otoroe, asahino, ikaribo abidé
Makeo, no waseo, warira, kaka ina,
Radio wasaki boe,
It, ni, san.

182

Figure 23 - Enclosure of sleeping Barracks in Kamp Banjoe Biroe
Imagebank WW2 - NIOD

Eventually, the exercises and singing were discontinued, either because of the rainy season or the growing number of patients.

At 9 p.m. all the lights in the camp had to be off, not that there were many lights. We in our little corner were mostly in the dark anyway. In our room we had one bulb hanging from a wire in the middle of the ceiling. We were happy to go to bed at 9, because sleep was a blessing, a state of being during which we could forget all our misery and didn't feel our empty stomachs. We were always dead tired from the day's hard labor.

Our nightly rests did not last when the Japs invented "walking guard." The night was divided into three parts: 9 to 12 p.m., 12 to 3 a.m. and 3 to 6 a.m. We took shifts in twos. The people who had the previous shift woke you up. Then you walked guard for three hours with your partner before you turned it over to the next couple. I had a nice partner, a young woman from one of the other houses. We had whispered conversations, very cautiously, because we weren't allowed to whisper, or even to stand still or sit down. This was supposed to be a measure against thieves, totally redundant in an enclosed camp. Japanese guards were sneaking around, and as soon as we saw one, we had to stand at attention, bow, and say our number (we were numbers), our block, and our street in Japanese. If they didn't respond, we bowed again and went on in silence, quite a task with a grumbling stomach! When we had sugar and coffee, a spoonful of *klop klop*, saved during the day, was delicious before going back to bed. I shared the bottom bunk bed with Paula. She was so little and thin that I easily fit beside her. Ronny slept in the top bunk.

They summoned us several times to hand in our money, jewelry and other possessions, like paper, pens and pencils. It was forbidden to own any of these things. I handed over a Japanese lacquered pen Fokko had received as a gift, which he liked very much. I hated it, however, and turned it in with pleasure, together with a cloisonné vase, Japanese art. I hid my good Dutch pen in Paula's doll. I didn't own much jewelry. I covered my gold bracelet with the same material as the belt of a certain dress, so it served as a buckle. I sewed my wedding ring into a pair of panties, which I quickly put on when they came to search our house. They always came unexpectedly. On such days we were ordered to go to the large field. I quickly donned my special underwear and dress, and had my treasures with me. I didn't have any money anymore, but Aunt Rita had once given me a bill of Fl.100 to save or, when needed, to use, and repay her after the war. I didn't hand it in, but folded it, wrapped it in a piece of cellophane. I molded it in some clay from the yard which I let dry, so it looked like a clod of dirt. When we had to assemble at the field, I put the clod under a bush, and they never discovered it. Because they knew that we never handed in everything, they repeatedly searched our houses and suitcases, which we had to open before we left. My large, but inconspicuously black diary was never discovered. Perhaps they always left our corner undisturbed.

And yet, these creatures were so cunningly mean they finally got my money in 1945. During another summons, the Japs announced that if we handed in the rest of our money there would be no punishment. They would use the money to bring more vegetables and meat into the camp. Many women and children were dying from malnutrition and disease. With hunger edema in our bodies and a funeral almost every day, I could not keep the money any longer. We were promised better food. I trusted their word, but it proved to be a grave mistake. They got their money, but the food remained the same. The villains!

The Nine Courageous Women

In August of 1944 we received the command that we had to help finish the infamous Japanese army caps. The six holes in the back for stringing laces had to be edged like buttonholes. Everyone received a number of them. I didn't work on the caps because an older woman in our house who could not do hard labor did it for all of us. I worked in the field every day with other women. When I came back, I was grateful for a little rest.

Nine officers' wives, who lived in one of the houses, refused to work on the military uniforms of the Japanese. Refusal? That meant disobedience of their divine Emperor! We were called to the field, not knowing why. When we were all together, we were made to witness something horrible. Several Japanese officers stood on a raised platform, while soldiers forced the nine women up there with clubs. The Camp Commander, Takahashi, started his usual screaming. He was bursting with anger, and his screams didn't sound human. We had to watch the women being clubbed. One elderly lady was hit in the face, and her glasses fell off, shattering on the wooden floor of the platform. When one of them stumbled, they kicked her with their boots. They were all beaten to a pulp. Japanese soldiers and *Heihos* walked among us with clubs raised to make sure we all were watching. They probably thought it set a good example. *Heihos* were young men, former KNIL soldiers (of the Dutch East Indian Army), natives, now employed by the Japs as guards. They were equally cruel, trained as they were in anti-Western ways. After the beating the women were led away, stumbling, to their home. We left too. It wasn't until later that I learned the reason for their punishment. It was only the beginning of their torture.

They were locked up in the front room of their home. Though it had a barred window, as usual in the tropics, the wooden shutters were nailed shut. They were holed up in a stuffy, hot, dark room, without water to wash themselves, without food or water, and without a toilet. To keep them alive, food and some drinking water were shoved through the door once a day, together with a bucket to serve all nine of them as a toilet. They were not granted much rest or sleep. At different times during the day or night they were dragged to the office to be questioned by members of the *Kenpetai*, the infamous Military Police, known for their devilish cruelties committed during interrogations, often executed by native helpers.

Although the women could hardly manage, they had to remain standing during the interrogations. Glowing cigarette butts were extinguished on tender parts of their bodies, needles were stuck underneath their fingernails and wounds were inflicted upon their bodies by electrical currents. After hours of collapsing and then being beaten until they stood up again, they were taken back to their home, only to be summoned again a few hours later. This lasted for several months. It was a heartbreaking sight to watch them come stumbling out of their house, deathly pale. Those who had children knew their children were being taken care of by roommates, but they never got to see them, for they were constantly guarded, and the door of their prison cell stayed shut. Were these women courageous? Maybe they were. But knowing that we were always on the losing end, I purposely, consciously, always behaved unobtrusively in order to live through those years as best as possible. What would our children do if we were half beaten to death? Nevertheless, the conditions and malnutrition were undermining our bodies. That was something we couldn't do anything about. Would my girls and I live to see the end?

The doctors and nurses in the camp took care of the nine women after they were released, giving them whatever medical care they could. At that time we didn't have vitamin pills yet. Although they were vitamins, their composition and their effect on health were still in the developmental stage. I'm sure the Red Cross packages must have contained some. They were probably only handed out to the doctors, who must have had better nutrition too, come to think of it, in order to be able to continue their work. Of the nine women, three died during the following months.

In another camp, a woman slapped a Jap in the face because he hit another woman mercilessly for no reason. That was considered a mortal sin. He kicked and hit her until she was half-dead. Locked up for weeks in a dark room, she was more dead than alive when released. How inspiring it must have been to observe her at that time, when she did what every other woman there would have wanted to do!

A heart-breaking story reached us from yet another camp. Several women were to be punished because they had obtained some fruit through the bamboo fence from the natives in exchange for clothing. The Japs caught them in the act and called all the women in the camp the next morning to witness the punishment. The poor wretches were told to kneel down, and a Jap put a heavy bamboo pole in the crook behind their knees, after which they had to sit back on their heels for hours in the burning sun. Two of the women had dysentery and just had to let it run down for the whole camp and the Japanese guards to see. Hours later, the poor women, totally exhausted, were told to get up and the bamboo poles were pulled away. All of them started screaming in agony, rolling on the ground in unbearable pain. The blood circulation in their legs, interrupted for so long, started up again. It was a way of torturing that did not leave any traces, an extremely cruel punishment, and it was used in many camps.

In November 1944 Paula got ill. She never regained her strength after the measles. Now she had dysentery. Since she was contagious, she couldn't stay in our crowded house but had to go to the hospital. The "hospital" consisted of several adjoining houses, which were quite full already, but Paula was admitted. Every day Ronny and I would spend time with her during the visitation hour. Paula, used to the dark little corner of our camp house, didn't feel very much at home there. By the time the visiting hour was over, she suddenly had to go on her potty. She knew I would help her, and tried to extend our visit that way.

During her stay in the hospital she turned four. We could only celebrate by giving her a small, homemade present, a braided headband. We didn't even have a lump of sugar to give. When we came to see her that day, I saw that the nurse had shaved off all her hair; she was totally bald. What a pitiful sight.

188

The nurse told us Paula was constantly twisting hair around her finger, until she had a bald spot on her head. I had shaved off Paula's hair myself for the same reason one and a half years ago, but I thought the nurse should have consulted me first, and I told her so. She said Paula was a difficult patient. She always wanted to go to Mamma, always cried after I went home. Poor Paula. She was such a sweet little thing, having a very bad time in that small "hospital" full of ill and dying people. Mamma wasn't there to take care of her, Ronny wasn't there either, and we were all she had! Rebuked by the nurse for crying so much, she was very miserable indeed.

The following day I was not allowed to see her. "It will be better for the child and also for the other patients if you don't come today," they told me. I walked home, crying, when I met Jopie Esser, who asked me what was wrong. She offered to visit Paula in my place, and read stories to her and a little boy who was in the same room. That was a great comfort to me. Paula eventually got well and came home again, thinner than ever. I worried about her. She hardly ate anything, yet she had to finish her plate.

New Year's Eve of 1944 arrived and, as I mentioned earlier, the wood for the fires was wet. No fires, no food. It was a bad omen. 1944 ended with hunger. 1945 would begin with hunger. We would learn the meaning of hunger edema.

Clearance Among Old Men

As I had experienced a couple of times, a lot of forced moving took place in the camp. No one knew why. Sometimes groups of women and children arrived from other camps, so our little houses became more and more crowded.

One day after the morning roll call we were told to go to work in another part of the camp. I slipped my feet into my wooden slippers (we frequently went barefoot to save our shoes for Liberation Day) and left, following the others to the paved road leading to a row of houses. When I reached the road, I noticed to my horror that it was covered with wriggling, yellowish-white maggots! I tried not to step on them—just the thought made me sick—and stepped my slippered feet criss-cross from one empty spot to the next all the way to the end of the road. When we arrived at the houses, parts of so-called Singapore beds were piled up everywhere: wide, metal beds, painted white, with bars and crossbars at the four corners for mosquito nets. In the tropics we sleep in a spacious, rectangular tent of netting, a mosquito net, to keep the mosquitoes at bay. The bed parts were old and rusty. Our assignment was to put them together.

Carrying the individual parts inside made us painfully aware that we weren't very fit anymore. We had no tools, and we should have had pliers and screwdrivers, but we had to work with our bare hands. Our job was to put one bed in each room of the recently vacated houses. We soon made a startling discovery: Each time a bed would hit the stone floor it would release a flow of bugs. All the beds were full of them. I had never seen lice before. Some women knew these houses were to be occupied by old men. What a terrible thought that their beds would literally be crawling with lice! At noon we had finished the job and, since there wasn't a Jap in sight, went home.

I was glad to be home. I worried about a sudden swelling of my neck and throat that day. I remembered seeing someone else with a swollen neck; it was called struma. This was the second sign I observed of my physical deterioration, the first being my discontinued menstrual cycle. My swollen neck scared me. I remembered hearing it was from a lack of iodine. We did have salt to wash our clothes, but very little in our food. To add to that, the hard labor in the tropics and drinking less than we did at home caused loss of our fluids through perspiration with not enough replenishment. To my relief, my neck was back to its normal proportions after a few days.

During 1945, we didn't have to work in the fields as much. We didn't know why. Other chores, like assembling those beds, were tiring too, but we didn't have to do those every day.

I could use these free hours very well. I had brought my sewing kit with embroidery thread and a piece of new material to make new smocked dresses for each of the girls for Liberation Day. I had to do it all by hand, of course, so it took a lot of time. At least it gave me an opportunity to be with my girls, and a little bit of rest was so welcome. When I got home after putting together the bug beds, they welcomed me happily as usual. Mamma was home again! Our joy was short lived. I had just stepped inside when the block leader announced that we all had to hurry back to the square. The Jap was furious because we had gone home without permission. On the way back I thought, *what will our punishment be this time? A day without food or standing in the sun for hours?* No, this Jap had invented something else. The hero climbed on a chair (all Japs were short), made us pass by him one by one, and hit us hard on the head with the butt of his rifle. After this punishment, we received permission to go home.

At times when no Japs were in sight and the women in our camp wanted to vent their feelings, we sang a song someone had made up about the Camp Commander. It went like this:

Ride along, Takahashi, ride along!
To the country of the Japs, where you belong!
All the women in this camp
Want to get rid of such a tramp!
Ride along, Takahashi, ride along!

**Figure 24 - Overcrowding in the camps continued after
the Japanese capitulation - Kamp Makasar**
Imagebank WW2 – NIOD

Even humming the melody could bring a smile to our faces
and made us long for the day the words of the song would come
true. We also did other things to boost our morale, to show each
other we had faith that the war would one day come to an end.
Some of us would wear clothes that showed the three colors of
our flag: the red, white and blue. A blue dress, a white belt, and
red shoes for instance, when we still had shoes. Or we would
hang the laundry on the line, blue next to white, next to red.
Those things were secret messages to one another of hope and
faith, which went unnoticed by the Japanese. The women in the
vegetable shift would smile at each other while cleaning carrots.
Orange, the color of Dutch Royalty, made them think of Queen
Wilhelmina, alive and well in Great Britain, who would
certainly be working toward our liberation.

The next morning I heard a noise that sounded like trucks driving by. I went outside and indeed saw trucks, loaded with old men, most of them Caucasian. All were standing up, packed like sardines. Their wispy white hair waving in the chilly early-morning wind, dressed only in thin white shirts, they looked chilled to the bone. They must have been on the road for a long time, transported from another camp. Many of the old men died during the following weeks. It was a feather on the cap of the Jap who had dreamed up this plan, "Job well done! Accelerated death for a great many at the same time!" Although the group grew smaller after a few months, it apparently didn't satisfy the Japs, and the men were put on another transport. We were working on the shoulder of the road. Coincidentally, I was close to one of the houses and saw a truck in the distance loaded with old men. Behind it, several jeeps with Japanese soldiers were lined up. In the last one an officer talked to the doctor, who disappeared into the house. A moment later the doctor re-appeared. Running toward the officer he called, *"Soedah mati!"* (Already dead). He announced it in a satisfied way, with a happy face, as if saying, "That's done and over with." The Jap nodded, and signaled the truck to get moving. I just stood there, trying to visualize what had just happened inside that little house. The group had to leave a dying person. They didn't want to wait, but they didn't want to take him with them either. That's how this old man died: "Hurry up and die, we have to leave." All that was left in the camp after the departure of the old men were the bugs. They spread everywhere, even to our bunk bed.

Hunger Edema, Illness and Death

When the year 1945 started, I thought, *it has been three years since the Japs invaded Java. Surely it can't last another three years before the war is over!* I felt my health diminishing and saw deterioration all around me. More and more people in the crowded houses became ill with dysentery, malaria, and jaundice. Only the worst cases were admitted to the hospital, their beds in the small rooms right next to each other. Paula had recovered, luckily, but she had lost even more weight. I was really worried about her. How much longer? Ronny, who had just turned six, developed round cheeks, too puffy to be natural. To keep her occupied, I taught her the letters of the alphabet, writing and reading. We were not allowed to have paper and pencils, but I had a slate and a slate pencil. She is smart and quickly learned the basics.

One night I discovered my ankles were swollen. Not sure of the cause, I waited until the next morning. They hadn't changed. On the contrary, the swelling was worse. In the weeks that followed the fluids kept creeping up in my legs, which became heavy when I walked. Hunger edema! One of my old neighbors from Soerabaja, who came to visit me at night while I was living alone with the two girls, asked me if I would visit her sister-in-law, who was in the hospital with a severe case of hunger edema. I went the next visiting hour and found Betty with an extremely swollen stomach and legs. The doctor had punctured them several times, releasing a bucketful of fluids each time, but two weeks later her stomach was swollen again. I had heard the fluids are destroying the intestines, and it is fatal when they reach the heart. I talked with Betty for quite a while. I felt so sad and so helpless. She wanted so much to get better, to see her husband again, together with her little four year old daughter, but it was not to be. She died a couple of days later from hunger edema.

Because of the great heat in the tropics, a burial in the Dutch East Indies took place on the same day as the demise if possible. Women had been dying since the beginning, but lately there was at least one funeral every day. Each time, the women who lived on the street of the deceased lined up on both sides of the road that led to the gate to render their last honors. The dead woman was put in a coffin that had a wooden plank for a bottom and a half-cylinder shaped lid made of woven bamboo. The coffin, put on an ox-drawn wagon driven by a native, slowly rolled to the gate, which had just been opened. Shaking, with the *block-block* sound of the large, slowly revolving wheels, it disappeared behind the gate. Upon the approach of the wagon, we were ordered to stand at attention, then bow and then straighten up again. Nobody was allowed to follow the wagon out of the gate. Children saw their mothers, and mothers saw their children, sisters and friends leave in the makeshift coffin without knowing where their bodies were taken. What helpless despair the survivors must have felt! The gate closed again, and we walked back to our little spot, full of sadness. How much longer?

It was not surprising that many women succumbed. The food had become worse. There were no more skins and bones for the soup, only dog meat. I heard later that the few vegetables we received were leftovers from the *pasar*, which closed around noon. Dried out and withered leftovers from the *pasar*, normally discarded, were sent to the camps. Once during that time we received a teaspoonful of liver paste, probably from a Red Cross package that got lost. The camp leaders were given permission to open the cans and distribute a bit of this unknown delicacy to each one of us.

We were not called upon anymore for labor in the fields or exercises, which had become impossible in our worsened conditions. Why? Was something going on or was it simply because they were obviously succeeding in their plan to destroy us all by starvation and disease?

Early 1945
Cocos Islands
Fokko

Toward the end of 1944, Fokko's friend, Jos Vermeulen, returned to Ceylon. He had been stationed on the barren island of Socotra in the Gulf of Aden. Part of the Dutch squadron was based there temporarily to accompany and protect convoys of ships. Jos told Fokko stories about the murderous heat in the tents they lived in. They ate their meals with a mosquito net covering their heads and plates because of the incredible swarms of flies everywhere. China Bay was a relief for Jos. The men lived in wooden barracks, two men to a room. Although Fokko and Jos didn't share a room, they often met between flights and during Fokko's free time. Sometimes they went to Trincomalee to see a movie. They swam and canoed and had long discussions about stars and the universe, in which they were both interested. Fokko had purchased several books in Colombo about stars and planets and how they came into existence, and Jos, being a flyer-navigator, was a good conversationalist.

Early in 1945 the Dutch squadron was given a new destination under utmost secrecy: the Cocos or Keeling Islands. The whole organization was transported to this atoll in the Indian Ocean, halfway between Ceylon and the Dutch East Indies. Fokko was part of the small group that was first flown to Colombo, and then transported to the Islands by a small vessel, together with a group of British male and female performers on their way to entertain the troops on the Cocos Islands. All Fokko's cases of spare parts were sent with him.

Figure 25 - Fokko's tent on the Cocos Islands

On one of the islands an airstrip had been constructed of steel mats. That did not pose much of a problem because the ground, consisting of hard coral, was easily leveled with bulldozers after the coconut trees had been removed. Soon British bomber squadrons arrived and then Dutch Liberators. The famous scouts, built of balsa wood with no other defense than their speed and armed only with photographic equipment, established a new speed record: they flew in twelve and a half hours from England to India. Once in a while Fokko had the opportunity to look at their espionage pictures, some of which were airshots of Soerabaja and the naval base. To his astonishment, all the buildings and grounds looked exactly as he remembered them from three years ago! How could that be? He himself had helped destroy them as part of the scorched-earth-tactics before the Japs invaded. Later he learned that the Japs had constructed new buildings and storage barracks on top of the old foundations.

The planes stationed on the Cocos Islands were to deter Japanese navigation in the Indies as much as possible. That was not too difficult to accomplish, since the Cocos Islands were

197

centrally located in the Indian Ocean between Ceylon and the Indies, and Java was within easy reach of their heavy bombers. Once an air raid warning sounded, but no airplanes were in sight.

The climate on the Cocos Islands was wonderful. A little breeze lowered the tropical temperatures. The only mammals, rats brought in by docking ships, were quite tame and would eat out of your hand. Fokko's tent was erected again, with the cases of airplane parts, to serve as his office. This time, the men had to do it all themselves, Englishmen and Dutch alike. There were no *koelies*. The Dutch had their quarters along the beach, a little ways from the airstrip. They slept on stretchers, three men to a tent. Other tents served as a mess hall and a canteen. They were surrounded by palm trees, growing everywhere along the beach.

A lovely white beach it was, about thirty-five feet wide. The coral reef stretched out to sea for about 150 feet, providing shallow water in which the men could bathe and swim, with care because of the sharp coral. Then a stretch of rocks, half-submerged, marked the enormous drop of the ocean floor to a depth of about three thousand feet. The surf, crashing on the rocks, caused twenty to thirty feet high white-crested waves, and the ocean breeze blew away the foam. It certainly looked like paradise, Fokko thought. If it hadn't been for the war, and for the realization that he was separated from the ones he loved most and didn't even know whether they were still alive, he would have been completely happy with his existence.

To get from his tent to his office, Fokko had to cross the runway, about two hundred feet. Since not much could grow on the coral base of the islands, especially no vegetables, the men lived on canned food. They caught fish as a source of fresh protein, and once in a while, the *Indos* in the group got a few pounds of rice to make fried rice, a feast for all Dutchmen. The British called it pig food and didn't want any part of it. Tankers brought in fresh water, and rations were small. After an ocean bath they each got half a bucketful to rinse off. Clothes were washed in the ocean with a special kind of soap. They always felt damp, but it didn't matter, since they wore few clothes anyway.

There wasn't much entertainment for the men on the Cocos Islands. Fokko missed the classical music programs he had so thoroughly enjoyed both in Colombo and in Trincomalee. There was much work to do. Occasionally heavy rain and thunderstorms at night would make it very difficult to assist Liberators, returning from their mission, in landing safely on the short, narrow runway. Once in a while they showed a movie under the palm trees on the beach, and sometimes a group of actors and actresses came to the islands. Once there was a magician who could do amazing tricks. One night, while two actors were doing a puppet show, a large number of beetles, attracted by the light, appeared and joined in the act. The actors improvised spontaneously and the audience couldn't stop laughing for half an hour. A few months later Gracie Fields came to the Cocos Islands and Fokko couldn't get over the fact that he had seen "the" Gracie Fields, free of charge, during wartime.

One night, in the far distance behind the palm trees, with a flash of light and the sound of an explosion, an airplane plunged into the ocean right after takeoff. Another night, at full moon, Fokko watched a miracle. He saw a rainbow across the sky, not in colors, but in different shades of grey. He had never seen it before, nor had he ever heard about it, and he never saw another one after that. Yet he was sure it was not his imagination, that it was real.

More Illness And Death

Soon after Betty died of hunger edema, a young woman in the house next to ours, who had lived close to us in the camp in Soerabaja, died of *Malaria Tropica*. A dangerous kind of malaria, it is often fatal, even on the outside, regardless of good care and medication, let alone in our situation. She left a little girl, three years old. It was another disease spreading throughout the camp. Many little children died from it after only a day or two. One morning, Annie, one of the women in the house next door, took a concerned look at Tineke, her little five year old, who was sleeping late, as she thought. She came out, screaming, Tineke in her arms, and ran to the hospital. It was too late; nothing could be done any more. Tineke was dead. Oh, I was so grateful I still had my little ones to take care of!

One of the rumors going around was that we would all be put on a transport to the island of Borneo to work in the mines. It was only a rumor, yet the transport from Soerabaja to this prison camp had started as a rumor too. We literally lived a day at a time.

In January, for my 35th birthday, I got a little homemade calendar from the thirteen year old girl in our room. I assume her mother had some paper and pencils for her three daughters. The little calendar was divided into little squares for each day of the month. Every night, with the thought *Thank God, another day has passed*, I crossed out another day.

Something else that spread, other than disease and rumors, was a bed-bug plague. We inherited the bugs from the old men and their Singapore beds. We never had them in any of my previous houses, but now they were bothering everyone. One night, just before we had to turn off the lights, Ronny, who was sitting with her doll on our top bunk, said, "Mamma, there's a bug on my doll, and another one on the mosquito net!" I wanted to put one foot on the bottom bunk as usual to pull myself up to get closer to her but discovered that I couldn't. It was a strange sensation. The fluids in my legs had risen up to my knees and I couldn't climb on the bed anymore. I gave Ronny a rag, and told her to kill the bugs with it as best she could. "The bugs will stink when you kill them Ronny, but it's better than if they would bite you." She was a brave girl, didn't complain, but had a lot of bug bites the following morning.

During the middle of 1945, we lived in a very small world: the world of our bunk bed and our suitcase. We knew nothing about the big world out there. Not too long before, when I was still able to climb on a chair or on the bed, I had noticed something strange in that other world outside the fence. I had climbed on the chair of one of my roommates and could see, across the high fence, at a distance, a flag. I saw the red and the white, but where was the blue of our wonderful Dutch flag? I didn't see it. I thought it was strange, but I didn't know then that this had become the flag of the Independent Republic of Indonesia. The Japs had assisted the Nationalistic Party in getting ready to proclaim the Republic as soon as the Japs would have abandoned the field. But that time hadn't come yet, and none of us in the camp knew anything about the course of the war. Sometimes I thought of the first victories of the Americans at Port Moresby and Guadalcanal. I had heard about them with my own ears, but what had happened after that?

Oh, how much strength it would have given us to live through those last excruciating months if we had only known that the Allied Powers in some areas in the Pacific, and the Americans in others, had driven back the Japanese step by step! If we had known of the capture of the Gilbert Islands in November of 1943, and that the capture of the Marshall Islands in January of 1944 had followed the capture of Midway in 1942. If we had only known that, in November of 1944, Japan was bombed for the first time from the Mariane Islands, and on March 10, 1945 the center of Tokyo was ablaze! If we had known that, on April 1, 1945, Okinawa was captured, unfortunately causing the loss of many young lives, we would have realized why we were left alone more often.

I used the hours at home to work on the girls' dresses and to make a romper for myself out of an almost new robe of Fokko's. It was painstaking work, since I had to do everything by hand. In the meantime, Ronny enjoyed the reading and writing lessons I gave her, and worked with her little pencil on her slate. She wasn't perky anymore. None of the children in camp were. Paula often didn't want to eat, and she was getting weaker and weaker.

Another tragic death, the death of a minister's wife, saddened our little community. According to her roommates, she had given most of her own rations to her three small children, who were always hungry as was everyone else. It wasn't surprising, considering that a day's ration consisted of a ladle of starchy watery porridge twice daily and a flat scoop of rice with a ladle of watery soup with an occasional small piece of vegetable in it. A diet like that was unthinkable for a growing child, and often fatal. Many elderly people, and infants and toddlers, died. The minister's wife paid with her life for her understandable desire to feed her children a little more. She grew weaker and weaker herself and died from malnutrition. In order to stay alive we each had to consume our own portions. And so, for her too, the ox wagon rattled out of the gate, leaving three children behind. Most of the deaths went by unnoticed. By then I didn't get out of our house much—only, together with Ronny, for our trips to the kitchen after the bell and, "Block five, get your food." That was the highlight of the day: food!

May 1945
Cocos Islands
Fokko

One day great news reached Fokko from across the oceans: Europe had been liberated on the fifth of May 1945. The Germans had surrendered. The war was over, at least in Europe. The men celebrated V.E. (Victory in Europe) day with an outburst of joy, remembering their relatives in Holland and England, and hoping for themselves, still in the middle of the war, that the end was in sight. Nobody could predict how much longer the war would last in the Pacific. Fokko immediately wrote a long letter to his parents and his in-laws, who were overjoyed that he was alive. He was unable to tell them anything about the situation in the Dutch East Indies, however, nor about Netty and his little girls.

The weeks and months passed with growing uncertainty and expectations. The Japanese were putting up heavy resistance, but the principal island of the Philippines, Luzon, was recaptured by the Americans in the beginning of March after two months of heavy fighting. Meanwhile, heavy fighting took place as well on one of the Bonin Islands, Iwo Jima, and on the island of Okinawa. The conquest of both islands took much more time than expected, and although it meant the Americans were well on their way toward Japan, it was obvious the end of the war was not yet in sight.

And then, on the 6th of August 1945, a very disconcerting message reached the Cocos Islands. A small but frightful bomb was dropped on Japan and had destroyed the whole city of Hiroshima and killed thousands of people for miles around. The news brought a lot of excitement. Fokko, who had read a lot during the past years about the stars and their nuclear fission, understood immediately that this bomb was so powerful because it had something to do with a similar enormous explosion of energy. The days that followed were filled with expectations and suppositions: what would happen next? The answer came very soon. On the 9th of August a second, similar bomb was dropped on Nagasaki, which six days later resulted in the capitulation of Japan. It was unbelievable but true, and the men on the Cocos Islands celebrated V.J. (Victory in Japan) day on the 15th of August 1945, with a bottle of beer each.

Finally, after another month, it was announced that those who might have survivors in the Dutch East Indies would have priority to leave for Batavia. Fokko was one of the first to leave on a Catalina flown by Jos Vermeulen. He handed his job over to another officer, mainly to finish things up. In due time, all Liberators, stripped of their most important instruments, were shoved into the jungle where they slowly deteriorated: lifeless bodies, quickly overgrown by the living jungle. Soon nothing indicated the buried remnants of the bloody war.

Anxious Days

My little calendar showed that the month of July 1945 was coming to an end. I was constantly worrying about little Paula, who was deteriorating noticeably. After being in the hospital around her fourth birthday for dysentery, she grew thinner by the day. Ronny and I had also grown thinner, but we had the deceptive appearance of still being normal because of the swelling of edema. To my utter grief Ronny was also showing the edemic swelling. Paula, however, was drying out; she had dry edema and became a skeleton, all her bones visible. She couldn't sit up anymore. She lay very still and weak in her corner of the bunk bed and didn't have much life left in her. I had been feeding her for weeks, with the greatest difficulty, because she couldn't eat, yet she had to. It was indescribable torment to feed that unpalatable food one way or another to that extremely weak little creature. After she swallowed some, she would throw it all up again. Her little body didn't want food anymore. I sat there crying and didn't know what to do.

One day my roommate with the three daughters called Nurse van den Borg, the nurse who visited patients with the female doctor or by herself. She arrived while I was trying to feed Paula, surveyed the situation for a moment and said, "Why don't you step aside? I will feed her." Right after swallowing a little, Paula threw it all up. The nurse continued to feed her the vomit. "She must take something," she said. "I'll ask the doctor if we can admit her. We must do something here." She returned the same day with the doctor and arranged for Paula to go to the hospital. I didn't dare carry her, with my heavily swollen knees and legs, afraid to fall, but the nurse didn't hesitate a minute and carried little Paula to the hospital herself.

Managing the hospital was the male doctor whom I had observed one day when he had announced the death of one of the old men to a Japanese officer. It seemed to me at the time that he sounded happy about it, and I had felt a dislike for him instantly. And now I was facing him. He said to me, "Lady, from what I have heard about the case, I can't give you any hope, but I'll see what I can do. Why don't you come back tomorrow morning?" I had to leave everything up to him. Again a human life was hanging from a thread, and again he was involved. As I turned to leave the hospital, I prayed silently, *Dear God, please help!*

It was one o'clock in the tropical afternoon when I walked back to our little spot with a heavy heart. Ronny was waiting for me. We sat down on our bunk bed together, and I told her that she probably wouldn't get her little sister back again. Big tears trickled down her puffy cheeks. I tried to comfort her by saying something I believed myself, that we wouldn't really lose Paula, because we would always treasure her in our hearts. And the doctor might even make her well again. In her prayer, before going to sleep that night, Ronny asked God if Paula could please get well again. I myself couldn't find the words to pray anymore. My whole heart was filled with an agonizing pain, a stifling desperation.

The hours of that day and night crept by with torturing uncertainty. It was still dark when I got up. I dressed quickly and silently so I wouldn't wake anyone and slipped outside barefoot (my wooden slippers were beyond repair). Over my head the night sky was lit with millions of twinkling stars. The silence was almost deafening. Step by step I approached the hospital. Step by step my heavy feet moved automatically across the cool surface of the road. There was the hospital, where I would get the news. Good or bad? In the front everything was dark, but a small beam of light came from the back of the building, so I walked around and stood still, totally enveloped by darkness. On the verandah, the night nurse sat behind a table, writing. A small lamp illuminated her work and nearby surroundings. Dead silence. I can hardly describe what went on inside me. My heart was pounding. I looked at the nurse and thought, *she knows, and I will have to ask her.* It would be kill or cure, yes or no. I had to do it. Now. Softly I asked, "Nurse?"

"Yes?"

"How is Paula doing?"

"Paula? Oh, she is doing fine; she already ate a piece of egg."

"Fine? *Fine?*" *That's what she said, wasn't it?* I walked over to her table and, whispering, she told me what had happened. As a last resort the doctor had injected a large dose of a medicinal saline solution into Paula's tummy. There were two possibilities: either her body would still be able to absorb it, or it wouldn't. It was kill or cure indeed. The liquid was absorbed, she was alive, and miracle of miracles, she ate a piece of egg. I heard later that this was given to emergency cases only, one piece per person. My feelings were indescribable. I was not to come back until the next evening, but I was so happy and so grateful! I looked up at the still-twinkling, starry sky with thanks to God, who had given His blessing from above to that emaciated little body. I went back to Ronny, who was still asleep. When she woke up and climbed down to the bottom bunk, I told her the good news. Again we sat, arms around each other, on the bottom bunk, happy beyond words because God had answered our prayers.

I was very happy that my little one was in the hospital, because she would receive better care there than at home. It wouldn't last long, unfortunately. When I went there again at night (there was no designated visiting hour), I was startled to find her bed outside on the verandah. She was asleep and I didn't wake her, but her nurse said she had cried for Mamma too often. It had disturbed the deadly ill women around her, so they had moved her outside, although the nights were quite chilly. Moreover, I was told she had to go home the next day. That frightened me. "Home" was the dark corner in the bunk bed, with nothing good to eat. We couldn't do anything about it, and the following day Nurse van den Borg carried her home again. She remained on the list of emergency cases, however, and every morning the nurse brought her a cup of milk and promised to bring a spoonful of cooked, ground liver once every three or four weeks.

Paula couldn't sit or stand anymore, and the situation couldn't last long, but we were living life a day at a time. We just existed. I went to the hospital once more to thank the doctor, and to tell him how happy I was. Other than that, we remained inside our house. We had no more field labor, not even a roll call. We were so tired; we frequently just lay on our mattresses. We couldn't have done anymore work anyway. "We" were all the women. Deaths became normal daily events all around us.

On the night of August 22, 1945, I crossed out another day on my little calendar. It would be the last time.

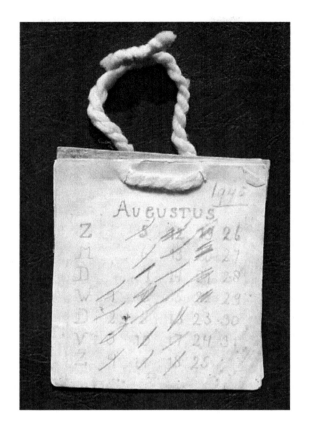

Figure 26 - The final days

August 23, 1945

The next morning, that day of August 23, I took little Paula outside as usual, into the freshness of the early morning, assisted by my elder daughter, whom I liked to call *me hieze Ronnetje*. It was her way of imitating me when I called her *m'n lieve Ronnetje* (my darling little Ronny), when she was still a baby. She was now six years old, but the long years of living in a camp and malnutrition had put their stamp on her and the other children. She, too, showed the signs of edema. Strangely, I'd had a fever off and on during the past week. According to the nurse, these were symptoms of malaria. There was no medication, so I just waited. Maybe it would go away by itself. We spent more and more hours on our bunkbed. However, it was always dark in our back corner of the narrow room. It had only one window, on the other side, because there were two other bunkbeds between that window and ours. So we sat outside as much as possible when it was a little cooler.

Ronny enjoyed helping her very weak little sister to stand between the two of us. Standing on her own two legs had become impossible for Paula; she had grown so weak. We tried to help her take a little step, and another, supporting her all the time. She was not able to sit up by herself either. I didn't know what would make her stronger. The injection in the hospital had saved her life, and now the small cup of milk a day would have to sustain her. We did not look far into the future, and took life a day at a time, and no more. We were a tightly knit trinity. The little ones had only me and I had only them. We were not in very good shape at all as we sat on the porch, Paula between the two of us.

Suddenly, in the distance, I heard a deep, droning sound approaching rapidly. I recognized the sound of an airplane, looked up, and there, flying low over our heads, was a grey

Catalina, a flying boat, a scout like Fokko used to fly in the Naval Air Force. Speechless, with wide-open eyes, I noticed on the wings the familiar round emblem: red, white and blue with the orange center. Was this real? In a split second the thought flashed through my mind: *Could it be the Japs up there? A trick? A captured plane?* Then, in the same second, after the initial total surprise, there was an explosion of excited voices all around us, crying, "That's our navy! Those are our men!" And then a mixture of exclamations, "Could the war be over? Could it be true?" We were afraid to believe it. We just couldn't believe it. It is indescribable what I felt. But there, after having veered to the left, the plane came back again. We waved and cried and then it was gone, leaving us behind with our emotions.

The girls didn't fully understand what all this meant, but they knew it must be very special good news. Their little faces beamed. Then the block leader appeared, telling us that the camp leader, Mrs. S., was summoning all of us to her office *now*. I left the girls where they were and hurried with the other women to the camp leader, who, standing on a barrel, officially announced that Japan had capitulated on August 15. She said, "Let us thank God that the war is over, and let us sing our National Anthem together." With a lump in our throats and tears flooding down our cheeks, we couldn't sing very well, yet our "Wilhelmus" sounded more beautiful than I could remember, with thankfulness and joy, but also sorrow for those who were gone. It was the last evil deed the Japs committed. Oh, how immeasurable was my contempt for them! They left us and the seriously ill ignorant for a whole week, seven long days during which women died without even knowing that the war was over.

Ronny had stayed next to her sister, and when I returned I took both of them into my arms and said, "It is peace. The war is over and our Pappa will come back soon." Ronny had said goodbye to Pappa when she was three and Paula was one year old. They probably could not remember him very well, but the three of us were very, very happy.

There was no immediate change in our situation. The Japs were still around, but we didn't see them often. Something did happen soon. Close to our little houses large holes were made in the *gedèk*, and there were natives on the other side with all kinds of wonderfully delicious merchandise. They had eggs, tomatoes, and oranges. They didn't want money in exchange, which we didn't have anyway, but clothes, which we didn't have much of either, but we did have some things. Even the most threadbare clothes were valuable, since, as we heard later, nowhere on Java was any material or clothing available immediately after Japan's capitulation. For the first time in years I had something nutritious to add to our spoonful of rice. Someone had a little clay barbecue (*anglo*) and some had charcoal, and they let me cook over their fire. We had to be very very careful with the additional food, however, for our intestines were no longer able to digest normal food after years of starvation, as we would find out later on.

Liberation did not mean everyone jubilantly walked out of the camp to go home. Far from it. During those first few days only a few women left the camp because they had lived in or around Semarang. There were some women from Soerabaja who boarded a homebound train with their children. I would have liked that, but couldn't. I couldn't carry little Paula and I didn't feel well at all. The fever had not left me. Besides, we were given orders that nobody was to leave the camp. We soon heard that it was done to protect us. Protect us from whom? From what? A few years ago the Japs had locked us up "to protect us," and now? We didn't know anything about the developments on Java during the war.

212

Figure 27 - Women keeping busy in the camp after Liberation
Imagebank WW2 - NIOD

Apparently, the red and white flag I had seen once to my
astonishment (where was the blue?) had become the official flag
of the newly proclaimed Republik Indonesia. Among the
natives, now called Indonesians, many groups of extremists
wanted revenge after three hundred years of colonial
government. Therefore, we wouldn't be safe outside the camp.
So what happened? The Japs were ordered by the Supreme
Commander of the Allied Forces to protect us inside the camps.
There was a temporary vacuum of authority. We thought the
Dutch authorities would establish themselves again immediately
but, as we heard later, the British prevented that. Not until the
16th of September did the first British warship appear in the
harbor of Batavia. For us everything remained the same those

first few weeks, with the important difference that we knew the war was over. As far as the food was concerned, a few more vegetables and more meat were brought in for the soup.

**Figure 28 – Japanese Soldiers from Formosa standing Guard
after the War**
Imagebank WW2 - NIOD

Some of the women and children who had traveled back to Soerabaja were killed. Intense fighting was going on among extremists and Japs, who had to protect women and children there too. Later, after the British had landed, fights erupted among extremists and Ghurkas. Extremists held up a convoy of trucks with women and children on their way to the harbor to escape and all were cruelly killed with knives and other weapons. We heard about this much later. We could have been among them!

214

One day a military doctor came to our camp to check our physical health. I can still see him standing there by our bunk bed, pronouncing my sentence. I had jaundice and had to be admitted to the hospital immediately. It frightened me: what was to happen to my little ones? Paula had become stronger during those few weeks and could stand now, and even walk, step by step, but how could I leave her alone? Mrs. G, the wonderful lady who lived with us for a while in Soerabaja on Moesistreet, whom the children knew, promised to take care of them, which made me very grateful. All of this happened during the weeks we were liberated, but not free.

Am I in Heaven?

Admittance to the hospital happened in a hurry. I had to get ready right away. Within a couple of hours the ambulance stopped in front of our little house. I could not climb into the car on my own, so I was put on a stretcher and shoved onto the lower ledge inside the ambulance. The last I saw of my little girls, they were standing next to each other, Ronny in tears and Paula with a straight face. Mrs. G, in whom I had total faith, stood behind them. I had no choice. The doors were closed and we drove out of the camp. During the trip a bug fell out of the upper stretcher on top of me. It didn't bother me. I was dead tired and must have fallen asleep immediately because I don't remember anything at all about our arrival at the hospital.

When I opened my eyes I thought, "Am I in Heaven?" Nothing could be more wonderful. I was lying in a real bed with white sheets in front of a large window. When I looked out the window I saw a large garden, bathed in sunlight. Nice nurses, nuns, pampered me, and a doctor prescribed a diet and medication. What could be more wonderful than resting my heavy, swollen legs in that soft white bed, dozing off, and realizing, when I woke up, that I wasn't dreaming! I was in St. Elizabeth Hospital in Semarang. I wondered where my girls were. I soon found out. One of the women from our camp house came to visit and told me they were in a convent. They were not allowed to visit me yet. I had to be patient.

One morning a military doctor came to my bedside, an Englishman, who asked whether I wanted to send a telegram to relatives. Of course I did. The dictated text was, "All well and in British hands," and I signed our three names: "Netty, Ronny, Paula." Some people jokingly said, "All well *but* in British hands." The telegram was sent to my parents. I didn't know anything about Fokko.

Later, I learned that my mother, when she received the telegram, immediately ran out of the house to meet my father on his way home from the office, and seeing him, waving the telegram, cried, "She is alive! She is alive!" It caused great emotion and joy for those two, who hadn't heard anything from us and had worried for years. In five years this was for them our first sign of life. Fokko had been able to reach them earlier, as soon as they were liberated from German occupation, but nobody knew anything about the children and me.

I still felt I was in heaven, and was overjoyed when my little angels finally came to visit, accompanied by the woman who had visited me earlier. They both sat on my bed and kept staring at me. Paula had been ill, and that's why it had taken them a little longer before they could come to visit. I took a good look at my little one. To my great relief she looked stronger already. They had been moved to a school building in Tjandi, the hilly area of Semarang, together with other orphans. The housing was probably better there than in the convent, in which their sleeping area was in an attic, to which they had to climb by means of a wooden ladder. They had to climb up and down that ladder every time, with Ronny helping her little sister. I still consider it a miracle that no accident happened.

I reluctantly let them go again. I had no choice. Tjandi was quite far, but I promised I would visit them as soon as I could. After a few weeks, sufficiently recovered to be moved to the "Eye Patient's Hospital" of the Salvation Army, I was given a bed in the garden pavilion, together with seven other women. I was ambulatory by then, and was allowed one afternoon to get out and go to my girls to tell them some very good news: a navy pilot had brought me a letter from Fokko. It was our first sign of life from him. He was already in Batavia, and wrote that a navy airplane would pick up the children and me very shortly. How happy I was! I got permission to go to the children, but the only way to get there was to get a ride with one of the military vehicles that sometimes went in that direction. I managed to get a ride and arrived at the school with a large lawn in front. After asking for directions a few times, I came to the building where my girls were supposed to be. Someone said, "They are in the bathroom." I walked over there, peeked around the corner and there they were, the sisters! Ronny was soaping Paula's head and then they rinsed off together.

I was so proud of Ronny! How tenderly and lovingly she took care of her little sister! When I stepped inside, I hugged two happy, wet little girls in my arms, then quickly dried them off, dressed them and took them outside. We sat on the lawn. I sat in the middle, with a girl on each side, and read Pappa's letter. I told them the whole story of the pilot who had handed me the letter, and that we would see our Pappa very soon now. Ronny said, "I am going to write Pappa a letter too," for she could read and write short words. I still have that letter. This time we said goodbye happily, because soon now we would all be reunited. That wouldn't happen according to plan, however.

217

In the Salvation Army Hospital the ambulatory patients were allowed to go outside during the day, but had to be in bed at night by nine o'clock. One night a few days after my visit to the girls, we heard loud screaming outside. It was coming closer—alarmingly closer. We sat up straight in our beds and saw, dimly lit by the outside lights, a group of shouting natives wildly gesticulating and running around our pavilion. They were waving *bamboe roentjings,* bamboo sticks with sharply whetted points dipped into a strong poison, over their heads. Stabbed in the stomach with one, their victim would die a very painful death.

We knew that the natives, especially the groups of extremists, freed from the colonial yoke (although it hadn't been all that bad), now considered us their enemies. We weren't safe anymore, and were afraid that while they kept yelling and running around our pavilion, they might at any moment come storming in to kill us all. A thought flashed through my mind: *Will I die here, now? So close to our reunion? And what about the children?* One flash, one brief moment, I was so scared. Then suddenly the yelling stopped.

The door opened and in came the director of the hospital in her white uniform with red epaulets. She said, "Don't be afraid, ladies. I talked to our gardener, who is with them, and they will go away." What a relief. We didn't sleep too soundly, however, because we understood how dangerous the situation was for us all. The fact that the director still had such influence on a group of these brutes proved the gardener was still loyal to her because he had been treated well in her service. We had always been on good terms with our servants. We were the masters and they were the servants, but they were always treated well. Anyway, the director had been able, by her authority, to calm down the wild group of natives for the moment. This time. There was no Dutch government to take charge of the situation.

There was no government at all; it was chaos, dangerous for the Dutch, and I was no longer in Heaven.

Two days later, the patients from the camps were called together and a British officer told us the situation in Semarang had become extremely dangerous for us. We had to be evacuated to Batavia that same day! My first question was, "What about the children?" I was assured that they would be brought to the harbor too. I collected the few possessions I had. We were not allowed to take a suitcase; only very small purses or parcels were allowed. The officer who took us to a waiting truck seemed nervous and in a hurry. His nervousness was not without reason, we heard later, since he knew what had happened in Soerabaja under the same circumstances. We got in quickly. With *Ghurkas*, their rifles ready, in all four corners of the truck, we drove through the city to the harbor at full speed. We were in British hands, protected during that dangerous trip by *Ghurkas*. They were strong fighters from Nepal, dark-skinned, and wearing turbans, who formed a courageous and useful division of the British army. We safely reached the harbor district after our wild drive through town. Not until later did we hear about the bloody massacre in Soerabaja, and only then did we understand the nervousness, the rush, and the fast ride. We could have been stopped and killed by extremists.

At the harbor a large hangar with mattresses on the floor served as our shelter for the night. We would not be leaving until the next day. Going inside, my legs still swollen from edema, I stumbled and fell over a threshold less than an inch high. A nurse treated the wound with a yellow powder, which was new to me: sulfa powder. Evening came and the children had not yet arrived. We all had mosquito nets over our mattresses on the floor and slept soundly, exhausted after the commotion of the day.

The next morning I stood on the lookout for my children, determined not to leave until they arrived. Finally, by noon, a truck full of children appeared. There they were, holding hands; in their other hand their few little possessions. Oh, the joy of seeing each other again! Preparations for departure were in full swing and I sat the girls down for a moment on a suitcase. An Englishman with a camera filmed them: two little war victims.

The ship, with odd-looking flat flaps that opened up, a landing craft, took us to a larger ship lying in the roads. Once on board I knew we were going to Fokko, at last, at last. We met old friends: Jos Vermeulen's wife, her sister and her parents. There was not much room for all of us on the crowded ship, but we were accustomed to hardship and anything was all right now. Dinner, some kind of solid food, was served in green army cans. Unfortunately, our camp stomachs were only used to watery food and none of us could digest these apparent delicacies. Diarrhea and vomiting were the result. Evening passed and morning came. It was the morning of my most important day in years: Batavia, November 27, 1945.

When the War Was Over

September 1945
Batavia
Fokko

Smoothly, the Catalina landed, and the touchdown on the familiar waters of Tandjong Priok, the harbor of Batavia, after three and a half years, was a great moment for the men in the seaplane. In Batavia they were put up in a former school building and slept on stretchers. They all had but one goal: to find out whether their relatives had survived the hardships in the camps and where they were at this moment. The next morning Jos and Fokko began their search together, on foot, trying to find an office where camps and names of interned women and children were registered. The situation in Batavia appeared to be chaotic. There was a vacuum of authority during the first month after the capitulation of Japan.

The Dutch government had not yet restored its authority, because the Dutch East Indies still fell under British military command. However, there was no British authority either until September 16th when the first British warship, *Cumberland*, arrived in the harbor of Batavia with authorities and troops. The Japanese were ordered to stay where they were, to maintain order and protect the people in the camps against groups of young extremists, who, after the proclamation of the *Republik Indonesia Serikat* just one month before, felt free and masters of their own country. They attacked, robbed and murdered Dutch people as well as the Japanese who were protecting them. Therefore, people had to remain in the camps for their own safety.

All this Fokko and Jos learned during the next few days, and what they saw in the streets was just as discouraging. On walls, homes, trams, bridges and viaducts anti-Dutch slogans were painted in big letters. Everywhere they encountered the word *Merdeka* (freedom) in big letters. Everywhere they noticed many red and white flags, the Dutch flag without the blue. They continued their daily search on foot, which was exhausting in the humid heat; talking to everyone they met, exchanging the little news they had. No one had any news about their wives. Employees of a newly established Welfare Organization couldn't give them any valuable information either.

In the meantime, the managing director of the naval base in Soerabaja had arrived in Batavia with his wife and daughter, and tried to assemble his officials. An important canning factory, as well as the building where the managing director and some of the officials were staying, had to be protected while fights were going on in an adjacent *kampong* between extremists and Japanese. More and more extremists, at first armed only with bamboo spears and knives, obtained guns from captured Japanese soldiers. Armed with Brenn-guns, Fokko and a few of his colleagues were assigned to guard these buildings close to the *kampong* day and night. Everyone, regardless of rank, performed different kinds of odd jobs. Return to the base and normal work was still out of the question. A real war seemed to be going on in Soerabaja as well, between groups of extremists and Japanese who had to maintain order. One day the frightening story of the bloody massacre of women and children in trucks, being transported to the harbor from the camps, reached Fokko and Jos, and they cringed at the thought that Netty and Annie could be among the victims. No news at all surfaced about the names of any of the women. Several weeks went by in devastating uncertainty.

October 1945
Batavia
Fokko

In October, Fokko, stationed in one of the local barracks, was given the marvelous job of invoice clerk, a sort of postmaster. He had a car with a chauffeur at his disposal. It was not exactly a limousine, but more like a tank; a vehicle with a hole on top, out of which most of Fokko's body appeared, complete with Brenn-gun at the ready, just to be sure. Every day he made two trips to the post office to pick up the mail, which was handed to him without any questions, and deliver it to the addressees. He and Jos Vermeulen, with a lot of time on their hands, kept looking for their wives. Most Dutch women they saw in the streets seemed to be in the later stages of pregnancy. However, they soon learned that the bulging stomachs were caused by malnutrition.

Everybody there talked to everybody else. One day Fokko met a woman who said, "Your name is Herman? Oh, your wife is fine. She is in the Eye Clinic in Semarang."

"The Eye Clinic? What is she doing in the Eye Clinic?" But it meant she was alive! How happy he was! The woman didn't know Jos's wife or her whereabouts, but she thought he might be able to find out from Netty. Immediately Fokko wrote her a letter, not knowing how to express his joy about this first contact. A pilot whom he knew well, who was to fly to Semarang a couple of days later, took the letter with him and promised to deliver it personally. Fokko went to the authorities on Koningsplein and tried to find out whether he could arrange priority for Netty to join him in Batavia. It was to no avail.

November 27, 1945
Batavia
Fokko

Every morning Fokko first delivered the mail, and then, still in the possession of the car and driver, he went to the harbor because ships arrived there occasionally from Semarang with women and children from the camps. One morning Fokko vaguely recognized a woman on the quay, and she recognized him. It was Jos Vermeulen's sister-in-law, who told him that she had just arrived on this ship and Netty and Annie were on board. He ran up the gangplank and moved quickly through the mob of women and children on the ship, searching for Netty. She was here! She was here! He recognized her the moment he saw her and stood motionless for a second. Then she saw him, too, and after only the slightest hesitation they locked in a tight embrace, overwhelmed with joy and emotion. Two little girls stood by, holding hands, watching this dark-bearded man hugging their mamma. Could this man be Pappa? Fokko squatted next to his two little daughters. How they had grown! To him these were the most emotional moments of the whole war. His little girls! He took them in his arms and lifted them high into the air. Together they went to say goodbye to Netty's friends on board, picked up their few belongings, and went ashore. Fokko sent his car and driver away, and the four of them, together with many others, climbed on a truck that took them to a camp in Batavia: Tjideng.

Netty and the girls were assigned a room in a large house together with other women and children. It was the happiest time of his life, Fokko thought. He got a week of "reunion vacation." It seemed as if they had never been separated, yet there was so much to talk about, so many stories to share. Supplies were abundant. Fokko brought pounds of meat, butter, white bread and sugar. They used the cans, bins and lids Fokko had collected for dishes and cups. For the first time in years they were completely happy. Little Paula was still very weak. Ronny went all out to please him. She was so proud to finally have a real father, whatever he looked like.

Later, when more and more people started to move out and more space became available, they moved from the small 9 by 9 feet room to a real pavilion, consisting of two small bedrooms, a kitchen and a covered porch. Those were glorious days indeed. There was enough to eat and the war was over.

Batavia Harbor
Reunion at Last

We saw a lot of people on the quay when our ship approached. I stayed close to the girls, five and six years old, wearing the dresses I had hand-sewn in the camp and saved for this big day. One and three years old when he left, they were now waiting for a father they couldn't remember. And then, suddenly, among all those people on board, there he was! I will never forget those moments. The greatest joy flashed through my whole being. The next moment I was in his arms and felt his kisses all over my face. Then he turned to his daughters, who curiously stared back at their father. Was this their Pappa? He kneeled down to have a good look at them, and full of emotion, he talked to them. Their little faces and bodies were marked by the past years of hardship. I saw tears in his eyes when he said, "Let's go."

After saying goodbye to my friends, we followed him through the crowd. Trucks waited to take women and children from the ship to a camp, to protect us from possible danger. Here, too, riots endangered our lives, like they did in Semarang, from where we had to be evacuated so suddenly. We climbed on a truck together. Fokko wouldn't let us get out of his sight and sent his driver home. When everyone was seated we left the harbor. During the trip from Tandjong Priok, the harbor area, to the city, Fokko told me that he knew we would be coming from Semarang and had gone to the harbor every day. We kept looking at each other. Three years and nine months of separation had not changed our relationship, and our joy included the children, sitting between Mamma and Pappa. The only obvious change was that Fokko had a dark beard instead of a blond mustache as when he left on March 2, 1942. But he was handsome as ever.

We came back to reality when we approached the city. I saw the red and white flags here and there, and the slogans painted on walls. One of them read, *Nica honden, wij eisen jullie bloed!* (Nica dogs, we demand your blood!) One word was everywhere, *Merdeka (*freedom). When we arrived at Camp Tjideng, many women had already evacuated the camp, so there was room for us now. The girls and I shared a large room with other women and children. We slept on army fieldbeds with khaki mosquito nets. After tucking us in early that night, Fokko went back to his room in the building of the Dutch Squadron, still under the command of the British Commander in Chief. Until the Naval Air Force at the naval base in Soerabaja could be operational again, work had to be done in Batavia. Fokko had the supervision of outgoing and incoming mail.

On the second day, our family was assigned a *goedang*, a small storage room of 9 by 9 feet, and a part of the annex of the big house in which I was placed. A room for the four of us! A palace could not have been more beautiful. We received our meals from the camp kitchen, but they were no comparison to the food the Japanese had given us. Fokko brought the most delicious things: white bread, butter, apricot jam and—oh, how divine—oatmeal! What a feast we had! Slowly the edema fluids disappeared from our legs, showing how skinny they really were. Ronny and I had legs like sticks. Paula, still looking like a skeleton, was gaining weight already! Fokko enjoyed his little girls. Ronny, with a bulging stomach over her skinny legs, did her utmost to please him, showing Pappa she was a big girl. Paula showed her affection in a different way. She looked at him with her big eyes and said at the most unexpected moments, "Pappa is back."

One day a ship arrived from Australia with frozen meat, which was distributed to the camps. All the women received an enormous piece, and in this tropical heat without a refrigerator I thought I'd better prepare it right away. We only had one *anglo*, shared by all the women, so I boiled the meat in a pan I borrowed. An hour later Fokko arrived with a great surprise for us, or so he thought: an enormous piece of meat, which had also been distributed to the men. We laughed about that, and gave it away to the central kitchen.

They served cool drinks at night on a patio on the village square. One night, while we were having a drink on the patio on the square, I noticed a little person in a nightgown walking barefoot among all the tables. It was *me hieze Ronnetje*, who had woken up and missed us. When you just got your Pappa back and Mamma has been the center of your life for years, and they suddenly disappear, you get up from your mattress on the floor to look for them, in the yard, or even in the street, where you hear a lot of voices. And there they were!

We went home with her right away. Pappa lifted his daughter high in the air and put her on his shoulders. A little while later she lay down on her mattress again and fell asleep, a happy child. Paula slept through all the commotion. How thankful I was that I could see her sleeping there, looking better already.

On other nights we sat outside our room together for hours. There was so much we had to tell each other, so much had happened. Once again we lived through night and day together, as we had dreamed. We enjoyed again the last embrace at night, the first cup of tea in the morning, and the knowledge that we were not alone. We lived again. Together. It was such an indescribable feeling to be free from starvation, from persecution, from fear of our fellow men. We were free to eat and sleep, to love and dream. We were free! The four of us were together again! What joy!

Fokko started looking for another place for us to live. He found a furnished pavilion, which is a little guesthouse on the grounds of many large homes in the East Indies. We lived there until Fokko had to go back to Soerabaja to resume his work on the naval base. First, though, he got a week's vacation to be with us. I remember one afternoon. The four of us went to a restaurant on Koningsplein (King's Square) to have ice cream, miracle of miracles! While we were enjoying our treat, there was so much to see. *Dogcars*, bicycles and jeeps, sometimes driven by Sikhs with the most beautiful headdresses, cleverly folded turbans of different colors with a vertical pleated crest. Sikhs were controlling the traffic. Everywhere there were other military men. Suddenly, a loud shot reverberated across the square. We told the girls it was a car tire, but we knew better. During the day as well as at night the extremists continued to fire shots. It was not safe in Batavia.

When Fokko left for Soerabaja, he went alone at first so he could survey the situation and look for a home for us to live in. The girls and I remained in our pavilion. Thank Heaven that didn't last long! After a few weeks I received word that we were to be picked up to fly to Soerabaja in a military airplane. What joy!

End of 1945
Soerabaja
Fokko

Fokko flew to Soerabaja. Still employed by the naval base, he was put to work as a supplies buyer. They needed many items at Morokrembangan, the naval base, and Fokko took a car to town on a daily basis. One day, returning to the base, he watched the landing of a Catalina out of which all his personal crates appeared, heavy loads, judging by the curses uttered by the boys who were unloading them. The ones filled with books in particular would be difficult to handle. Fokko smiled, remembering the wonderful hours he had spent in Colombo, selecting them. He marveled at the thought that all his possessions were shipped after him, first to Trincomalee, then to the Cocos Islands, to Batavia, and now to Soerabaja. Incredible that nothing got lost. He smiled again when he thought of the surprised faces of Netty and the girls when he would give them their presents.

Soerabaja itself had only been recaptured by the British a couple of weeks prior to Fokko's return. The rebels had withdrawn, their scouts hiding in trenches just across the Wonokromo Bridge. Darmo, the area of town where Fokko and Netty had lived before the war, was deserted. Fokko drove around in the afternoons, sometimes with Jos Vermeulen, also stationed in Soerabaja and happily reunited with his wife Annie. Natives had moved into the house on Brouwerstreet during the war. Fokko didn't see any of their belongings. Besides, had he discovered some personal items, he had no right to claim anything. He found a large home on Tjimanoek Street that he liked instantly, with a large yard in the front and back. The only drawback was the continuing noise of grenades dropped on adjacent Wonokromo by the British warships lying off shore, fighting off the extremists. But that wouldn't last forever.

There was no public transportation yet. The men were picked up for work and taken home by military trucks with benches. One of Fokko's colleagues had discovered an old Ford Ten at the dump and had fixed it up so it could drive. When he left for Holland a few weeks later, he offered the car to Fokko. After a fifteen-minute driving lesson, Fokko drove it home through the still disorderly traffic of downtown Soerabaja. Cold sweat covered his forehead and his stomach felt tight, but he made it home safely. A few weeks later he received a military driver's license, and much later the police issued a real driver's license, all without taking a driving test. In his job as a buyer, he drove all kinds of military vehicles, the only ones available at that time.

Soerabaja: A Deserted City

We looked forward to finally go home again after so many years. The girls could hardly wait for the big day. Our best friend, Jos, a pilot with the M.L.D. (Naval Air Force), came to pick us up. He accompanied us to the base and led us to a Catalina, a long-distance scout. We sat in the "blister," a plexiglass dome through which we had a marvelous view of Java below us. In those days they flew at a much lower altitude than they do nowadays. The girls loved their first flight with Uncle Jos. When we arrived at Morokrembangan, we heard to our disappointment that Fokko was in the hospital ward after minor surgery on a dangerous boil, and had to stay there a few more days. Jos took us to the house Fokko had found for us, about fifteen kilometers south of the harbor. During the long ride I saw all the familiar streets and buildings, but hardly any people. The city seemed deserted.

Heavy fighting had taken place only recently, when a British general was murdered. The Ghurkas, the strongest battle unit of the British Army, drove back the extremists, who regrouped outside the city. Jos stopped at the District Office to inform them we had arrived. Before the war there was no such thing as a District Office, but many things had to be organized in this post-war chaos. It was late in the afternoon. It would be dark by six, so they asked me to return the next morning to register. Then Jos took us to the house, which was empty like all the others in the neighborhood. A man from the District Office, a former Marine sergeant, arrived soon thereafter. He asked us to call him "Uncle Ben." Jos said goodbye and left. Uncle Ben told us that the front and back doors couldn't be locked because the locks were broken, but he would take care of that the next day. He said because of the barracks behind our house we could expect to see some *Ghurkas* around. Then he left too.

The house, nice and spacious, with a large front and back yard, had a garage on the left. It was obvious our house was *gerampokt* (plundered). Everything portable had been carried out after the locks had been forced. I looked around while it was still light, and saw it was empty except for a large sideboard and three large wooden beds with mattresses. The girls found a silver hand mirror and a silver salt dish underneath the sideboard. I visualized a nicely furnished home that its owners had to leave behind, after which the extremists stole everything in it. A few crates from the yard could function as a table and chairs, and we ate the sandwiches I had brought. After that, there was nothing to do but go to bed. My suitcase, sent after me—first to the hospital in Semarang, then to Batavia, and now to Soerabaja—would be delivered the next day.

We didn't care about the lack of sheets; we didn't know any better. The children quickly fell asleep. I didn't feel very safe in an unlocked house, even though it was close to *Ghurka* barracks. But the night passed, daylight came, the sun shone brightly, and the locks were fixed. A few days later a *Ghurka* appeared in the front yard. It scared me momentarily. I went outside and said with my most stern look that this was my house and he had to leave at once. Otherwise, I would contact his superiors. He left. Perhaps he thought he could get to his barracks through our yard. When Uncle Ben arrived with a native locksmith, I discovered to my astonishment that his wife was no one other than *Tante* Marie, the helpful sailor's wife from my first little house in Camp Halmahera!

They lived close by, and she came by a little later in the day. It was a very special moment for me to meet her again, in my empty house, free at last. I could only offer her a crate for a chair. Again she came to our rescue. She told us that they were to leave for Holland soon and that we could have their furniture. They had moved into a large house, almost empty, like ours, and had collected some furniture from other homes in the neighborhood. Her husband had told her that a mother with two little girls had moved into 19 *Djalan* Tjimanoek (Tjimanoek Street), after interment in Camp Halmahera in Semarang. She remembered my name and came to see me. We told each other our stories. Mrs. H's husband had returned safely, and they were repatriated together with their daughter Yvette on one of the first ships leaving Batavia. Many more ships were to follow, taking ex-internees and their families and ex-prisoners of war back to Holland.

She also told me that the *pasar* at Kepoetran, about three kilometers in the direction of the city, had just re-opened. After everybody had fled to the *dessa*, the *pasars* remained empty. Now several natives had come back with their merchandise, vegetables, fruit, meat and eggs. We received rice and other rations from the District Office, and when, to our great joy,

Fokko came home from the hospital a few days later, he brought several cans of food with him, rations distributed on the naval base.

Neither the electric tram, which used to go through the whole city, nor the steam tram, which went to many places as well, was operational yet. There was no public transportation at all and, as in Semarang, we hitchhiked with military men, often *Sikhs* and *Ghurkas*. Once I was the passenger of an officer in a jeep, who had a hair net around his black beard. Another time I climbed on a truck, and the black-eyed, turbaned *Ghurka* said to me, "You come into my camp." Thank heavens he dropped me at the *pasar* instead. I noticed a lot of merchandise on the *pasar* was obviously stolen from the homes. I collected my dinner china and added a few plates from one merchant, and dishes and glasses from yet another merchant.

In our kitchen I found a stove in working order. One day an old native woman, Marning, arrived at the door and asked if I needed a Kokki. She didn't look very healthy, but when I hesitated she told me she had been to Holland once with her former employer to look after the children. To my astonishment, she remembered the address, Sweelinckstraat in The Hague. When she mentioned a few dishes she could cook that I hadn't thought of in years, I hired her. The next day she brought a Baboe for the laundry, Sima, a very nice woman, and both of them worked for us a long time.

Slowly, a normal life pattern developed again. The District Manager took me to the former camp, the area of town, still fenced, where we used to live, to see whether there was anything left of my belongings in the garage that the girls and I had occupied. There was nothing. He did let me take a few chairs, a table and a few wall decorations. Together with *Tante* Marie's furniture, our house began to look very nice. The homes around us came alive as well. Indonesian doctors and their families moved into the large corner homes. Across the street a *dogcar* appeared once in a while with some furniture. The Chinese, great traders in the East, opened a grocery store and a vegetable store in the neighborhood. Soon an elementary school opened up with a few classrooms, where our girls went for their first education.

I no longer needed to hitchhike to the *pasar*, because Kokki Marning did the errands before she came in the morning, and both the electric tram and the steam tram had started up again. Slowly but surely the city came back to life. A lot of Dutch families had left. We were eligible for a furlough, for a whole year. Normally, we would go on a furlough of six months after six years of work. It was ten years ago since we had left Holland. Therefore, in 1947 it would be our turn to go. Our parents, anxious to see us again and meet their granddaughters for the first time, had to be very patient. It wasn't easy for them, since they heard many people had already returned to Holland. I resumed my correspondence, we sent pictures, and were happy to know that everyone was alive and well.

Life Continues—Another War Ensues

In 1946, volunteers arrived, Marines and soldiers, red-cheeked, obviously straight from Holland. Several young men came to visit us with greetings from their parents and our parents, and we listened to their stories. Some of them brought a friend, or stayed for dinner. They liked being in a home with a family for a change. The so-called 7th December Division, on their way to liberate us from the Japanese and restore order on Java, had not been allowed by the British to land, but was sent to Malakka instead. Finally on Java, the boys had to fight the extremists of the new *Republik Indonesia*. They had to patrol Java, waylaid by snipers and ambushed in unfamiliar territory.

They saw comrades atrociously mutilated, their bodies tied to rafts, floating down the river.

Together with Dutch soldiers and Marines, teams of medical doctors and nurses arrived in Soerabaja. Some of them came to live in our neighborhood, since conveniently, both the Roman Catholic Hospital and the Salvation Army Hospital were just around the corner. A Dutch nurse moved into the pavilion next door. A young couple with a child moved into the house directly across the street from us, and a Dutch physician who soon got married to a rosy-cheeked, red-haired nurse occupied the pavilion across the street.

Tom, the district manager, became our friend. After the capitulation of Japan he immediately left the internment camp in search of his wife, who was pregnant when she was put on a transport, and their little girl Corrie. He returned to Soerabaja and arrived in the midst of heavy fighting between the fierce young extremists and the Japs (later joined by Ghurkas), who had been summoned by the British Commander in Chief to protect the Dutch people in and outside the camps. He did not escape their cruelties. They took him, together with many other Dutchmen, to the building of our Dutch club. They were beaten and tortured. From the clubhouse they had to walk to waiting trucks, bent over, between two rows of extremists, armed with clubs, rifles, spears and knives, who attacked the already injured men. One of them fell. They stabbed him to death. Tom stumbled once but, knowing he was fighting for his life, managed to keep going, thus escaping a cruel and very painful death. They were put in prison, with so many men to a cell that there was no room for them to lie down.

Later on, he learned that his wife had tried desperately to survive for the sake of her little girl and her unborn baby, but had died in the camp before giving birth, leaving behind her little four year old daughter. Corrie had watched her mamma being wheeled out of the camp in an oxcart. Although he found his daughter, the loss of his wife was a heavy blow for Tom. Men, women and children who had survived the death camps, and *Indos*, who had been free during the past years, were interned again; this time, to protect them from the *pemoedas*, young fighters with the war cry, *Merdeka*. They were finally rescued by troops of the British Army. The *pemoedas* were driven out of town, across the Wonokromo Bridge to Wonokromo, on the other side of the *Kali* Soerabaja (Soerabaja River), the southernmost boundary of the city. From Wonokromo inland the Indonesians carried on a guerilla war under the command of *Boeng Tomo* (Brother Tomo).

At home a Baboe took care of little Corrie and a neighbor sewed a few dresses for her. Corrie had her father back and he loved her, of course, but his work kept him busy, and Corrie missed a loving mother. She loved to come to our house to play with Ronny and Paula. Once, when those two were absorbed in a game, she climbed onto my lap and put her arms around my neck. "I wish you were my Mamma."

I held her in my arms and hugged her. That's what she needed so very much. I felt so sorry for that little one. After a while, Tom, appointed manager of the District Office, married a nurse on the Dutch team. Wil, his bride, continued her work in the hospital until she had fulfilled her term. Corrie left for Holland to live with her grandparents.

The time for our furlough approached. We loved making preparations for "going home" after ten years. Our parents had never yet seen the girls. I made nice dresses for them, and from the material Fokko had brought home for me from Colombo, linen and silk, I had several beautiful dressed made by Madame Claire, a well-known French seamstress who had resumed her work in Soerabaja.

Wil, knowing we were looking for someone to housesit for us during our furlough, recommended a Dutch sergeant and a young student-nurse who were planning to get married and needed a home. Our housesitters arrived on the day we left, and the Baboe*s*, Marning and Sima, stayed on to work for them. That was the situation when we went on leave in May of 1947.

To Holland And Back

Many ships had already made the five-week trip during the past one and a half years, transporting many people to the Netherlands. The "Liberty ships" were built in America for England, to replace its many lost ships sunk by the Germans. (Said Winston Churchill, "Give us the tools and we'll finish the job.") America built the ships to carry goods and materials. They always sailed in a convoy, at a slow speed, protected by war ships and aircraft. When Holland was in need of ships to transport its troops to the Dutch East Indies, Liberty ships were used as troop ships after converting their holds into enormous dormitories with triple bunkbeds. Now they were used to transport men, women and children back to Holland. We expected to share a cabin, the normal accommodation on board. That turned out to be different, however. There were still too many applicants on the list. Our ship, *Johan van Oldebarneveldt*, had two- and three-level berths in her holds. The cabins were for the old, weak and sick people and perhaps a few V.I.P.s. Being none of the above, we didn't get a cabin, yet it was a joy to go home. Imagine that moment for the four of us. We boarded the ship and began a journey that would take more than a month. To the girls everything was new and exciting.

After weeks with only the view of the wide ocean, we approached the Red Sea. With Egypt to the left and Saudi Arabia to the right, we headed for Suez, at the entrance of the

Suez Canal. In Suez, those passengers who had been interned were invited to go ashore in Ataqa and report to an official in a large hangar, where, upon showing their registration cards, they were given shoes, clothing and underwear. Fokko went with us. We could choose anything we wanted, free of charge. There were no people in rags, but coming from the tropics and going to Holland where the temperature even in May can drop to the thirties at night, we all could use some warm clothing. We gratefully chose warm underwear, a navy blue coat and knit caps for each of the girls, and a coat for me. It was a welfare outreach that we appreciated very much.

From Ataqa through the Gulf of Suez, followed by the Suez Canal, was an interesting part of the journey. At the end of the Canal, in Port Said, it is customary for the ship's captain and crew to change their uniforms from white to navy blue. It meant we were approaching Europe! Needless to say we were anxiously looking forward to getting the first glimpse of Holland, the dunes.

Everyone was on deck, eyes eagerly skimming the horizon. Finally, there it was, our homeland, after ten whole years! We shared our excitement with the girls and showed them the coastline. It was wonderful to approach Hoek of Holland. We saw the green grass, the typical Dutch houses coming closer and closer. Holland! In the Northsea Canal, on our way to the harbor of Amsterdam, a pilot-boat came alongside, looking like a nutshell in comparison to the enormous passenger ship. Someone on the little boat was waving an orange banner. We waved back. I bent over the railing to take a closer look. There was Jan! Our Jan, always "in" for a special performance, waving her banner, dancing up and down from excitement when she recognized me. I looked at Fokko and couldn't hold back the tears. I put my arms around the girls, pointed at the little boat and said, "Look, over there in the boat is *Tante* Jan, Mamma's little sister." These were unforgettable moments. Jan and my sister-in-law, who was with her on the boat, had begged the pilot to take them for the short ride along the big ship, so they would be the first ones to greet us. We looked and waved.

Then there was the pier full of people: our brothers and sisters, waving a flag to welcome us back. From high above on deck I showed them our girls, looking so well now in their nice dresses. A little later, going down the gangway, someone welcomed us with a small basket of ripe cherries from Dutch orchards. Then we set foot ashore. We enjoyed embraces and laughter when Jan and Tini came back from their boat tour through the canal. My brothers had rented a van, which took all of us plus our luggage to Middelburg, where our parents were waiting. There was the familiar house. The front door opened, and there they were, Mother and Father Kees, my parents-in-law, and Mina, Mother's domestic help of thirty-five years, always sharing in the family's sorrows and joys. The first meeting of grandparents and their granddaughters, now seven and nine years old was all too good to be true.

All this was the beginning of a wonderful furlough in Holland. I was back in Middelburg. I treasured the freedom to scan the sky, the fields, the canals; the freedom to walk in the wind along the dyke with my little girls; the ability to look each month at a new full moon without asking, how many more days before the war is over?

A Miraculous Story

We quickly felt at home in the big house in Middelburg. Fokko and I shared the large front room on the second floor with three windows overlooking Londense Kade and the Canal. Ronny and Paula shared the little bedroom right next to it, and enjoyed playing on the four different staircases in the house, a new experience. They went to school and made new friends.

All ex-internees received food stamps on a weekly basis at an office in Middelburg. One day, when Fokko went to get the stamps for us, he was helped by an *Indo*, who said, when he read my name on the camp registration card, "Sir, did you get married to this lady in Middelburg in 1937?"

When Fokko, totally surprised, answered affirmatively, the man said, "Well, in that case I may have your Wedding Bible at home. I'll bring it with me tomorrow." The next day Fokko and I went back to the office and there was our Bible. I couldn't help but think of my grandmother. It was as if she was telling me again, "Do as I do, my child, read one page a day."

The man told the incredible story of the journey our Bible had apparently taken. As soon as the women had left Soerabaja for the camp in Semarang, the Japanese had opened the trunks that were left behind. They took whatever they wanted and sold the rest to the natives. Before the war, native women, mostly from the island of *Madoera*, walked the streets with a basket on their heads, buying and selling almost everything people wanted to get rid of, such as empty bottles, magazines, and used clothing. Javanese women sold meat, vegetables and fruit, which they carried in their baskets in small quantities. Our Bible must have gone from my trunk to the *pasar* and was bought by a *Madoera* woman. One day, an *Indo* lady, Mrs. K, sitting on her front porch, wanted to see what the *Madoera* woman had in her basket and called her over. *Indos*, if they could prove one of their grandparents was a hundred percent native, were allowed to stay outside the camps. Therefore, Mrs. K and her husband, who kept his job, lived "outside." In the woman's basket she found a Bible that had two names inscribed on the first page, and the name of the town of Middelburg. That got her attention. Her brother-in-law had left for Holland before the war, and he had settled in Middelburg with his family. Wondering what had become of the couple who owned this Bible, she bought it. The war went on. When the Japanese capitulated and the Republic of Indonesia became a fact, the large group of Indo-Europeans had a hard time. The extremists of the new Republic looked down upon them as *Belandas* (Europeans), regardless of the fact they had native grandparents, and put many of them in camps for a while. When, after that, they were given the opportunity to go to Holland, and the Dutch government was willing to advance the money for the voyage, the majority of them left, including Mrs. K and her husband. They took our Bible with them and settled down in Middelburg. Mr. K found work in the office distributing food stamps to ex-prisoners of war, and one day he met Fokko and returned our Bible. This was truly God's hand at work, and I thought again of my grandmother, reading her Bible, and my grandfather saying grace at the noontime meal.

Encounters with Jos Fokko

One day, during our furlough in Holland in 1947 at the train station in Dordrecht, when Fokko had to change trains, he walked into Jos Vermeulen once again. They only had a few minutes to talk and took up where they had left off, reaffirming their friendship once more. Eight years later they met again, at the airport in Batavia, when Fokko, Paula and Netty returned from another six months' vacation in Holland. Jos had left the Naval Air Force by that time, and he left the Indies for good shortly afterwards, while Fokko remained there to leave among the last group of Dutch people. They visited each other in Holland occasionally over the years; both changed jobs several times, and discovered during one of their visits that they had both officially retired on May 1, 1976. Miraculous coincidences in the lives of two men....

Figure 29 - Our family in 1947

The Final Years

We had a wonderful furlough in Holland, a very happy reunion with all our family members, friends and acquaintances. The year went by quickly. Unfortunately, we could not travel back together because the ships to Indonesia were still overcrowded. The industry needed people in every branch, and both they whose furlough had come to an end and they who were newly sent had priority over women and children. Therefore, Fokko went ahead, and we followed several months later. This time, we traveled on the old ship *Sibajak*, which had taken Fokko and his group of pilots to the Dutch East Indies in 1937. Again, the girls and I had to sleep in one of the holds with many other women and children. Loekie Vierhout and her three boys were nice company. The children knew each other well since we had lived in the same house at the beginning of the war. Cas, her husband, had survived the camps too, and we celebrated our families' reunions.

Amazingly, we felt like we were going home after our furlough in Holland. Indonesia had become our second native country. It was wonderful to go ashore at the first port of entry, Sabang, and to smell the familiar, fruity scents. In Batavia the ship stayed overnight and we spent the day ashore with cousin Ad Wisse, whom I had visited in the military prison camp in Soerabaja when I was still free. Ad survived by the narrowest of margins, and moved back to Batavia after the war.

Two days later the white building of the harbor office in Soerabaja came in sight. Fokko came on board to welcome us back, and I was happy again.

At first we had to share our home temporarily with the family who occupied it while we were in Holland. They hadn't been able to find another place to live, because there was a shortage of houses. However, that too came to pass. We made our home cozy with things we had brought with us from Holland. The children attended a normal school, and it seemed that things in the city were as they had been before the war.

Outside, the threat of the extremists still existed. Occasional shots were still fired at night. The year of 1949 passed quickly. Queen Wilhelmina had promised the new republic its independence, planning to make it a gradual change. The extremists, however, led by Soekarno, wanted their independence immediately and were ready to fight anyone and anything. Two police actions by our military men had taken place, and discussions had been held between representatives of our government and those of the *Republik Indonesia*, but the transfer of sovereignty did not take place until the end of 1949. The sovereignty of Dutch New Guinea remained a controversial issue for a while, but for us it went by unnoticed.

One day I met Jopie Esser, who was very happy to see me again. She told me that Henk, after some time in hiding, had been interned, too. When entering the military service with the Navy Submarines, he had sworn allegiance to the Dutch Queen. In the camp, at the command of his camp commander he had to pledge allegiance to the Emperor of Japan. He refused. The Jap then prepared to decapitate him. They took him to a field outside the camp, where he had to dig a large, rectangular hole in the ground. They made him kneel at the edge of the hole and told him one more time to pledge allegiance to the Emperor. Again, faithful to his oath, he refused to obey their order. The sword hit the back of his neck as he shouted his last words: "Long live the Queen!" It was a heavy blow.

For a split second he thought, "My head is still there." The Japanese officer must have admired him for his loyalty to the Queen, a loyalty he could understand because of his own blind obedience to his Emperor, and had hit him with the back of the sword. A Japanese officer with human feelings... He spared Henk's life. Henk and Jopie were reunited after the war and returned to Soerabaja.

It slowly but surely became clear that all Dutch government officials would have to leave to make room for the Indonesians. So in 1952, when Fokko was offered a job replacing the president of an Import Company for a year and to stay on as Vice President, he accepted and said goodbye to the Dutch Naval Air Force. He worked in that capacity for six years, our last years in Indonesia.

Farewell, Indies!

In the beginning of 1958 things were not as they used to be. Our situation had changed, which was obvious everywhere. Even our Dutch Club was put under Indonesian management, so no one attended anymore. Street names were changed, and the attitude of the Indonesians, who felt superior now, was downright unpleasant. The Dutch schools were closed, so the girls had left for Holland to continue their studies. At Fokko's company, like everywhere else, young Indonesians were trained to take over the jobs. It became clear that for us, too, the moment to leave was approaching. We started preparations for an auction. We had to sell most of our belongings within a short time, and since everybody else was in the same position, we didn't get good prices. Finally the moment arrived. We had a moving farewell in our front yard. Our neighbor, the Indonesian doctor's wife, cried her heart out. The servants had a difficult time too.

Although the ships were still overly crowded, we had a stroke of good luck. We booked passage on a freighter with passenger accommodations: only twelve passengers and all conveniences. The ship docked at several harbors where it stayed for several days, so we were able to go sightseeing. A few remaining friends came to the harbor to see us off. Then the hawsers were untied, and we watched Soerabaja's white harbor building disappear slowly in the distance. When the very last part of the Indies, Sabang, disappeared from view, I was standing at the railing of our ship. Sabang, the last spot of green, the last emerald in the *Emerald Girdle*, became a mere dot in the blue of the ocean – then it was gone. A lot of feelings went on inside me. We had lived there for twenty-one years. We almost died there. We had experienced highs and lows, and it had become our second native country. Farewell Indies. I turned around and joined the others while our ship steamed its way through the Indian Ocean to a future yet unknown to us.

Author's Note

The misery of all those years is long past, but the events still live on in the minds of many as a recurring nightmare. For some, the psychological consequences are far from over. Bitter feelings of hatred for the Japanese still exist, and understandably so. After more than sixty-five years, the Japanese government still refuses to acknowledge responsibility for the mass atrocities they committed in WW II, much less offer apologies and compensation.

Time does not erase all wounds. Most survivors say that they could forgive, but not forget. For a long time, speaking about the war years in the Dutch East Indies to people in Holland was taboo. They had just survived a war of their own, and were not open to the problems of the masses of people who landed on their soil from the colony.

Many of the repatriates had a difficult time getting settled in the Netherlands after the war and moved on to other countries with warmer climates. Others struggled for years and made the most of it.

Part Two

Rising from the Shadow of the Sun

Autobiography and Memoir of

Ronny Herman de Jong

Life on a Roller Coaster

The bulging skin popped open amidst the smooth feathers. Pappa held the white-and-gray dove upside down so I had access to the opening I had just slit with the scalpel. I scooped a spoonful of undigested slimy seeds out of her gizzard, then another one. Interestingly, there was no blood. It didn't seem to hurt either. Neither one of us could detect a cause for the blockage she seemed to have developed in her digestive tract. After some deliberation, Pappa handed me the large curved needle already threaded with cotton yarn. It was about four inches long. I had to tug hard to get it through the dove's skin back and forth across the gap. *Poor dove*, I thought. I closed the wound and Pappa put the dove inside the pigeon-house, where she would stay for a few days so we could keep an eye on her.

On a Saturday afternoon, just after the sun dropped behind the roof and shaded the back yard, we walked to the chicken coop together. Two of our Australorps had developed some strange growths around their beaks and nostrils. Although Pappa didn't know whether they were malignant, he knew they were contagious, so we had to treat them. A brief chase resulted in a good catch and I sat down on the upside-down feed bucket with one of the affected black beauties in a firm grip turned over on my lap. Her dark legs kicked wildly in the air in protest as Pappa wound a piece of rope around them. Dabbing iodine on the growths on her red face made her screech with pain. *Poor chick*, I thought. It was a quick job, and she ran off in a flurry when we set her free.

From the time I was twelve and still lived in Soerabaja, Pappa involved me in all kinds of medical hands-on tasks. He trained me to become a doctor.

I wanted to be an actress. From the time I was a little girl and we lived in Soerabaja after the war, I performed puppet shows for the children in the neighborhood. In high school I won leading roles in several plays. I wanted to go to acting school. "Acting school?" said Pappa. "Nonsense. As an actress you will have a very uncertain future. You will not have a happy marriage." He was adamant.

I adapted. I lived according to my parents' expectations. My high school education prepared me for Medical School, focusing on math, science and biology. At the end of the second furlough in Holland in 1956, my parents returned to Surabaja with Paula. I stayed behind in The Hague to continue my education. It was not until I graduated high school that I thought about my future as a doctor. The idea all of a sudden terrified me. I didn't want to be a doctor. Acting School was still out of the question. A vocational guidance test showed I would be a good teacher or social worker. "What?" said Pappa. "A teacher or a social worker? Nonsense. They need teachers and social workers, but *you* will be a doctor, and a good one Ronny. Trust me."

But ultimately, the choice was mine. Since I knew next to nothing about the profession of a social worker, I decided to go to college, major in English and take it from there. A Math student, I had no education whatsoever in the ancient languages, Greek and Latin, a prerequisite for Language studies. Undaunted, I took evening classes in Greek and Latin and a secretarial course during the daytime. I also learned to make patterns and sew. After my high school graduation, Pappa gave me an old electric sewing machine he had found in Chinatown in Soerabaja. He had personally sanded all of its 12 x 8 x 12 inches and painted it a soft yellow. It must have been one of the very first electric sewing machines ever, so it needed a transformer. It could only sew forward but it had a light. I worked wonders on that little machine for many years. I still have it.

"Do you want to dance?" The voice belonged to a curly-haired, blue-eyed young man who reached out his hand. After the performance in Amicitia, The Hague, the chairs had been removed and Dixieland music filled the auditorium. We danced and talked all night and I fell head over heels in love. Meindert de Jong happened to live about five blocks from where I lived and he took me home on the back of his bike after the party. It was five in the morning and we were still kissing goodbye outside my front door when the milkman put two bottles of milk on the porch with a sideways glance at us. We parted reluctantly. After college, Meindert had lived in The Hague for just six months, and was drafted a month after we met, starting boot camp in Amsterdam in April 1957. "I want to see you again," he said and left me his radio so he had a reason to come back. We stayed in touch through letters and phone calls, and got engaged in February of 1960.

Figure 30 – Engagement in 1960

"Ronny Herman, Number One." I stood up from the attic floor where two hundred and six freshman students were hunkering down. It was our first roll call of the three-week rush of the sorority V.V.S.L., the *Vereniging van Vrouwelijke Studenten in Leiden* (Organization of Female Students in Leyden), and nobody else volunteered to be first. In 1957, after one year of Greek and Latin studies in The Hague, I started my college education at Leyden University, the oldest University in the Netherlands. Twice a week, at night, I rode my bike from Leyden to The Hague, some fifteen miles each way, for additional Greek and Latin classes. In Leyden, I went through three weeks of initiation. Her Royal Highness, Princess Beatrix Van Oranje Nassau, had enrolled at the university one year before me and was one of the five women serving on the initiation committee. The daughter of Queen Juliana of the Netherlands, she was heiress to the throne. It was very special to be so close to royalty. We took different classes, of course, but we ran into each other at times on the street or at our sorority Clubhouse.

After I passed my State Exams for Latin and Greek in the summer of 1958, I could finally fully engage in college life. I spent a summer as *au pair* with a wonderful family with four children in England to improve my conversational English, and traveled with them to the South of France. Meanwhile, Meindert had left the army as a 1st lieutenant and worked in Amsterdam in the buying department of Holland's most famous department store, The Bijenkorf. He applied for and was accepted in a business exchange program through The Netherlands America Foundation with offices in Amsterdam and New York. Scheduled to leave on January 13, 1961, he would be gone for a year to a year and a half.

In the train on our way to our parents' home for Christmas, we realized the full extent of the situation. "Eighteen months without you will seem like an eternity," I said.

"They only recruit single people. But if we get married, I could just tell them I *had* to bring my wife along since we got married over Christmas."

"You're leaving in three weeks! I need a passport and a ticket, and I'll have to move out of my apartment. Tomorrow it's Christmas. When can we possibly get married?"

"You can store your things in your parents' basement, get your papers and come by boat as soon as you have everything arranged. We'll get married before I leave."

"Really?"

"Of course, Ron! Let's do it!"

Anything was possible. We were jubilant at the prospect of going to the United States together. We knew we could overcome every hurdle. We were in love. Life couldn't be better.

Our parents, when we informed them of our decision, were shocked to say the least. "You need to build a future before you can get married," Meindert's father said with a frown.

"You don't have to do *everything* together," his mother said to me. "Meindert will be back in a year and you can get married then." But with the exuberant confidence of youth, we told them we did not want to compromise. We would get married *now*. We had ten days to make it work. We jumped on a roller coaster.

On Tuesday, December 27, we borrowed his father's car and drove to the south of Holland to get Meindert's birth certificate in the village where he was born. On the 28th, just in time, we posted the announcement of our intended marriage, which had to be posted at least ten working days before the actual wedding, on the bulletin board in City Hall in Nijmegen, my parents' domicile. We found a minister and a charming little ivy-clad church in Beek, a nearby village. I bought yards of white lace and satin, from which Mamma and I, in a week's time, fabricated a lovely wedding dress and a veil. To get white shoes in January in the Netherlands initially posed a problem, but I did find a pair my size in the basement of a shoe store in Arnhem. They had been in the window all summer, so they had lost their purest white sheen, but they would have to do. We sent out invitations, asked four of our friends to be our witnesses and Meindert's two younger sisters to be our flower girls. Our wedding took place on January 10, 1961 at City Hall in Nijmegen, and was blessed right afterwards at the little church in Beek. A lovely reception at a restaurant overlooking the Waal River completed the day. We thanked our parents for all of their efforts and cooperation in spite of their disillusionment at our "irresponsible, wily whim." Our day was perfect. We were free. Life couldn't be better.

Figure 31 – Church in Beek

Figure 32 – Our wedding day, 1961

New York, New York!

January 1961

After a short, two-day honeymoon in Holland, we had a long, year and a half, wonderful and adventurous honeymoon in the United States. We learned many things by trial and error. We rented a small, one-bedroom apartment in Corona, a then-

Italian neighborhood on Long Island. It didn't matter that the black-and-white TV set had no frame. It worked fine without one. Around the corner, an Italian bakery provided fresh bread straight from the oven. Our landlady, Mrs. Beetz, a motherly woman with nine children, was not exactly the right person to ask about birth control, but since I didn't know any other women yet, I did anyway. "Mrs. Beetz," I said one day. "I went to the doctor to ask him about birth control, but he didn't give me anything."

"I know," she said. "The doctor is Catholic. I am using a gadget that you put in, you know?" In my four years of college I had not learned the word *gadget*. Birth control pills had not yet been invented, and at 22, I was not familiar with condoms. Ah, the innocence of youth in those days!

Meindert went through the Executive Training Program at Bloomingdale's on 57th street. Nobody could pronounce his name correctly. It was "Mindert," "Meandert," or "Maynard." Finally one day someone called him "Mike." He has been Mike ever since.

After a couple of months I found out through the Dutch Consulate that the Dutch Cheese Exporters in Rockefeller Center were looking for a bilingual Dutch-English secretary. I fit the bill. My visa was changed to give me a work permit and I became the secretary in the one-man office under Jan Klinkert. My first job! Jan was a wonderful boss. I felt God's hand in all of this. My diverse education had prepared me for this country and this job. Life couldn't be better.

New York is a wonderful place to live, especially when you are young. We went to Broadway and off-Broadway shows. We saw the Rockettes and had whiskey sours in the Rainbow Room. We bought an old Plymouth Station wagon from a friend who was returning to the Netherlands. We camped in the Catskills and went to Washington DC to see the cherry blossoms, the White House and all the monuments. After six months at Bloomingdale's, Mike continued his training at Sears Roebuck on Thirty-Fourth Street for another six months. Through Sears, he found a job in Los Angeles with a Sears' supplier of women's sportswear. In between jobs, we took a month to travel from the east coast to the west coast via Washington DC, New Orleans, Tucson, Phoenix, Flagstaff, and Las Vegas. We had to bypass the Grand Canyon. A sudden snowstorm dropped three feet of snow in front of our motel in Flagstaff and the road to the Grand Canyon was closed to all traffic. Weather in Las Vegas was balmy. Upon entering one of the casinos, we were stopped by a guard, who pointed at me. "I'm sorry Sir, but you have to be twenty-one to get into a casino."

"She's my wife."

"Doesn't matter, she has to be twenty-one." We had to produce my passport to show that I was twenty-three, and we all had a good laugh.

In Highland Park the apartment complex we found, to our delight, had a pool. We easily made new friends and enjoyed the casual outdoor lifestyle that is so unique to southern California. Mike worked for a women's sportswear manufacturer, and I found a job in the Primary Elections with the *Gibson for Assessor Campaign*. On weekends, we explored the National Parks with our newfound friends and barbecued steaks at the Salton Sea. They were glorious, carefree days. Life couldn't be better.

In July of 1962, our honeymoon was coming to an end. We boarded a roller coaster again and drove back to New York in our Plymouth station wagon via the Grand Canyon, Bryce and Zion National Parks, San Francisco, the World's Fair in Seattle, and Yellowstone National Park. We looped from the Black Hills in South Dakota, where we visited Mount Rushmore and

Crazy Horse, to Denver, through Kansas to Chicago, Detroit, and finally New York. We sold our car to a poor Dutch immigrant for $75 and boarded the New Amsterdam to sail back to the Netherlands.

The Rapids

August 1962

A textile company in Enschede, a town in the East of Holland, hired Mike as Managing Director. We rented an apartment in the center of town. The small makeshift kitchen of the one-bedroom apartment doubled as a bathroom. Right of the entry door the toilet had a pull-down chain. On a small table along the left wall stood a double gas burner. Against the wall between the toilet and the table with the gas burner a large bathtub was the focal point of the room. The faucet over the bathtub only provided cold water. Once, and only once, I tried to run a bath. I filled a large pan and a kettle with water and heated the water on the stove. When the water boiled, I emptied both into the bathtub and started the second round of pan and kettle. By the time I emptied those two into the bathtub, the first supply of water had completely cooled. I could not keep up. "How in the world can we take a hot bath in this bathtub?" I asked the landlady. "There is no warm water."

"You are not supposed to," she answered. "You should go to the bathhouse for your showers or baths."

Yes of course. I had always gone to the bathhouse in Leyden because the three-room student apartment I shared with two other girls had only a small sink in the hallway with cold water. It didn't have a kitchen either, and we had a single gas burner on a table in the living room. I went once a week to the local bathhouse, as was the custom in Holland, with a towel, soap, and shampoo. Very few homes had a built-in bathroom with a tub or a shower. But hey, at least every house had a toilet, and that was more than we had in the camps.

As much as possible we continued the lifestyle we had come to love in America. We had orange juice, bacon and eggs for breakfast, a drink before dinner, and pie or ice cream for dessert. Within two weeks, our whole monthly salary was depleted. Whoa! That was a rude awakening. Quickly, we cut down on our expenses and adapted to the Dutch standard of living. That is what life is about anyway, isn't it? Adapt to your environment. Adjust, and be happy with the blessings you have. But we made a vow that one day, after our mandatory two years back-to-our-country-to-spread-the-goodwill were over, we would return to America. Ten years later, we made it happen.

During the ten very happy years in Holland, we started a family. In July of 1963, our daughter Annemieke was born in the local hospital. While Mike was with me in the hospital that night, his bike was stolen from the place where he had parked it and he had to walk home. Annemieke's baby bath was small enough to be filled with warm water from the stove, but the landlady soon became too meddlesome and the apartment too small. We moved to a lovely new two-story home in the suburbs of Enschede. But not for long. In the summer of 1964, Mike's promotion to Managing Director of a daughter company of the company in Enschede, a knitting mill in the south of Holland, made us move to Son, near Eindhoven. Jacqueline, our second daughter, born at home, according to the custom, made her entrance in February of 1966. A Chow-Chow puppy we named Roy completed our family.

In 1970, we landed on a roller coaster once again. Mike was offered the position of President of a manufacturer of children's wear in Tilburg, a city not too far from Son. It was tempting. He accepted. In October of 1971, to my absolute joy, I became pregnant again. At the same time, Mike received an offer from John Fulmer, whom he had worked for in Los Angeles in 1962, to come over and be his production manager. John had started his own company after we left in 1962 and remembered Mike's exceptional qualifications.

We were so excited. This was our chance. We could do it. The time was right. A job was waiting. The fact that Mike's sister and brother-in-law in Kalamazoo had just been sworn-in as U.S. citizens gave us priority in the emigration process. In less than three months our papers, prepared at the Consulate in Rotterdam, were ready. We waited for the birth of the baby. It was a boy. It couldn't be better! Dennis was born on the 5th of June 1972. We sold the house in a matter of weeks and flew to Los Angeles on August 21 with two daughters, a ten-week-old son in a bassinette and a Chow-Chow. Another big adventure awaited us, an adventure together with our family. An adventure that is still ongoing, with new developments every day.

California, Here We Come!

August 1972

In the months preceding our big move, we had contacted a real estate agent in Pasadena, California, where we decided to settle down. She had found us a motel on Colorado Boulevard, on the east side of town. It would be our home base for a month. We discovered a lovely, three-bedroom California ranch style home with a pool overlooking Pasadena and Altadena. At only fifteen hundred square feet, it would serve us for the time being, but we planned to add on as soon as we were settled. At the end of a cul-de-sac, it came with a second lot, which rose steeply behind the house, all the way up to the street above. The lot was virtually inaccessible, but gave us privacy. We closed escrow a month later and gave our home the name Shangri-La.

Figure 33 – Shangri-La

Mike bought a car to go to work at John's company, located in the heart of the garment district in downtown Los Angeles. I needed to get some groceries and said to the motel clerk at the front desk, "I have to go to the supermarket. The dog and the baby are both asleep in our room. I will take the girls, and I'll be back soon."

"Ma'am, that's against the law," she said. "You cannot leave a baby by himself. You need a babysitter."

"Well, I leave him home alone all the time. He will not wake up, I'm sure, and he is too little to get out of the bassinette on his own. He never cries either. Would you please check on him once in a while?" But she did not budge, and I had to go to the store later, with all three kids, on foot, in the mid-day heat.

Our Pasadena friends Fred and Sandy, whom we had met by the pool in our Highland Park apartment in 1962, recommended their pediatrician for our children, so I made an appointment for the following day. I studied the map of Pasadena and saw that his office was only four blocks west on Colorado Blvd. and two blocks south on Sierra Madre, about twenty minutes from our motel. Or so I thought. With little Dennis in the sling against my chest and a girl on each side, I started down Colorado Blvd. We walked and we walked, and there was no end to the first block – and then no end to the second, and the third.... An hour and a half after the appointed time we arrived, hot and thirsty, at the doctor's office.

"I am sorry," I said to the nurse. "We walked here because I thought it was not far. We are immigrants from the Netherlands and the distances there are quite different. My husband has the car to go to work in Los Angeles."

"Well, welcome to Pasadena", she said. "It is a sprawling city indeed. The doctor can check the baby in half an hour. Where is your motel? On Colorado Blvd.? Oh, but then you can take the bus home." And so we did.

That night, I said to Mike, "What an impossible situation! The distances here are immense. I have to take the children everywhere, because the motel owner won't let them stay in the room by themselves. Even if I had my bike, I could not take all three. The schools are starting in a week. I think I need a car too."

So we went car shopping and bought a yellow station wagon. We called it *The Yellow Submarine*. Our "happy car" fit all five of us plus the dog, and we had fun with it for many years.

At the end of September we moved into the house. Our furniture did not arrive until a month later, but we borrowed camping gear from Fred and Sandy. Our first purchase, a television set, we put on the floor in the den. After school, we set the girls down in front of the television to watch children's programs to their heart's content. They quickly learned the English language. So quickly, in fact, that Annemieke, after only six months in fourth grade, won first prize in an essay contest.

Almost immediately after moving in, under my supervision, we added a master bedroom with a bathroom, a guestroom and a laundry room to the house. Our original construction loan had to be enlarged because there was no money left for carpeting, but then we were the proud, albeit poor, owners of a five-bedroom house with a pool and a view. Life couldn't be better.

When Dennis was two years old and potty trained, I had to go to work. We found Annette, a wonderful, caring lady with a two year old girl of her own to take care of Dennis every morning. I answered an ad in the local paper for a part-time secretary with CSC, Computer Sciences Corporation, a contractor of NASA (National Aeronautics and Space Administration) in La Cañada- Flintridge. One requirement for the job, the ability to work with an electric typewriter, posed a problem. I had never used an electric typewriter before, but I needed the job. So I had a salesman at an office supply store explain to me the ins and outs of an electric typewriter. At the interview the next day, I could type a letter, very slowly, but without any mistakes. I got the job. For two years, I worked with the CSC team on the Viking to Mars project in the NASA Space Program. My math education came in handy now and then in editing the engineers' reports.

Acting and Modeling in the greater Los Angeles area

After two years on the job, I could embark on my lifelong dream: acting. A course with John Robert Powers gave me the confidence and contacts for ramp modeling and tea-room modeling in the greater Los Angeles area. Acting classes at Pasadena City College, Cal State LA, and in Beverly Hills led me to getting my first agent, then a better one. A member of AFTRA, the American Federation of Television and Radio Artists and SAG, the Screen Actors Guild, I did print work, won small parts, then lead roles in several plays, and did extra work on television series like *Archie Bunker* and *General Hospital.* Oh joy! Life couldn't be better!

In due time, however, I discovered that I could not do it all. I was spreading myself too thin. My family had to come first. I adjusted. That's what life is all about. Instead of doing plays, which required weeks of evening rehearsals, I went into commercial acting. I could manage a day for an audition, a day for the call back if I was lucky, and a day for the shoot in a studio or on location. It was fun as well. When he was five, Dennis joined me in doing print work and commercials and earned a nice sum of money to start his college education.

The children, bilingual by then, all attended Pasadena Public Schools. In 1982, a deacon at La Cañada Presbyterian Church in charge of supporting fifteen families, I realized that my life had been so full of *Life,* that I would not know how to help people with *Death.* I think there comes a time in life for everyone that he or she starts thinking about his or her own mortality. So, when the opportunity presented itself, I trained to become a Hospice volunteer with Verdugo Hills Hospice.

For six years, I entered the home of a different person for weeks or months at a time until death separated us. It was, for me, an intensely gratifying task. I visited my patients more often than the required one hour per week. I became their friend. I listened to their stories and their family's stories. I comforted them, helped restore broken relationships, and cried at their funerals.

One time, at Rose Hills Mortuary in Whittier, the family and friends of my latest patient had gathered in the funeral parlor to await the arrival of the minister. After waiting for over half an hour, people started to get restless. Several phone calls by the mortician to locate the minister provided no results. "I'm an ordained Presbyterian deacon. I could perform a service for your Mom," I said to the anguished daughter.

"Oh, would you do that please?" she said, dabbing her eyes.

"You'd better keep it short and sweet," said her brother nervously.

I really did not intend to give a long sermon on the spur of the moment. At the graveside, after being handed a Bible, I started a brief service with the Lord's Prayer. Again, I felt God's direction in my life. I had learned to listen deeply in my acting classes. It prepared me for the task of listening to my dying patients and their families. Some of my patients lived longer than expected. Saying goodbye to them became more and more difficult. After six years, I could not cope with the losses any more. When a new project presented itself, I left the Hospice Volunteer program.

In 1985, I received Mamma's diary and two years later I began translating it for posterity. Our children could all speak Dutch, but reading it was a different story. In 1989, something exciting happened that changed our lives yet again and put my manuscript on a back burner.

After we celebrated our 25th wedding anniversary with our family of five, Mike and I went to Hawai'i. We visited Maui, Kauai and the Big Island. We loved especially the Big Island. So in 1989, we took Dennis with us and went back for a visit at

Figure 34 - 25th Wedding Anniversary, 1986

Easter. We explored the island, looking at real estate, with the thought in the back of our minds that perhaps in due time, we'd like to retire in Hawai'i. Just north of Hilo, on the rainy side of the Big Island, along a country road in Onomea, a For Sale sign got our attention. When we left the island a week later, we were the proud owners of a beautiful house on five acres, overlooking the Pacific Ocean.

What to do now? Dennis had a year of high school left. Mike still had his job. Retirement seemed a ways off. But we owned a beautiful house in Hawai'i. We rented the house out for a year while we worked out our plans. When Dennis graduated and went to college the following year, Mike resigned from his job as Vice President, C.O.O. of the company and in August of 1990, eighteen years almost to the day after we moved to California, we moved to Hawai'i.

Figure 15 - Hale Kea Akai

Hawai'i No Ka 'Oi

August 1990

The most wonderful years ensued. Every time I saw tourists on our island, I thought, *I live here!* And it filled my heart with joy. Our house in Onomea, one mile from the Hawai'i Tropical Botanical Garden and surrounded by sugar cane fields, overlooked the Pacific Ocean. Onomea, the location of a Japanese homestead in the early days of the sugar industry, wraps around the beautiful Onomea Bay, a cane harbor in those days. The cane was harvested every other year. First, one field at a time, the workers set fire to the cane to burn off the leaves. Instantly, a layer of sticky soot covered our white house and everything in it. A few days later, large sugar cane trucks dug up the cane and hauled it away, working around the clock, rain or shine. And rain it did. Sometimes we got fifteen inches of rain in twenty-four hours. The dirt roads around the house turned into muddy red clay, with parts of sugar cane roots and leaves scattered everywhere. The first year, two hundred and twenty inches of rain turned everything green—our shoes, leather belts, purses, wallets—everything. Mildew grew on the walls; our clothes felt continuously damp and acquired a musty smell. "Is it always going to be like this?" we asked a newfound friend at our first Thanksgiving dinner.

"As long as it does not get green between your toes, you'll be all right," she said with a big grin. Rain, mildew, cockroaches, centipedes and other bugs, and geckoes on the walls were all part of living in rural East Hawai'i. We adapted. We grew to love the rain. Many hours of warm sunshine in between the showers made up for muggy nights and damp, dark days.

Our beautiful white house needed a lot of maintenance in the rainy climate. We derived our water from a spring across the highway. The old, rusty pipes leading to our house and to the four other homes down the road often sprang a leak. The first house on the street, ours was also the first to run out of water. We searched across the property, across the road, along the creek bed up to the highway, sometimes underneath the highway, all the way up to the spring, cutting our way through the dense, tropical jungle, listening for the sound of rushing water. Mike was very good in finding the leaks. He then called Lito, the Philippino servant of the neighbor in the last house down the street, and Lito came with wire, rope, and pieces of wood and tape to fix it. It would hold up for a while and then break again, or the line would spring a leak somewhere else.

The water quality had to be tested at the lab in Hilo on a regular basis. Sometimes, the watered-down manure of the cows in the field across the highway seeped through the wooden trap doors of the spring and polluted the water. At times like that, we had to boil all our drinking water for a while. After a few years, the doors of the spring were replaced with steel trap doors, part of the pipeline was replaced with PVC pipe and we had clear spring water again. We finally understood why the previous owner, when we came to look at the house and asked for a glass of her fresh spring water, offered us a glass of "fresh rainwater" from a bucket on the lawn instead. There must have been a leak in the water line when she was showing the house, so she could not offer fresh tap water from the spring.

We rescued a two-year old Doberman-pincher, which we named Koa, The Fearless One, from the humane society. Another dog, Lani, The Heavenly One, we also rescued, from her owner. We found her on a heavy chain in the carport of a small house in Puna, a district in the southern part of our island. She was advertised in the paper as a Rottweiler, but she was really a mix, a "poi dog," as so many dogs in Hawaii are. She had her tail cut like a Rottweiler's, and she had the Rottweiler character, but she never grew to be over fifty pounds.

Along the bedroom side of the house, meandering around the back, a seasonal stream cascaded along the rocks on its way to the ocean. It took a while before we discovered it because it flowed about ten feet down a steep bank, surrounded by dense tropical rain forest. We found a variety of colorful *Heliconia*, yellow *Calathea* or rattlesnake plants, all kinds of ferns, and a forest of young palm trees in different stages of growth among the boulders in and around the creek. It was fascinating. My vision of making a small sitting area down by the stream where I could retreat with a good book proved to be mainland-naïve. Every time I went down to pick flowers or leaves, thousands of mosquitoes wanted my blood.

Underneath our bedroom window, and in groves farther down the creek, banana trees growing on the slippery slope of the streambed were weighed down with large bunches of apple bananas. Lani and I would drive around the property in our Jeep Cherokee to a place where a banana grove seemed somewhat accessible, armed with a machete. Spotting a tree with yellow bananas, I cut a path through the dense vegetation, slid down the muddy slope, braced myself and, with a few blows, chopped down the banana tree. Inevitably, the whole tree would fall on top of the enormous bunch of bananas, and inevitably, some of the bananas would be crushed. Lani was right there to eat a few, right from the tree. So did I. Apple bananas, the most delicious bananas I ever tasted, are small and slightly tangy. Lani running ahead, I hauled the whole bunch of over a hundred bananas to the car, lifted it inside, and together we drove back to the house. As is customary in Hawai'i, we gave away many bananas. But the supply was always so enormous that I made banana bread, banana muffins, banana-ginger jam, and banana cheesecake, to eat, freeze for later, or give away.

Adjacent to the entrance of the trail to the stream, a *guava* tree grew next to a *lilikoi* vine, and when they were in season, I harvested *guava* and *lilikoi* for jam, *lilikoi* sauce and cheesecake, delectable foods right from our own yard. Eleven white pineapple plants produced the sweetest kind of pineapples in August. From the carport, we looked through a grove of tangerines and grapefruit to a huge *Lichee* tree across the lawn, loaded with fruit every other year. One day, after we had lived in our house for a couple of years, Lani came to the front door with a two-pound avocado in her mouth. She put it on the doormat, waited until we came outside and then ran ahead of us to a part of the property behind the tall fishtail palms, where we found another avocado, already half-eaten. A huge avocado tree towering overhead, loaded with one to three-pound avocados provided us with many delicious, creamy fruit for many years thereafter. A large banyan tree in the corner of the front lawn provided a sleeping place for many birds, and at sundown, if it didn't rain, we often listened to their lullabies. Underneath the banyan, a white sign with blue letters hanging from a heavy chain across two rock pillars displayed the name of our house: *Hale Kea Akai* (White House by the Sea).

When we had adapted to our new environment, I started working on my manuscript again. I befriended Erik Hazelhoff Roelfzema, a famous Dutch war hero, who happened to live on our island. He had written a book about the resistance in Holland during WW II, in which he was active. *Soldier of Orange* even became a movie. And in October 2010, *Soldaat van Oranje, de Musical* premiered in the Netherlands. Erik, I knew, also born in Soerabaja, had also studied at Leyden University, albeit about twenty years before I did. I gave him my manuscript to read. "Erik, I'm looking for a publisher. Would you happen to know someone who would be interested in this story?"

Figure 35 - First Book, 1992

Erik put me in touch with a Dutch-Canadian Publisher in British Columbia, and in 1992, my book appeared in print: *In the Shadow of the Sun*, a true story of life in Japanese concentration camps on Java during WW II, based on my mother's diary.

In Hawai'i, where a large part of the population consists of Japanese Americans, the subject of my book was delicate, to say the least. But with an invitation from a Japanese-American friend, I spoke to the local Rotary clubs and was invited for an interview on the *Television News Hour* in Honolulu. The book was generally well received. It revealed a part of history not many were familiar with. Libraries on all the Hawaiian Islands ordered copies, and teachers discussed the subject in middle schools.

For my parents' fifty-fifth wedding anniversary we took a small suitcase filled with the first one hundred copies of the book to Holland. On the desk in the living room they opened it and burst into surprised exclamations and tears. They had known of course that I was working on a book, but to see the finished product—a real book with their names in it and their story of love and endurance and suffering and survival—was just too much. I love surprises, especially unexpected, heart-warming surprises that touch the soul. My parents became distributors of the book in Holland; it opened a window to the world in their later years. After a television interview about the book just before we returned the United States, they were inundated with calls and letters. People called from all over Holland to talk about the camps, other survivors, and friends who had died. Friends from Soerabaja they had lost touch with called out of the blue and came to visit. It was a real blessing for them, and they loved it.

At Schiphol, Amsterdam's International Airport, before our flight took off, my publisher had arranged an interview for me with Shin'ichi Harada, a Japanese journalist at the London branch of the *Hokkaido Shimbun Press.* Shin'ichi, born in 1951, knew next to nothing about the role his country had played in the Second World War. Japan has methodically destroyed all historic evidence by eliminating periods in history where it played a scandalous and aggressive role. Typically, Japanese school and college textbooks have given only half a dozen or so pages to WW II in its entirety, with phrased and sanitized language officially enforced by the Ministry of Education. Japan is described as the victim of Western aggression, and the atrocities of the war begin and end with Hiroshima and Nagasaki. World-scale atrocities like the rape of Nanking have been reduced to "incidents."

Shin'ichi was shocked. After our interview, he wrote an article about *In the Shadow of the Sun* in the *Hokkaido Shimbun Press* and sent me a copy. I had it translated into English. It had four titles (chapters):

Title 1: *Narrative of a Dutch Woman in an Indonesian Internment Camp*
Title 2: *A Detailed Account of the Japanese Army's Heartlessness*
Title 3: *Many Die in Poor Environment*
Title 4: *Recreated From Her Mother's Diary and From Her Own Memories*

I asked Shin'ichi the meaning of the words of the Japanese song we had to sing in camp Halmahera at roll call every morning. I spelled it phonetically from memory, but it did not make sense to him. "I will ask my father," he said. Several months later, he sent me the words, correctly spelled and interpreted. They are: *Odoru, asahino hikariwo abite, Mageo nobaseyo wareragateasi, Rajio wa sakebu ichi ni san.* I still remember the melody. It was a song about the beauty of the sunrise.

Knowing first-hand now the limited knowledge of the people of Japan about their country's role in WW II, I started to investigate possibilities of a Japanese translation and publication of my book in Japan. Over the course of several years, I corresponded with Father Gerard Salemink, a Dutch Priest living in Kyoto. Father Salemink was most helpful in contacting several Japanese publishers, who were not exactly eager to engage in such a project, based on the virtual impossibility of getting the book marketed. Besides, the astronomical cost of translation, about 3000 yen per page, was something I could not afford. I did not pursue it further but donated a copy to the Osaka International Peace Center and the Ritsumei Daigaku Peace Museum, both specializing in education and promoting peace.

Indonesia Tanah Airku

Back in Hawai'i, I grew restless. For five years, my thoughts had been on Java, in Soerabaja, Semarang, Batavia. I had written about places and experiences from my early years, but they were mainly memories of my parents. I longed to go back to the country of my birth. I wanted to take in the country, the places where I had lived, through the eyes of an adult. I needed to experience everything myself. I felt I had to talk to people, observe their ways, smell and taste their foods again. I wanted to see parts of my island where I had not yet been because the war and the ensuing *Bersiap* had made traveling too dangerous. I wanted to share all these things with Mike, so he would understand where I was coming from. I *had* to go back.

In June of 1992, we made it happen. We planned a trip to Bali, Java and Sumatra. The journey left an indelible impression on me.

From Hawai'i we flew to Tokyo. In our hotel room an invitation was waiting from Minoru Hayasaka, representative of the *Hokkaido Shimbun Press* in the Tokyo office. Minoru, an associate of Shin'ichi Harada, born after the war, like Shin'ichi, was equally ignorant about WW II. He took us on a tour of the town that evening. A sea of umbrellas undulated under bright neon signs as we walked from one restaurant to the next. We washed down sashimi, sushi and Japanese barbeque in three different restaurants with sake, sake and more sake. Yet, in spite of all the hospitality extended by this young man, who was unaware of the crimes committed by his country, I could not keep myself from thinking back to the years of suffering and death in the Japanese death camps.

Figure 36 - Bali

Bali

We landed at Den Pasar airport on the island of Bali at dark. After collecting our luggage we looked for a taxicab to take us to town. Three young men, smoking cigarettes, squatted close to the exit of the baggage area. Like magic, words came to my mind as I walked up to one of them. *"Bisa tulung?"* (Could you help us please?) I asked one of them.

The answer came readily. *"Bisa"* (Yes I can), he said, and helped us take our luggage to a waiting taxi. Along dark roads we drove to our hotel. Everywhere little lights danced in the darkness, like the fireflies in *The Pirates of the Caribbean* in California's Disneyland: oil lamps in the *kampongs* (native shantytowns). Once in a while, delicious smells from a *warung* (eating place) along the side of the road drifted through our open windows.

The next morning, a 7 a.m. telephone call woke us from a deep sleep: Our guide was waiting to show us around. "What guide?" said Mike. "We didn't order a guide, did we?" I could not remember having ordered a guide either, especially not this early on the first day, but after a quick breakfast of fried rice we traversed part of Bali with Amman. The scenery was absolutely beautiful. *Gunung Agung* (Mount Agung), its top shrouded in mist, towering in the background of the terraced *sawahs* (rice fields), looked exactly like a typical Balinese painting. But almost everywhere we went Bali was extremely commercialized and we often felt threatened by the people's attitude. Ignorant tourists the first day, we were taken to tourist attractions we did not really want to see, everyone tried to sell us merchandise we were not interested in, and my attempts to speak the few words I remembered in *Bahasa Indonesia* immediately branded me as Dutch, which was apparently no asset. Pollution was rampant. From the beaches to the mountains, smoke was everywhere. From incense to burnt offerings to the burning of trash, Bali was smoking. In the evening, exploring on our own, we enjoyed a ride around the town in a *dogcar*. The price seemed far too high, so I bargained with the driver. It was my first experience with bargaining in thirty-eight years, but it worked, and was accepted with a smile.

It is only an hour's flight on Merpati Air from Den Pasar, Bali to Soerabaja, Java, but a three-hour delay due to mechanical problems made for a long day. Once on board, Mike couldn't sit down. The plane was obviously made for short people. His long legs didn't fit, and we had to change seats with the people in the front row. They announced the safety precautions in *Bahasa Indonesia*, of which I only understood a few words, and English with such a heavy accent, that I understood just about the same. We each received a small carton box containing a napkin, a cup with fruit juice, a piece of *roti kukus* and two *rissoles*. It was fun to taste these childhood delicacies again.

More and more I began to understand what people around us were saying. I recognized words, and I could translate bits and pieces of an article in the in-flight magazine. The thrill of it! What a fantastic computer is our brain. Slowly but surely, the language I had learned as a child came back. A sign in the bathroom said, *Dilarang Merokok*. I understood *No Smoking*. I was delighted with every new word I recognized.

Back in my seat, during our descent into Soerabaja, I looked through the window at the darkening sky. Huge clouds ballooned over a flat landscape. I could discern patches of water: streams, lakes perhaps? I searched my mind. *Sawahs* (flooded rice fields) of course! Suddenly, tears came to my eyes. My chest filled with an indescribable feeling of joy. It had been so long. This was Java, the island where I was born. Déjàvu, déjàvu. Life couldn't be better.

Soerabaja, Java

A Pilgrimage

Darkness had settled as we landed. A gentle rain, *hoedjan*, diminished our view. Our host, Robert, had patiently waited three hours at the airport, used to the fact that planes were often delayed. He spotted us right away as the *Belandas*, the Dutch couple he was expecting. Robert, an *Indo* our age, was forced to remain in Indonesia with his father, who had assumed the Indonesian nationality at the time Sukarno took over. Driving through different districts of Soerabaja in the dark, Robert mentioned street names, some of them familiar. He took us to a spacious, air-conditioned room on the first floor of his Bed and Breakfast place in *Gubeng*, a neighborhood of Soerabaja I did not know well.

It was late by then, and we were hungry. Across the street we found a little *warung* (eating place) still open for business. The stir-fry, made to order in a huge *wadjan* (wok) over an open fire close to our table tasted delicious. We each had a beer served over ice and knowingly took a chance. Water, and therefore ice cubes, is contaminated in all of Indonesia. But it was very hot and we needed a cool drink. "Perhaps the alcohol will kill the germs," Mike said to me. It probably did, because we had no ill effects the following days.

The next morning when we awoke, a deluge came down in translucent sheets. The *slokans* along the side of the road overflowed and brown water gurgled in every direction. We watched the traffic passing our window at the early hour. Cars and motor scooters, brightly colored *betjaks* and bikers, lifting their feet high as they splashed through deep water, made for a lively picture. Sounds of honking and bells, the laughter of soaking-wet little boys, and the slush-slush of water completed the scene. Everybody seemed in good spirits. The unexpected June rain brought a refreshing change of the summer's heat.

After fried rice for breakfast, we bought a street map of Soerabaja at the corner bookstore and took a *betjak* to Darmo, the neighborhood where I was born and grew up. We sat cramped together in the *betjak*. A plastic sheet covered the opening to protect us from the rain, but prevented us from looking out. The driver, peddling behind us, braved oncoming cars and motorcycles and crossed streets, weaving through throngs of pedestrians to make right turns from the left lane without any hesitation, all the time loudly ringing his bell. It was a death-defying experience. Traffic in Indonesia is still on the left side of the street, which made everything even more confusing for us.

We got out at the corner of *Djalan* Bengawan and *Djalan* Darmo, paid our driver and continued on foot. The one long block to *Djalan* Tjimanoek had no sidewalk. The rain had stopped. We passed large white homes behind huge white fences. A row of trees lined the road and a deep *slokan* separated the street from the fenced homes.

We arrived at the corner house, which used to be Dr. Sutedjo's. Dilapidated and deserted, it now had a high metal fence around it. Full of expectation, I turned the corner. It was a very emotional moment. I was prepared to see my old house in a very run-down condition. Would anyone be home? Would we be asked to come inside? Memories came flooding back. In my mind's eye, I saw the back yard as it was when I left Soerabaja, and the wall adjacent to the fire lane, covered with ivy. Red carpenter ants used to build nests in the large ivy leaves, and we would cut those out and quickly throw them in the chicken coop, where the chickens tore them open and devoured the eggs inside.

The street, lined with shade trees, looked friendly. A grassy berm separated the street from the *slokan*. The street name in white letters on a green background showed the new spelling: Jl. Cimanuk. I had not anticipated what I saw next. I was stunned. For a split second I thought we were in the wrong place. A brand new white building with a red tile roof was partially visible behind a white wall, in which a grey metal gate gave access to an invisible driveway. On the front wall of the house, a large silver colored number 19 clearly showed there could be no mistake. This was *Djalan* Tjimanoek 19. I recognized absolutely nothing. Even the layout of the house seemed different. I climbed on a three-*foot*-high wall across the street to see more of the new house that had taken the place of the home I grew up in. A smaller wooden gate to the left of the metal gate opened momentarily and a man appeared. He looked at us, closed the gate, and then disappeared around the corner of Jl. Bengawan.

The house to the right of number 19 looked like it had been replaced some years ago. A young woman brooming the front porch told us number 19 had been torn down eight months ago. We would probably be welcome to go inside and look around. But what sense was there in looking around inside a new house? I felt immensely sad. I was one year too late. The house across the street, number 18, was still the original house and I was grateful for that. Through the barbed-wire-topped fence I could see three steps leading up to the front porch, surrounded by a low brick wall. The double front door with narrow windows to the left and right was a mirror image of my own old house. To the left, the wall adjacent to the fire lane still stood, and beyond it the higher wall surrounded the William Booth Hospital.

We continued our pilgrimage on foot. It was strange to see all those homes walled in and fenced. It was strange, too, to walk streets without a sidewalk, dodging among the junk piles.

Many of the tall fences and walls were topped with cut glass or rolls of barbed wire, safety precautions against burglars. Dust whirled up almost continually because of the never-ending stream of traffic that engulfed us wherever we went. Cars, *betjaks* and motorcycles zoomed by. Pedestrians were crossing everywhere. In the shade, along the streets and on street corners *betjaks* were parked, some with their owners in them, asleep or just resting. We found that to be the case everywhere else we went on Java, an incredible number of *betjaks* standing idle on street corners, waiting for business.

My old grammar school had been replaced by a two-story building. The recess bell sounded when we arrived, and the now-paved playground filled quickly with youngsters in red and white uniforms, the colors of the flag of the *Republik Indonesia*. When I told a couple of little girls that this used to be my school many years ago, they actually understood me and in no time at all I was surrounded by jumping, yelling kids, waving notebooks, scraps of paper and notepads, pencils and ballpoints for my autograph. A teacher gave me a little peacock and a hobbyhorse made by the students to hang on the wall. She showed me around and took me to the principal. I signed my name in an alumni book, which dated back to 1972. One teacher addressed me in Dutch. They complimented me on my use of the Indonesian language, and I proudly said, with a big smile, that this was the school where I had first learned it.

Figure 37 - Betjaks and a dogcar

We crossed the former Coen Blvd. and came to Brouwerstreet. Nobody really walked in the middle of the day like we did, and we were very hot. Number 2 Brouwerstreet, where I spent the first two years of my life, was no longer there. In its place stood a white three-story house behind a tall fence. On the third-floor balcony someone was hanging laundry. At the end of Brouwerstreet, a friendly young woman in the *warung* next to the entrance of a Chinese temple asked whether we wanted to visit the temple. *"Boekan,"* we said. "But we do want to sit down in the shade and we need something cold to drink. Do you have a beer?" We always asked for beer since we knew the water was contaminated.

"Boekan," she said, but she had iced tea and four bottles of red Fanta. We were so hot; we drank all four bottles of Fanta. Of course they were not cold, so she served them over ice and we took a chance a second time. It was wonderful to sit on the bench in the shade and talk. I was delighted as I remembered more and more words. I jotted some of them down so I wouldn't forget them again. By that time I could actually understand people well and make myself understood, an incredible experience.

Figure 38 – Drinking Fanta in a Warung

Both high schools we visited were partially rebuilt and partially still the way I remembered them. In the hallways, the walls covered with pictures of decorated military men framed openings giving access to the classrooms. The furniture consisted of large, heavy, old-fashioned benches. Over the blackboard in each classroom hung pictures of the president and vice-president of Indonesia.

We took a *betjak* to Musistreet 44, Loekie Vierhout's home before the war. In the beginning of the war, Mamma, my little sister Paula and I occupied her garage for a year before we were put on the transport to the camp in Semarang. The house we saw was a newer, two-story white building, surrounded by a white fence, but the garage was still on the right and I could envision our quarters as they used to be.

Soerabaja was celebrating its 700th birthday with a display of flags in front of City Hall. A large statue showed the fighting shark and crocodile (*Sura 'n Buaya*), from which Soerabaja derives its name. The *kali* (river), its water a dirty brown with all kinds of objects floating in it, was being used for a toilet even as we passed. The whole city was chaotic and dirty. A lack of traffic lights in Soerabaja made traffic unbelievably hectic.

Robert, our host, told us that most of the people I knew, including my piano teacher, had passed away. "Business in Indonesia is for a large percentage in the hands of the Chinese, and Indonesians dominate in government," he said. "Although Indonesia's economy is progressive and regionally important, the problems of widespread corruption, poverty, illiteracy, political instability and regional separatism remain major issues hindering national development. With a population of over 200 million, it is the world's fourth most populous country and most populous Muslim-majority nation."

We continued our pilgrimage the next morning and took a plane to Semarang, where Mamma had known the deepest despair under Japanese oppression and also the greatest joy when victory came at last.

Semarang

The barred doors and windows of our hotel in Semarang made it look like a prison. Our room, which we surely thought to be the cheapest room in the whole place, actually was the best, and came equipped with a window air conditioner, a TV and a small refrigerator. The beds were clean but hard. It felt like I was lying on a *baleh-baleh*. Semarang, warmer and more humid than Soerabaja, had more bikers, but traffic in general was less hectic. Exploring the street scene, both enjoyable and informative, we arrived at the *pasar*. I recognized *mangga, sawu* and *mangistan,* and we tasted them on the spot. Delicious! One type of fruit looked familiar but I could not place it and I asked the vendor, "*Apa namanja itu?*" (What is the name of that fruit?)

"*Srikaya,*" she said. *Srikaya!* Yes, of course, that was it. We had a *srikaya* tree in the front yard in Tjimanoek Street, and I remembered it had sweet, white meat with lots of black seeds. To her amusement, I asked "*Boleh tawar?*" (Is it all right if I bargain?)

"*Boleh.*" (Yes, you may.) The woman wanted 750 *Rupiahs* for a pound. By pretending to walk away and calling prices back and forth, I finally got it for 500 *Rupiahs,* the value of a quarter. It wasn't about the money; it was about the mutual understanding of the sport. She had fun too, and was surprised that a tourist could bargain in her own language. Merchants around us joined in the laughter.

The following day we rented a car and driver and went to Kali Banteng, the cemetery just outside the city, where almost 3000 victims of the war have found their final resting place. Maintained by the *Nederlandse Oorlogsgravenstichting* (the Dutch Foundation of War Graves), it looked very well kept. Rows upon rows of white crosses of different shapes marked

288

the graves of hundreds of men, women and children. Unexpectedly, we came upon the sculpture of a stone coffin in memory of *De Onbekende Vrouw* (The Unknown Woman), 1942-1945. It made a deep impression on us. Toward the back of the cemetery a large statue depicted two women supporting each other, a small child between them. The plaque said: *Hun Geest Heeft Overwonnen* (Their Spirit Was Victorious). On another bronze statue of a skeleton-like little boy, in memory of boys' camps, we read, *Zij waren nog zo jong* (They Were Still So Young).

Moved to tears, with gratitude in my heart for being alive, I thought of Mamma. She endured the suffering and kept us alive for almost four years. I mourned those men, women and children who did not survive, but whose graves with white crosses remind visitors of the cruelties of a horrible war.

Halmaheira

Many people, including my mother, still associate the name Halmaheira with the camp on the outskirts of Semarang where they suffered beyond endurance at the hands of the Japanese. But in fifty years a lot has changed. The original name, Halmahera, had the letter *i* added to it, and Halmaheira today is a district of the city of Semarang. We went there in a *betjak* and drove narrow streets through a *kampong* (native shantytown) until we crossed a river and came to a street bearing the name Jl. Halmaheira.

I tried to evoke a picture in my mind of how it used to be. The river must have been one of the boundaries of the camp, with an entrance gate across the street. On the other side Jl. Halmaheira ended in a busy cross street: the perfect place for another barrier. In the middle of the block, a small village square fingered out into several narrow side streets, called

289

Halmaheira I, II and III. The ramshackle homes, butting up against each other with small front yards, could not have been the same as the small brick homes we were confined to fifty years earlier. The whole neighborhood, full of shade trees, greenery and flowers, looked friendly, and it was difficult to imagine that fifty years ago, Mamma, Paula and I had lived here and walked to the camp kitchen for our daily scoop of rice. Fifty years ago, this was the scene of cruelties of the most inhuman kind, of severe bodily punishments, hunger, starvation, despair, diseases and death.

Figure 39 - Woman in Halmaheira

Figure 40 - Old Woman with Tjaping

In the tropical heat we walked the narrow streets back and forth. I hoped to recognize something Mamma might have told me about. An old woman, *tjaping* on her head, was rummaging through a trash bin. She glanced briefly at us over her shoulder and then resumed her activity. A couple of little boys stared at us and then ran away when Mike took their picture, roaring with laughter. Two homes across the village square were larger than most and I wondered whether those used to be the hospital. The camp kitchen? The Camp Commander's office? But no, that could not be. They looked too new to be over fifty years old. In Halmaheira, time has erased all traces of the bloody past.

Leaving Semarang for Dieng the next morning, we drove south through the hilly area of Tjandi (now Candi) and made a brief stop across the street from the William Booth Hospital where Mamma had been treated for jaundice and *beri-beri* (hunger edema) right after our liberation.

Central and West Java

We drove south to Tjilatjap (now Cilacap), from where Pappa had left with his squadron on the *Tawali* in 1942. It was hard to believe that we were walking along the same beach, standing on the same pier, where Pappa had stood and walked fifty years earlier. We took a boat up the river and sat among local people with all kinds of merchandise, including baskets with live chickens and large, odoriferous *durians*. It was like sitting on a bus. After a couple of stops to let off and take on passengers, our driver picked us up on the other side, and we continued our tour through Java, to include the beautiful ninth-century Buddhist and Hindu temples, Borobudur, and Prambanan. I loved to converse with the people. In general, people evedrywhere were very friendly. The small gifts— pencils, pens, note pads, rulers, strings of beads and bracelets I had brought—proved to be an immense source of joy for everyone involved. In a small village before Tasikmalaja, where we stopped to look at a very colorful display of *tapioca* wafers drying in the sun along the road, I was surrounded in no time at all by children and adults, eager to receive a keepsake from me. I kept telling everyone I was from Soerabaja and was very proud that was really true.

Figure 41 - The Prambanan

Figure 42 - Stupa's of the Borobudur

Figure 43 - Drinks at a Warung

The uplands of Java are the nearest thing on earth to paradise. The beautiful, hilly landscape consists of terraced *sawahs* with *padi* in different stages of growth. I love those *sawahs*, bordered by stately palm trees and clusters of bamboo, separated by narrow dikes used as footpaths. At the higher elevations people were hard at work in tobacco, potato and tea plantations, men and women alike in boots, their *sarongs* hitched up to prevent them from getting wet.

We drove through places whose names I could suddenly recite, in order, from memory. Volcanoes, dormant as well as active, loomed here and there on the horizon. In the cities, we noticed the sharp contrast between neighborhoods with castle-like homes, mostly owned by rich Chinese, next to *kampongs* with unpaved roads and bamboo shacks, occupied by the poorest natives. The great majority of the population is out of work or earns just enough money for one meal a day. There is often no money for food, let alone education. Many people are homeless. How rich in beauty is this country, yet how great her pollution and poverty, and how immense her problem of overpopulation!

Hawai'i My Home

The Island of Hawai'i somewhat resembles parts of Java, where I was born and grew up. Hilo Bay, the old buildings in town, the small villages along the coast, the simple lifestyle, the fruits and flowers, the smells and the climate all contributed to the feeling that I was home. I was *senang.*

Exploring the ocean that surrounded it was the most wonderful part of living on the island. The warm waters of Hawai'i invite whales to return between October and March to spawn. We could often see them playing and spouting from our kitchen window. In the curve formed by the reef at Richardson's Beach Park, a small local black sand beach not yet discovered by tourists, beautiful underwater coral gardens teem with all kinds of colored fish and beautiful anemone, hiding in crevices of the dark lava or swaying in the current. Many of the beaches in Hawai'i are black-sand beaches, fashioned of black lava rock crushed by the waves over centuries.

Figure 44 - Richardson's black sand Beach

When all the Hilo rain became too much for us, we drove to Mauna Kea white sand beach, one of the best beaches on the island, on Kauna'oa Bay. The sand is a perfect crescent shape and extends for almost a quarter mile. A natural lava rock reef provides some protection from the surf. Snorkeling out to sea along the rocks I often spotted a large sea turtle below me, flying like a bird. Looking up, close to the surface, I saw a school of translucent needlefish. Brightly colored parrotfish and an occasional yellow trumpet fish sometimes diverted my attention from what was almost invisible on the ocean floor. There! A sole, a perfect mimicry in the sand, and a school of yellow-stripe goatfish, lying motionless on the bottom amidst the rocks like a ghost fleet-in-waiting. An octopus suddenly camouflaged itself in a jet-black cloud when my shadow hovered overhead.

Figure 45 - Kauna'oa Bay, Mauna Kea Beach

Other times, at Mauna Lani Beach, I swam in the open ocean. Mauna Lani Beach Park, south of Mauna Lani Bay Hotel, is a short fifteen-minute walk away along the ocean, across a grassy area. One day, I decided to swim from the shallow waters in front of the hotel to the Beach Park. Mike would walk along the shore and keep an eye on me. It proved to be a scary adventure for both of us. Beyond the surf and the coral reef, where the water was deep, I swam. I swam and I swam and I swam. I didn't see Mike, and he didn't see me. Distances are deceptive on the water. I thought of the recent shark attacks and imagined the headline in the paper: *Haole Woman Lost Leg in Shark Attack*. Thankfully, I did not see sharks that day. I was greatly relieved when, after about half an hour I rounded a corner and saw the clubhouse in the distance. The only time in my life that I swam faster was when I actually spotted a small shark below me while snorkeling off a boat somewhere in the waters around Tahiti. "It's just a pup," the driver of the boat said. But the nine-*foot* shark pup, in my opinion, could have easily chewed off my foot for lunch.

In 1991, Mamma, Pappa and Paula came to stay with us for a month. It was a journey they never repeated because of the immense distance and their advanced age. "We have a surprise for you, Mamma," I said when we drove to the nearby Hawai'i Tropical Botanical Garden. "You will plant a tree today in the Garden. It is a *Sea Putat*, and it loves the ocean, just like you."

Under supervision of the owners of the Garden, Mamma planted a three-foot slender tree stalk, close to Turtle Bay along the ocean. It was our way to honor her memory and thank her for all she has done for us. At its foot, a turquoise sign states her name, the date, and the name of the tree.

Figure 46 - Mamma plants a Sea Putat

The Hawaiian culture is captivating. The Hawaiian language is again taught in schools. *Kumu Hula* in many *Halau* on every island teach again the ancient art of Hula. "Hula is the language of the heart, and therefore the heartbeat of the Hawaiian people," they say in Hawai'i. The annual *Merrie Monarch Festival* in Hilo, celebrated the week after Easter, honors King Kalakaua, (1836 – 1891) known as the Merrie Monarch. Kalakaua almost single-handedly restored many of the nearly extinct cultural traditions of the Hawaiian people. These included myths and legends, and hula, forbidden by the missionaries for over 70 years. The hula festival draws

298

competing dancers and their musicians as well as spectators from the mainland and all over the world, even from Japan. We immersed ourselves in the Hawaiian culture. I learned to make leis from all kinds of flowers, leaves and seeds. For nine years, I learned to dance *Hula*: "the art of Hawaiian dance expressing all we see, hear, smell, taste, touch and feel" (Maiki Aiu Lake, *Kumu Hula*). One of my dear hula sisters gave me my Hawaiian name: Makalani. I loved to get up and dance wherever live musicians played a song I knew. Life couldn't be better.

Figure 47 - Hula in Hilo, 1995

Exploring Kalaupapa

In 1999, the United Church of Christ organized a weekend retreat in Kalaupapa, on the island of Moloka'i. I decided to participate and flew from Hilo International airport on the Big Island to Kalaupapa in a small plane.

When I arrived at Kalaupapa's little airport, Lon Rycraft, Kalaupapa's Pastor and our host for the weekend, and five of the participants were already there. We all climbed into a ramshackle van, with a side door that could not close anymore, and we surely felt one with nature as the wind blew through the van and the misty rain sprayed us from time to time through the open door. We drove to Kalaupapa town, a short ride through a small, dilapidated industrial center and past the Mormon Church. On our right, an endless stretch of weathered gravesites along a narrow white sand beach bordered the road. Across the bay, steep cliffs towered about 2000 feet above the water, inaccessible except for a narrow mule trail.

Since 1866, Kalaupapa has been a place of exile for people with leprosy or Hansen's disease, as it is officially called today. In 1873, Father Damien, a 33 year old priest from Belgium, came to Kalaupapa and worked among the patients until he himself died of leprosy in 1889 at the settlement in Kalawao. In 1883, Mother Marianne Kopp, and others after her, came to live on the peninsula to care for the patients. By 1900, a decline in the number of leprosy cases was evident. Strict isolation finally seemed to have worked and a newly developed drug, Dapsone or DDS, made it possible to "cure" leprosy. By 1940, the number of cases was down from 1,213 at its peak to 350.

Two stone pillars marked the entrance to a cluster of three buildings: Kana'ana Hou Church, the fellowship hall, and the parsonage. Kana'ana Hou Church was a Hawaiian church until the last original residents of Kalaupapa left and the settlement of patients moved from the original site at Kalawao to the Kalaupapa side of the peninsula in the 1920s. As we entered the fellowship hall, two participants, Pastor Dean and Pat Brown, came hiking down the trail from topside, as locals call upper Moloka'i. The two-and-one-half-hour hike had been strenuous, especially in slippers, the customary footwear for Hawaiians.

Before dinner I walked around in the little town, which had a library, a post office, a bar, a Catholic Church, and a store. The store was for residents only, because supplies are scarce on the peninsula. They have to be brought in by small plane, by mule from topside, or on a barge twice a year. Facing the ocean were the old Visitors' Quarters, which, until 1949, had a fence running through the middle to separate the visitors from the patients. To the left was a little hospital. Twelve nurses still worked there, and a doctor came down from topside twice a week. To the right of the Visitors' Quarters I found some shelter from the wind in a sailcloth-covered lookout. Next to a warehouse, the pier, an enormous block of cement, jutted out between huge boulders of black lava rock. The wind had become increasingly stronger and ominous clouds had gathered over the steep cliffs across the bay. The ocean looked dark and dangerous. It made me think of the creation of the world as described in Genesis. It felt like God's power was ever-present.

Supper consisted of rice, Portuguese bean soup and salad. I was part of the clean-up crew and dried dishes in the kitchen. (The two dishtowels were used for drying dishes as well as hands during the whole weekend and I could envision germs everywhere!) We held Vespers in the fellowship hall. Eight participants were from Maui, one from Oahu, one from topside, and I from Hawai'i. One, Puna, was a resident and the wife of a patient. After Vespers, people brought out cots and pillows, creating a place to sleep. "You may also sleep in the sanctuary," said Pastor Lon. Pat, Dean and I decided to do that. Two long foam pew pillows served as my mattress. Just as I slipped into my sleeping bag, I saw a large cockroach planning to do the same. I went after it on hands and knees and killed it with my shoe. Pastor Dean joined us a little later and bedded down in the front of the sanctuary.

Throughout the night, rain pounded on the metal roof, windows squeaked, and a tree branch kept knocking against a wall. At 2:00 a.m., Dean's alarm went off. I woke again before 6 a.m. on Saturday and was the first one in the shower. The bathroom was outside the fellowship hall. To get there, I tiptoed past sleeping Dean, through a little door in the front of the sanctuary, and across the lawn. Rain continued to fall and my slippered feet made a slush-slush sound on the waterlogged grass.

I helped prepare breakfast, which consisted of coffee and orange juice, sausage, bacon, scrambled eggs and fried rice (nobody seemed concerned about cholesterol). We also had cereal with powdered milk. "Add less water; then it's richer," said Puna. After breakfast, the wind still strong, the clouds dark and threatening with intermittent downpours, we packed our backpacks and piled into the van. "I don't have a cell phone," said Lon. (If he had had one, I doubt it would have worked on the peninsula.) "So, just in case something goes wrong and the van gets stuck somewhere in the wilderness, Puna will follow us in her pickup truck so she can get help." We all agreed that was a good idea.

Wherever we drove in the open van, we noticed low rock walls crossing the landscape. After about twenty minutes on a bumpy jeep trail through wooded, rough terrain, we arrived at the base of an enormous rock pile named Makapula Pai. Lon said, "We'll climb to the top to look at some interesting plateaus with petroglyphs." I couldn't believe the people in our group would be able to get up there. Most of the ladies were in their seventies and Albert was in his late eighties. Makapula Pai rose higher than a two-story house, without anything that even remotely looked like a trail. We made our way through scratchy bushes and clambered up the Pai, using hands and feet. Unbelievably, we all reached the top.

Once there, we had little time to enjoy the view. It was extremely windy. It started raining harder. I took my new poncho out of its pouch and started to put it on. I got as far as putting the hood over my head, but I was still wearing sunglasses, so I couldn't see. I should have tried it out at home. I tried to protect my camera from the rain, all the while struggling to get the poncho over my backpack and around my body. It was all in vain. The poncho flapped around me like a sail in the storm and I could see myself flying off the rock. I thought of Icarus. He would have *wanted* some rain, though. In desperation, I took a step back and squatted behind a bush for some protection from the wind. Sitting there, dripping wet, the notion that I had brought my curling iron to look pretty on Sunday suddenly made me laugh.

From our vantage point on top of the ridge we could see several rock plateaus, carved out by early Hawaiians. David, Pat and Dean crawled a few yards farther to look at the petroglyphs, but for me one plateau was enough. We helped each other climb down the Pai again and drove to Ho'olehua Beach nearby. As the sun and the warm wind dried our clothes, we walked along the shell-covered beach. Up on the hill stood a lighthouse, its light blinking every so often. The ocean appeared dark, but the waves crashing on the black lava along the white sand beach showed a brilliant aqua, topped with white foam.

After lunch, we boarded the van again, with Puna following in her truck in case of emergency. We passed a very old tree-shaded cemetery and stopped at a *heiau*, an ancient Hawaiian sacred temple. A trail led up a high hill to a huge white stone cross, surrounded by very old gravesites, many of the gravestones unidentifiable. It rose up on the edge of Kauhako Crater. "Early Hawaiians lived eight hundred feet down at the lake inside this crater," said Lon. We marveled at the view of the whole peninsula below. In the distance we could distinguish parts of the mule trail zigzagging down the cliff. The grandeur and spirituality of the place filled us with awe.

From the crater's edge we drove to another plateau, the original location of the Leper Settlement Kalawao. Standing at the edge, Lon pointed to an area high up on the hill behind us, across from Waileia Stream. "That's where we are heading, to look at ancient rock formations and old fishing shrines," he said.

We hiked across a narrow plank bridge spanning a dry creek bed far below us. From there, we crossed an area with ironwood trees and remnants of the pharmacy and doctor's quarters, dating back to the early 1900s, when they opened the U.S. Leprosy Investigation Station in Kalawao for a brief period of time. We trekked a steep, narrow trail, slipping, sliding and holding on to sisal plants, roots and branches, all the way down to Wai'aleia Valley. We stood on the rocky beach looking at the islets Mokapu, the rounded one, and Okala, the triangular one, rising out of the ocean in front of us, shrouded in mist. The Waileia Stream splashed down from the towering cliffs behind us. *How was it possible?* I thought. It was hard to imagine that sick, deformed people, hurting and scared, were separated from their loved ones and dropped off on this inaccessible, desolate, rocky beach, destined to die because for them there was no cure, no hope. Almost eight thousand people were sent to this peninsula to die.

From the beach, we followed the stream uphill until we came to a place where it seemed relatively easy to cross, jumping from one big boulder to the next. We formed a chain until the whole group was safely on the other side. From there it was straight upwards again, holding on to anything that was firmly rooted. It was a strenuous climb. It rained off and on. The wind kept blowing. The team spirit remained strong, and we all made it. As we traversed the plateau, covered with bushes and Christmasberry trees, we passed two ancient rock formations. Pat spotted two goats on the rocky beach deep down below us. After a short rest, we went back the same way, slipping and sliding, for the ground was muddy here and there from the rain. We made it back to the van and drove the short distance to the two churches we had passed on our way in. "Siloama Church, or Church of the Healing Spring, was the first church at Kalawao, founded by 12 women and 23 men in 1871," explained Lon. "St. Philomena Church was originally a wooden chapel built in Honolulu. It was transported to Kalawao in 1872. This historic church is commonly known as 'Father Damien's Church' because Father Damien enlarged it twice." Their breathtaking physical setting and nearby graveyards illustrated both the peace and the tragedy of Kalawao. We spent a few minutes at Father Damien's gravesite, which now holds only his right hand. His body was exhumed and returned to Belgium in 1936.

Two of the ladies, Mildred and Kats, had been looking forward to free time so they could go fishing. They had brought their bamboo rods all the way from Maui and hurried to the pier after we arrived. "I will join you, ladies," said Dean.

"I'm so tired, I'm going to take a nap," I said, and I crawled into my sleeping bag in the back of the sanctuary. Two hours later, dinner was upon us. Everyone was excited, because Dean and friends had actually caught two nine-inch and one six-inch fish. Alfred prepared them with lots of onions in a large frying pan. I don't recall what else was for dinner, except rice and bean soup again, even better the second day, as everyone said.

The three fish, surrounded by the fried onions, lay on a large platter, looking sadly at me (perhaps beaming at the others). As I skipped by them in the line, Lois, behind me, said, "I would love to have the eyes." But then she gave them away to the next person. How generous! Espe, next in line, said, "I like the brains the best." I believe she got them. It couldn't have been more than half a teaspoon full, from all three fish combined, poor thing! I didn't look back but headed for the soup, in my eyes the better choice.

After Vespers, the three of us retreated to the sanctuary again. Sitting in our sleeping bags, we conversed until midnight when the second cockroach appeared. This one scurried faster than the first one, and I had to dive underneath the pews with Dean's slipper, the only weapon at hand, before I got it. It took a while before I fell asleep. Dean's alarm went off again at 2 a.m. *Are pastors always waking up at 2 a.m.?* I wondered. Dean explained the next morning that somehow he can't turn the alarm off.

Sunday morning, Palm Sunday, dawned as a glorious day. The rain had stopped. After breakfast, we drove to Siloama Church for a service of celebration and thanksgiving. The church was decorated with palm fronds and large bouquets of beautiful flowers. Several resident-patients attended the service with us. Part of the singing and scripture reading was done in Hawaiian, linking us to the past. Here we were, witnesses of God's grace: Hansen's disease, finally conquered, in His time. *He nani no*, "How Great Thou Art!" One of the resident-patients sang harmony. The hymn sounded so beautiful it moved me to tears.

After the service, we drove to a place near the ocean, which Puna had single-handedly cleared over the years and made into a lovely, shady place to walk or sit and meditate. Nailed to one of the trees was a copy of *Footprints*. In the sand below, leading up to the tree was a trail of strangely shaped rocks, "like the deformed feet of many patients."

When the little plane lifted off later that day and I watched the lighthouse disappear in the distance, my thoughts lingered. Many patients lived and died on Kalaupapa, the beautiful, yet inhospitable peninsula of crosses. Only twenty-four patients are still alive today. They are allowed to leave the peninsula. But for them, Kalaupapa is home; they were born there. They came to love it. They stay by choice. Kalaupapa is now a National Historical Park. A few more years, and the reality of Kalaupapa will be reduced to memories and written history.

Pele

According to Hawaiian lore, Pele, Goddess of Fire, occasionally rises up out of her home in Kilauea Volcano in an explosive eruption, throwing molten rock high into the air, higher and higher in a fountain of fire and smoke. *Pahoehoe*, the red-hot fluid lava, cascades down the *Pali* (cliff) toward the ocean, a ruthless river destroying everything in its path. Thick ripples of viscous lava, or *'a'a*, in an effusive eruption, tantalizingly slowly move across the land, unstoppable, leaving a trail of skeletons of blackened trees and homes.

As the blistering hot lava meets the cool ocean water, it shatters into a million pieces with sprays of steam creating fine threads of glass that settle on everything: Pele's hair. New lava banks over time solidify into new land. Standing as close as I could without getting singed by the hellish heat of the *'a'a*, I watched the miracle of creation.

Figure 48 - Lava field

Later that night, as I drove up the Chain of Craters Road, a light rain drizzled from a cloud in the otherwise clear sky and misted the window of my car. Suddenly, I could not believe what I saw. I parked the car on the side of the road, got out, and stared at the heavens. There, with a full moon over the ocean behind me, a rainbow in shades of gray was visible against the dark sky: a lunar rainbow. I thought of Pappa, who saw one on the Cocos Islands in 1945. We shared the miracle of a very rare occurrence.

Pele has sent her lava to the ocean continually since 1983. The three hundred different gases that are spewed into the air on a daily basis cannot be seen or smelled but they affect the health of many people; they did Mike's. We decided to leave Hawai'i.

Prescott, Arizona
Everybody's Hometown
2001

Again, we had to adapt to a new environment. We moved from a tropical jungle at sea level to about 5600 feet elevation of a high desert with a forest of pine trees. From our home, we see the Bradshaw Mountains. I often think, *beyond those mountains, if I would travel far enough, is the ocean, and at the other side of the ocean is Hawai'i.* We miss it. When we moved here, our realtor told us Prescott has a mild winter. Well, that may be true for people coming from Chicago, but we still freeze every winter, and shoveling snow so we can get out of the garage with the car is no fun. If we almost got mildew between our toes in Hawai'i, in Prescott our skin cracked and peeled for about six months. That first year, we looked forward to the July monsoon. Monsoon? It does not deserve the name! Compared to Hawai'i, where we sometimes had fifteen inches of rain in a single weekend during the monsoon, Prescott's monsoon is like a mild summer rain. But we adapted. That's what life is all about.

When, in 2003, the government of the Netherlands passed a law that we could not acquire dual citizenship but had to choose between the two countries, we decided we would become American citizens. Two years later, we made it happen. In Phoenix, Arizona, on July 15, 2005, together with hundreds of people from other nationalities, we were officially sworn in as United States Citizens. Once again, my soul filled to overflowing with enormous gratitude and joy on that momentous occasion. Another wish was fulfilled; another dream came true. I am so proud to call myself an American.

We will always miss Hawai'i. Prescott is a nice place to live and it looks like we'll be here for a while. Until life's roller coaster takes us on another wild ride.

Epilogue

During World War II Japan totally ignored the rules of international conventions and human rights. Japanese military forces committed genocide, murder, rape, torture and other cruelties of the most inhuman and barbaric kind. They sacrificed prisoners in military experiments. Imperial Military Forces conducted serial rape of more than 200,000 women in Japan, Korea, China, the Philippines, Burma, and the Dutch East Indies. A Dutch "comfort woman," Jan Ruff-O'Hearne, now a resident of Australia, writes in her book *Fifty Years of Silence* that she had been raped day and night for three months by Japanese soldiers when she was 21.

On March 1, 2007, a U.S. House of Representatives committee called on the Japanese Government to "apologize for and acknowledge" the role of the Japanese Imperial military in wartime sex slavery. Japanese Prime Minister Shinzo Abe denied the facts, stating, "There is no evidence to prove there was coercion, nothing to support it." His comments caused negative reactions all over the world. America is not the only country interested in seeing Japan belatedly accept full responsibility. Korea, China and the Philippines are also infuriated by years of Japanese equivocations over the issue. However, until today, the Japanese Government has neither confessed to committing these atrocities, nor offered its apologies. Japan claims to be a civilized nation with a superior culture and has become one of the most affluent nations in the world. Yet, unlike Germany, Canada and the United States, who apologized and compensated the Japanese Americans who were unfairly interned in detention camps for the duration of WW II, Japan has never adequately compensated its victims in proportion to the crimes committed. In 1956, Japan agreed to pay each ex-prisoner of war and internee a meager sum of less than $200 and considered that to be the end of its responsibilities.

Fifty years after the war, the *USS Missouri*, then anchored in the Puget Sound Naval Shipyard in Bremerton, WA, was re-opened for WW II Veterans and other visitors to commemorate the 50th anniversary of the end of the war. I was there. It was an incredibly moving experience for me. I actually stood on board the ship where the Instrument of Surrender was signed to end the Second World War. I was among a group of about fifty men and women, all camp survivors. Everyone related stories about lost loved ones, and terrible scenes they had witnessed and could not put out of their minds even now, fifty years later. I cradled a total stranger in my arms, who was overcome with emotion and could not stop crying. We saw the round memorial plaque in the middle of the deck, and touched one of the nine 16-inch gun barrels. We took the tour of the inside of the ship, and looked at pictures of the table at which the signing of the document had taken place. This is where the promise of a new life originated.

In August 1996, the Navy selected the non-profit USS Missouri Memorial Association as caretaker for the battleship, and Pearl Harbor as its permanent home. On May 4, 1998, the Navy made it official, transferring *Mighty Mo*'s care to the retired military veterans who have served their country in conflicts throughout the world and patriotic citizens and volunteers. The Battleship *USS Missouri* is now a museum in Pearl Harbor. It is open to the public, and in close proximity to the USS Arizona Memorial, the USS Oklahoma Memorial and the Pacific Aviation Museum.

The NARA Files

My life was saved by the atomic bombs. Sixty years later, I discovered what else the atomic bombs prevented: Mass execution of millions of captives, not only on Java, but on all other islands of the Dutch East Indies and the Philippines, as well as in Burma, Singapore, Korea and Japan, according to the 1942 'liquidation plan' of the Japanese Ministry of War: Death for all. This top secret information was declassified in the year 2000. I found out about the Japanese War Crimes files when I did research for this book.

The NARA Files
Japanese War Crimes

More than a half-century after the end of World War II, the demand for information to fill in many of the missing details of that era remains strong. Although a huge body of information has become available, including wartime and post-war military and diplomatic records, much information held by U.S. intelligence agencies that could shed new light on events of the World War II remained classified.

For several years, it has been one of the special concerns of the National Archives and Records Administration (NARA) to work with other agencies in the Federal government to meet the demand for more information about Nazi war crimes and those who committed them. This has been done through our chairmanship of the Nazi War Crimes (NWC) and Japanese Imperial Government Records Interagency Working Group (IWG). The IWG has a simple mandate: Declassify as much as possible the remaining classified U.S. Government records about war criminals and crimes committed by the Nazis and their allies, specifically including the Japanese, during World War II.

Its authority is derived from two acts of Congress: the Nazi War Crimes Disclosure Act of 1998 and the Japanese Imperial Government Disclosure Act of 2000, which confirmed that declassification of documents pertaining to Japanese war crimes is among IWG responsibilities." (Quote from *Declassifying the Secrets of War Crimes by* John W. Carlin, Organization of American Historians (OAH))

Among the papers that survived the fire at the headquarters of the Japanese Imperial Army in Taiwan, set intentionally at the time of surrender in order to destroy all evidence, top military secret documents were found that were declassified not too long ago. Among them, two documents pertain specifically to the internees in the Philippines and the Dutch East Indies. They are, Document No. 2697, certified as Exhibit "J" in Doc. No. 2687, the **Order telling guards to flee to avoid prosecution for war crimes.** The other, designated as Document No. 2710, certified as Exhibit "O", was the **Order to kill all the POWs.**

Order telling guards to <u>flee to</u> avoid prosecution for war crimes Order to <u>Kill all the POWs</u>

N.B. The Japanese had plans to murder all prisoners starting (link) in September of 1945

Exhibit "J" - The order authorizing brutal guards and commanders to flee

Source: NARA, War Crimes, Japan, RG 24, Box 2011

Page One of authorization for Guards to flee because of mistreatment of POWs Dated 20 Aug 1945, 5 days after the surrender. For larger image, 72 dpi, 72 Kb file, click on image

Translation of Exhibit "J"

Complete text as submitted for trial.

If you want higher resolution files (300 dpi), of document, please contact us.

Page Two of authorization for Guards to flee because of mistreatment of POWs Dated 20 Aug 1945, 5 days after the surrender. For larger image, 72 dpi, 87 Kb file, click on image

Doc 2701, Exhibit "O" - The order to murder all the POWs

Source: NARA, War Crimes, Japan, RG 24, Box 2015

While some claim the author of this "policy memorandum" from the war ministry did not have the authority to issue order such an order, this "policy" was transmitted to every POW Command and POW prison camp commander. Other documents in

315

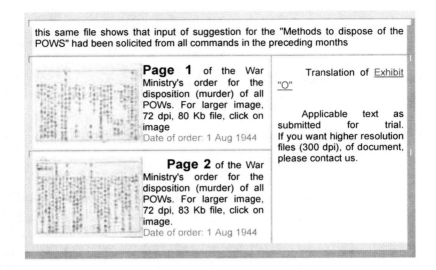

this same file shows that input of suggestion for the "Methods to dispose of the POWS" had been solicited from all commands in the preceding months

Page 1 of the War Ministry's order for the disposition (murder) of all POWs. For larger image, 72 dpi, 80 Kb file, click on image
Date of order: 1 Aug 1944

Translation of Exhibit "O"

Applicable text as submitted for trial. If you want higher resolution files (300 dpi), of document, please contact us.

Page 2 of the War Ministry's order for the disposition (murder) of all POWs. For larger image, 72 dpi, 83 Kb file, click on image.
Date of order: 1 Aug 1944

Following are the original documents and their translation.

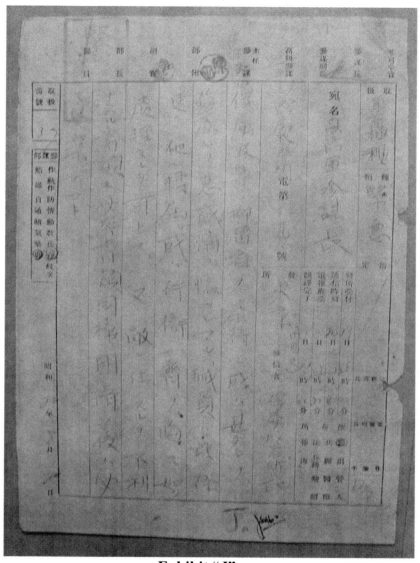

Exhibit "J"

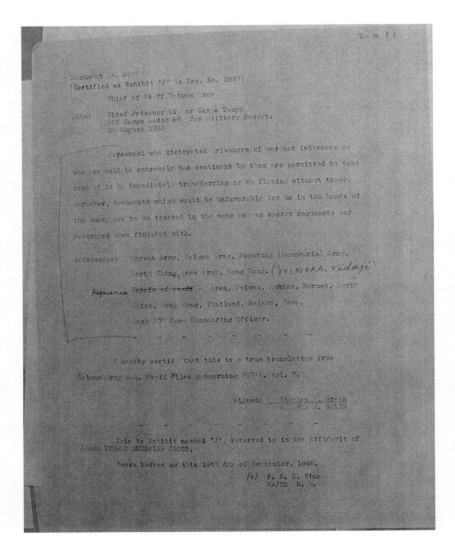

Translation Exhibit "J"

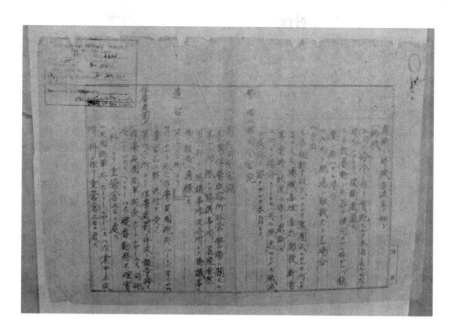

Exhibit "O"

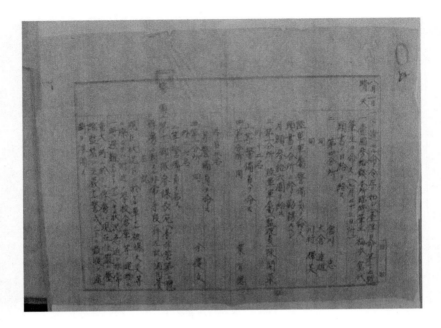

Exhibit "O" page 2

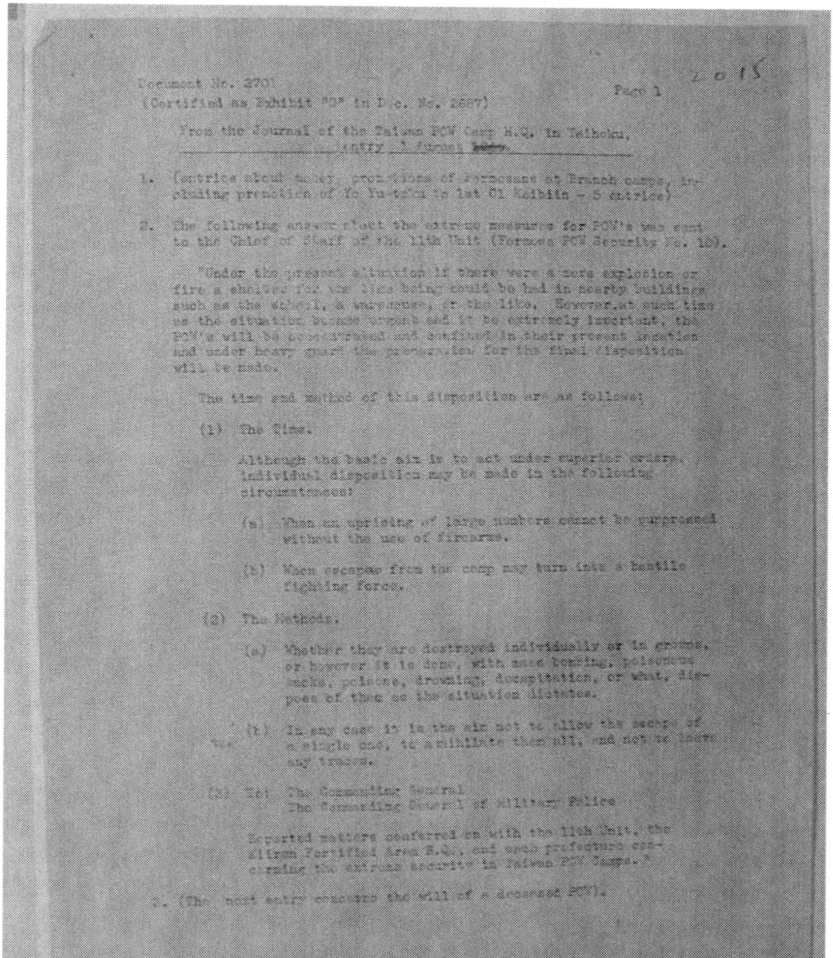

Translation Exhibit "O"

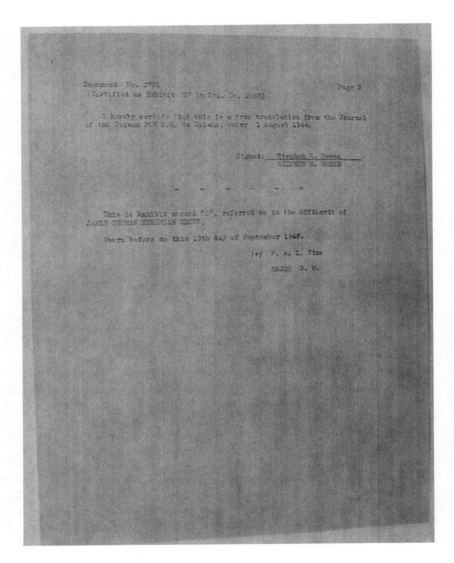

Translation Exhibit "O" Page 2

These documents clearly indicate that the POWS' and Internees' Execution dates were set before the Atom Bombs were dropped and that the Japanese had plans to murder all prisoners starting in September of 1945. "Methods to dispose of the POWS" had been solicited from all commands in the preceding months.

In a detailed order for a camp in Northeast Borneo, all prisoners were placed in one of four categories and were to be liquidated in the following manner by September 15, 1945.

1. Women, children and nuns were to be given poisoned rice
2. Interned men and priests were to be blindfolded, shot and burned
3. 500 British, American, Dutch and Australian POWS were to be marched to the mountains to be shot and burned
4. The sick and weak were to be bayoneted and the entire camp was to be destroyed by fire.

On the densely populated island of Java, the last designated island to be 'treated', remote impregnable rainforest jungles where more than 80.000 prisoners could be disposed of without leaving a trace were non-existent. So the army resorted to a different strategy: provocation of the prisoners to smuggling, revolt and attempted escapes in reaction to severe punishments. Rioting and fleeing prisoners were to be shot. In the spring of 1945 large trenches were dug outside several camps: mass graves, obvious to all. The strategy did not work. The prisoners were simply too tired, too sick, and too lethargic, to rebel or even notice an open gate and attempt an escape. Besides, where would they go?

It is a good thing that we could not look into the future. Mamma, and thousands of men and women with her, would have been desperate had they known about the orders of the Imperial Army to kill all prisoners in all the camps on all islands by the end of September 1945. It would have killed their hope of survival. The way it was, knowing nothing, the women kept going, day after day.

They kept going for the sake of their children. They kept hoping for the end of the war, reunion with loved ones, freedom. The freedom to look at the trees, the rice paddies, the mountains without seeing barbed wire on bamboo fences; the freedom to walk wherever they wanted to go and no guards to stop them; the joy to get up every day without asking, *how many more days before the war is over?* The freedom to go home.

And finally, freedom came.

Dénouement

Last summer, I paddled for over two hours in a little red kayak down the Deschutes River in Oregon with a good friend. It was my first time alone in a very small craft on a body of water that seemed to have a life of its own. When I started out, I could float on the calm water without using my paddle. As the river snaked around bends and rolled through forested canyons, the change of terrain seemed to change the speed and direction of the current. I had to consciously steer my kayak in the direction I wanted to go if I did not want to end up at the mercy of the river. Dorothy, paddling beside me, watched out for me and showed me how to use my paddle.

Life is like being alone in a little kayak on a river. If you don't consciously direct your own mind to where you want to go in life you may end up where you don't want to be.

My life started on a little tributary with calm water, a small stream on a long trip towards the ocean. Before long, a raging torrent crushing all obstacles in its way threatened to overturn my kayak. But Mamma was by my side, guiding me, protecting me through the roller coasters of whitewater until we reached calm waters again and found peace. She waged a desperate battle with great determination and coached her two little girls through the perils of war.

In a letter diary, Mamma related our experiences and stories of the people who were near us during those four years. To my knowledge, of all the people mentioned in her diary, only five are still alive today. They are Mamma, Paula, Corrie den Hoed, Rob Vierhout and I. All of them, except me, live in the Netherlands.

Mamma's parents and siblings all died even before Mamma's diary was published in 1992 as *In the Shadow of the Sun*. Tante Jan, Mamma's favorite little sister, got married in

1957 and emigrated to New Zealand, where she and her husband adopted two baby boys, John and Carl. At the age of seventy-two she died of Scleroderma.

Our parents visited us each a year for a month when we lived in Pasadena, and once when we lived in Hawai'i. Pappa had a little vegetable garden after he retired and enjoyed many years of cultivating the soil, planting and harvesting his crops. After a three-month illness, he died peacefully at home in September of 1998, a week after his 85th birthday. Mamma, Paula and I were with him during the final three weeks of his life.

Jos Vermeulen died of colon cancer in November of 1978. After Oom Henk Esser passed on, Tante Jopie moved into a retirement home in the province of Zeeland, where she was from. Until her death, Mamma visited her on occasion. Loekie Vierhout, in whose garage we spent the first year of the war, had a little girl in 1949 and lived in Vlissingen, a harbor town near Middelburg, in the province of Zeeland. She and my parents visited off and on through the years. She died in the same month as Pappa, September 1998.

Cas Vierhout, Pappa's friend, under whose leadership 7000 military men escaped from Tjilatjap to Australia in 1942, survived three-and-a-half years in a POW camp in Thailand. Queen Juliana of the Netherlands honored him in 1947 as *Ridder in de Orde van Oranje-Nassau met de Zwaarden* (Knight in the Order of Oranje-Nassau with the Swords, an honor specifically for the military). He retired in 1960 and died in March 1962.

Casper Vierhout, the eldest of their three sons, a journalist with a Dutch Television Station for seven years, died in 1966 on the spot in a car accident beyond his fault.

Eric Vierhout graduated Nautical College in Vlissingen and in 1959 became an engineer on board of the *Straat Banka*, one of the ships of Royal Interocean Lines sailing between Japan and Australia. From 1970 he mainly worked on small coasters for trading companies in Europe. In 1974, sailing on the Coaster *De Blauwe Tulp* from Kiel, Germany to Bergen, Norway, a fire broke out in the engine room. Eric yelled "Fire!" and, without a moment's hesitation, ran to get one of the CO_2 extinguishers to extinguish the fire. It failed. Panic ensued among the crewmembers as the fire spread rapidly throughout the engine room. Eric's clothes were on fire. It seemed like his whole body was on fire. The second fire extinguisher failed as well. The whole engine room was ablaze. Two of the crewmembers panicked, jumped overboard and drowned. Eric made a narrow escape. A rescue helicopter of the Norwegian Coastguard airlifted him to a hospital in Stavanger. For two months they treated him for second and third degree burns. Then he was taken to the Burn Center in Beverwijk, the Netherlands. During the following years, Eric underwent many surgeries, including plastic surgery, to make his face presentable again, and multiple smaller surgeries on his hands.

The ship's engine room burned out completely and the ship was towed to Stavanger to be repaired. They found that the extinguishers had failed due to lack of proper maintenance.

After the accident, Eric was traumatized and claustrophobic. At the age of 36 in 1975, he was disqualified and lived on disability. After his release from the Burn Center in Beverwijk he lived with his mother for a short while until he moved into his own apartment in Vlissingen. He enjoyed occasional visits with Mamma and Paula until he got severely disabled and was no longer ambulatory. He refused all scans and tests, and died at the age of 66 from unknown maladies.

Rob Vierhout, Eric's brother, is alive and well. He graduated the Royal Netherlands Naval College in Den Helder in 1963. He worked as an Engineer and Training Coordinator in fluid dynamics and the design of heat exchangers for nuclear plants in the Netherlands. This led to a career in design and construction of alternative energy installations after the Dutch government decided to discontinue construction of nuclear plants in 1979. Rob and his wife Henny, their son and two daughters lived near Amsterdam while the children grew up. After his retirement in 2005, they moved to a town in the eastern part of Holland.

Corrie den Hoed, the daughter of the District Manager in Soerabaja, lives near The Hague. She has two daughters and four grandchildren and has been an active volunteer with organizations for the elderly. Tom, her father, contracted Alzheimer's, from which he died. Several times a year, Corrie comes over to visit Mamma to talk about old times and exchange news about things happening in their lives.

My sister Paula, too young to remember anything about the horrors of the camps, left the Indies in 1957. She lived with our grandparents in Middelburg to finish her high school education. After studying English and German, she specialized in the Hotel and Catering business and got certified in Office Management. In 1962 she got married and settled in the same village our parents would move to in 1972.

Paula's son Martin, whom I call my favorite nephew although I have only one, holds a Bachelor's Degree in Computer Science and Telecommunications. He and his wife Helen moved to Norway in 2000. Their two sons, Bart Fokko and Tom, and daughter Anniek complete the family. Bart Fokko was named after his great-grandfather, who died four months after Bart's birth.

Our three children are our pride and joy. Our daughter Annemieke holds a Ph.D. in Clinical Psychology. She has a private practice in the San Francisco Bay area, California. She and her partner Leslie have two children, Jack Michael and Morgan Claire.

Our daughter Jacqueline holds a Master's Degree in the field of Education and Administration. A gifted educator serving children with special needs for over seventeen years, she and her partner Ann currently reside in Western Canada.

A musician with a Master's Degree in Music, our son Dennis performs regionally as a freelance trumpet player and maintains a full-time teaching position as Music Program Coordinator at a Community College in his area. He resides in North Carolina with his wife Stephanie, who has a Doctorate in Voice, and their three sons, Chandler, Luke and Grant. They make beautiful music together.

Mamma has been blessed with a long, happy and healthy life. It is because of Paula's unselfish character and loving dedication that Mamma has been able to live in her own home until she was one hundred years old. Every week for four years, Paula made the three-hour drive to Mamma's house and spent three days to shop and cook for her, and plan meals for the remainder of the week. Tirelessly, she took Mamma for doctor and dentist's visits, hair and nail appointments, hearing aid checkups and much more. She still does all the necessary administration since Mamma cannot see well any more. Macular degeneration slowly but surely prevented Mamma from enjoying the many activities she loved. She stopped riding her bike at 92. She gave up her fitness class at 94, but she still loved to walk. For years, listening to English audio books and doing the most difficult crossword puzzles and cryptograms kept her mind sharp. Her neighbors Jo and Piet invited her over frequently for a cup of tea or coffee or a glass of wine. Mamma always sees the clouds with a silver lining. She has a true Pollyanna outlook on life and does not feel like a centenarian, although she often calls herself *an ouwe doze* (a golden old'un).

She is content. She has a thankful heart and her motto continues to be "On we go!"

Figure 49 - Mamma with Ronny and Paula

On January 27, 2010, Mamma celebrated her 100th birthday. What a festive day it was! We had a luncheon in a nearby restaurant for the relatives and a reception in the afternoon for all the neighbors and friends in the village. The Mayor came to the house for a personal visit and presented her with a copy of her original birth certificate. In March, Mamma moved into a new assisted living facility in her village. She adapted quickly and says, "Now I'd better stay healthy, so I can go on living here for a while longer."

In January 2011, Mike and I celebrated our Golden Wedding Anniversary with a special dinner and dance in a cozy restaurant. In May, we will cruise to the Netherlands to celebrate with Mamma, Paula, relatives and friends, and we will rent a home on Lake Tahoe this summer and celebrate the occasion all over again for a whole week with our children and grandchildren. Fifty years of marriage is worth celebrating all year, wouldn't you say?

On January 27, 2011, I was in the Netherlands again to be with Mamma on her 101st birthday. I stayed with Paula, who now lives in Mamma's old home, and we had a great time together. Three times a day I walked to the special wing of Laarstede, where Mamma lives in the company of four other ladies and one gentleman. They each have their own spacious bedroom but are together during the day in a combined living room/dining room/kitchen. Family members, neighbors and friends visit off and on, bringing flowers, cookies, wine and other treats for all to share. I got to know many of them on this my third visit to Laarstede. Mamma and the gentleman like a small glass of red wine, a *"pimpeltje"* as Mamma calls it, with some nuts during happy hour. The word got out. On her 101st birthday, the room was decorated with flags and beautiful flower arrangements. Radiant in the orange chair in the corner that has become her special place in the room she received eight bottles of wine and six bags of nuts. The following day she quipped, "I hope that the people in town won't say every day, let's go to Mrs. Herman for a *pimpeltje.*"

I fully enjoyed the privilege of visiting Mamma three times a day. Because it was extremely cold, I could only take her out in her wheelchair once. But I found some large domino tiles, which she could still see, and we played dominoes. We did crossword puzzles with me asking the question, Mamma giving the answer and me writing it down. Her memory is still relatively good. Her eyes, sadly, are not. But she never complains and is very satisfied with her new environment, the food, the company and the care she gets. Each night I tucked her in, after the half-hour ritual of washing herself, changing into her pajamas, brushing her teeth, and taking out her hearing aids – all of which she still does herself – she said, "Oh, I am so blessed. I have my two daughters by my side, and they are taking such good care of me. I will sleep like a rose. I can do that really well, you know, sleep." And with that, she closed her eyes and slept.

Figure 50 - Mamma, 2011, 101 years old

To Mamma

When you held me in your arms for the very first time
You loved me, and you gave me love for life and for the world,
But above all, you gave me
Love for you.

And in those precious baby years, with Pappa home,
You taught me how to smile and how to walk, and gave me
All the little things a baby needs to feel secure.
But above all, you gave me
Love for you.

Then, in the terrifying years of scarcity and fear, with Pappa gone,
You showed me courage, perseverance, love for God
And never-ending hope; protecting me and loving me.
But above all, you gave me
Love for you.

And in my – sometimes trying – teenage years,
Together as a family again,
Those years of growing up with heartaches, joys
And constant change, you were my friend and ally.
But above all, you gave me
Love for you.

Throughout my childhood and my adult years,
you showed me values: yours.
I feel so privileged to be your child and watch you live your life,
So privileged to have you for so long.
And most of all, I want to say,
I love you.

Ronny

GLOSSARY

Dutch words are marked with a **D**
Hawaiian words are marked with an **H**
Japanese words are marked with a **J**
All other words are Indonesian/Indo words or expressions or an explanation of terminology

Aloha - H - Hello, goodbye and Love. Aloha is the most Hawaiian word in the Hawaiian language.
Ada siempen radio - J - Is there still a radio kept somewhere?
Amoebic dysentery - An intestinal infection.
*Anglo -*A clay barbecue.
Arang - Charcoal.

Baboe - A female servant, usually hired for the laundry and general cleaning duties
Baleh-baleh – Hard, bamboo cot, native bed.
Bamboe roentjing - A bamboo stick with a sharply whetted point, dipped in a strong poison.
Batavia - D. The colonial Dutch name for the Indonesian capital Djakarta, now Jakarta
Bersiap - Native Indonesians' fight for independence after WW II
Betjak - A bicycle taxi
Belanda - A Dutch person
Bisa - I can or can you?
Bisa toeloeng - Can you help?
Boekan - No
Boeng - Brother
Boleh tawar – May I bargain?
Borstplaat - D, Fondant, sugar candy

Copra - The dried meat of the coconut from which oil is pressed.

Dessa - A native village located in a rural area.
Dettol - Disinfectant mouthwash
Djalan - Street, currently *Jalan or Jl.*
Doerian - (now durian), a succulent, creamy, tropical fruit that smells like stinky socks
Dogcar (dog-cart) - A light, two-wheeled, horse-drawn vehicle

Emerald Girdle - Name for the Dutch East Indies, as is *Insulinde*. Dutch author E. Douwes Dekker (1820 - 1887) wrote in his book 'Multatuli', *Insulinde, dat zich slingert om de evenaar als een Gordel van Smaragd.* ("Dutch East Indies, wrapped around the equator like an Emerald Girdle.")

Fl.- D - Abbreviation for *Florin,* Dutch Guilder, the monetary unit of the Netherlands, equal to 100 cents
Flitspuit - D - A manual pumping device used for spraying D.D.T., an insecticide.
Gedèk - A fence made of woven bamboo
Gerampokt - Plundered, see also *rampokken*
Goedang - A large storage room outside of the main house, connected by a breezeway
Ghurka - A soldier from Nepal, serving in the British army, sent to help restore law and order in Indonesia after the Japanese occupation ended on August 15, 1945

Halau - H - Hula school
Haole - H - White person, Caucasian
Heiho- J - A young native, a former soldier of the Dutch East Indies Army *(KNIL)* who was employed by the Japanese

Hoedjan - Rain
Hula - **H** - Hawaiian dance for men and women

Indo - **D** - A Eurasian, a descendant of a relationship between a European and a native of Indonesia.

Kampong - A small native village within the city limits
Katjong - A teenage male servant, usually hired for odd jobs
Kebon - A gardener.
Keirei- J - Left (a Japanese command).
Kenpetai- J - Japanese military police force (sometimes spelled kempetai)
Kiwotsuke- J - Stand at attention (a Japanese command)
Klamboe - A mosquito net used over a bed
Klop klop – D - Literally meaning, "whip whip", a process to whip sugar and coffee extract into a fluffy treat
K.N.I.L. - **D** - Abbreviation for *Koninklijk Nederlands-Indisch Leger,* Royal Dutch East Indies Army
Koelie - A coolie, an unskilled native laborer
Kokki - A female cook
K.P.M. - **D** - Abbreviation for *Koninklijke Paketvaart Maatschappij,* Royal Freight Line Company.

Lida boeaja - Aloe plant (literally translated, the tongue of an alligator)

M.L.D. - **D** - Abbreviation for *Marine Luchtvaart Dienst,* the Dutch Naval Air Force
Malaria Tropica - An infectious tropical disease transferred by mosquitoes
Mandi bak - A large tiled container of water, part of a shower room, used for dip-bucket cold showers
Mandi kamer - A shower room

Mantri - A head nurse
Merdeka - Freedom
Mijter - **D** - A mitre, a bishop's headdress

Naore - **J** - Stand up straight (a Japanese command)

Oliebollen - **D** - Dumplings cooked in oil, a Dutch New Year's Eve treat
Oma – **D** - Grandma
Opa - **D** - Grandpa

Padi – *grains of rice*
Pan bakaran - A pan oven
Pasar - An open-air market
Pemuda - A young man, an Indonesian extreme nationalist
Pimpeltje – **D** – A little booze

Rajaps - White ants; wood-eating insects; termites
Rampokken - Plunder
Razzia - A military (or police) raid
Roti Koekoes - (now roti kukus) Steamed cake
Rissoles – Meat-filled pastry
Rupiah - Monetary unit in Indonesia, equivalent to 100 cents

Sado - A light, two-wheeled, horse-drawn vehicle (see also entry for dogcar)
Sago - Starch derived from the pith of sago palm stems
Samurai - **J** - Sword, weapon used by members of the Japanese Military Police *(Kenpetai)*
*t*o injure or decapitate prisoners
Sarong - An ankle-length wrap-around batik garment for women and men
Senang - Happy

Sereh oil - Citronella oil, a mosquito repellant
Sinterklaas - **D** - A derivative of *Sint Nicolaas,* or St. Nicholas
Slokans - Cement ditches along streets
Srikaja – Tropical fruit, resembling a pinecone, with sweet, custard-like white meat covering many black seeds
Soedah mati - He already died
Stroop - Indo term for a sweet, red beverage that resembles cool-aid
Soera 'n Boeaja – (now Sura 'n Buaya) The shark and the Crocodile, emblem of the city of Soerabaja.

Tante - **D** – Aunt
Tapioca - a flavorless, colorless, odorless, almost proteine free starch extracted from the root of the cassava plant
Tjaping - a pointed straw hat
Toet-toet – **D** - The sound made by honking a horn or sound of sirens

Wilhelmus - The Dutch National Anthem, named after William of Nassau, Prince of Orange, nicknamed "the Taciturn"

LIST OF JAPANESE CAMPS IN THE DUTCH EAST INDIES

During the Second World War in the former Dutch East Indies, from March, 1942 to August, 1945, about 100,000 Dutch civilians were detained by the Japanese in internment camps. Men were separated from women and children. Starting in 1944, older boys were interned in either men's camps or separate boys' camps.

All non-Asians were confined to designated areas or buildings, initially ranging from residential neighborhoods, houses and barracks, to schools, convents, hospitals and prisons. Eventually a large number of concentration camps was specially built throughout the occupied territories. Some camps were only used for a short time and the prisoners were transferred to other, often larger camps. The following list of camps has been gleaned from a Dutch doctoral thesis, titled *De Japanse Burgerkampen* (The Japanese Camps for Civilians) by D. van Velden, PhD (1963). The information was used with permission from Uitgeverij Van Wijnen, Franeker in the Netherlands.

SUMATRA
Atjeh
Lae Butar, March 42 - June 42, M/W/C, to Singkel
Singkel, June 42 - July 42, M/W/C, to Meulaboh
Meulaboh, July 42, M/W/C, to Kutaradja
Kualasimpang, March 42 - April 42, M/W/C, to Bireuen/Langsa
Langsa, March 42 - June 42, M/W/C, to Bireuen/Kutaradja
Lhoseumawe, March 42 - April 42, M/W/C, to Bireuen/Langsa
Takengeun, March 42 - April 42, M/W/C, to Bireuen/Langsa
Bireuen, March 42 - June 42, M/W/C, to Langsa/Kutaradja

Sabang, March 42 - June 42, M/W/C, to Kutaradja
Kutaradja, March 42 - June 42, M/W, to Kuta
Alamkamp/Keuda
Kuta Alamkamp, June 42 - August 43, M/B, to
Lawesigalagala
Keuda, June 42 - September 43, W/C, to Lawesigalagala
Lawesigalagala, August 43 - October 44, M/B, to Siringoringo
Lawesigalagala, September 43 - October 44, W/C, to Belawan
Estate

Tapanuli
Sibolga, March 42 - May 42, M/W/C, to Pematangsiantar
Taratung, March 42 - May 42, M/W/C, to Pematangsiantar
Padangsidempuan, March 42 - May 42, M/W/C, to
Pematangsiantar **Pangururan**, March 42 - April 42, M/W/C, to
Pematangsiantar
Balige, March 42 - December 42, M/W/C, to Hephata/Medan
Hephata, June 42 - December 42, W/C, to Pulauberajan

East coast
Medan Pulauberajan, April 42 - July 45, W/C, to Aik
Pamienke/Glugur II
Medan Glugur I, April 42 - May 42, W/C, to Pulauberajan
Medan Glugur II, June 45 - July 42, W/C, to Aik Pamienke II
Serdang, April 42 - October 42, W/C, to Tandjungmorawa
Tandjungmorawa, October 42 - June 43, W/C, to
Pulauberajan/St. Jozef School **Kampong Baru**, November 42 -
March 43, W/C, to Pulauberajan/ St. Jozef School
St. Jozef School, April 42 - October 44, M/W/C, to Belawan
Estate/Glugur II **Belawan Uniekampong**, April 42 - July 43,
M/W/C, to Belawan Estate **Tebingtinggi**, March 42 -
November 43, M/W/C, to Uniekampong/Pulauberajan
Pemantangsiantar, March 42 - April 43, M/W/C, to

Sungaisengkol/Berastagi **Tandjungbalai**, March 42 - February 42, M, to Uniekampong/Sungaisengkol **Tandjungbalai I/II**, March 42 - April 45. W/C, to Pulauberajan/Aik Pamienke **Bindjai**, March 42 - October 44, M. to Uniekampong Belawan/Padanghalaban **Bindjai Bangkatan**, March 42 - January 43, W/C, to Pulauberajan **Kabandjahe**, April 42 - May 42. M, to Uniekampong Belawan **Berastagi**, April 42 - July 45. W/C, to Aik Pamienke **Belawan Estate I**, July 43 - October 44, M, to Aik Pamienke I/Padanghalaban **Belawan Estate II**, October 44 - May 45, W/C, to Aik Pamienke I **Sungaisengkol**, March 43 - October 44, M, to Aik Pamienke I/Siringoringo **Siringoringo**, October 44 - October 45, M/B **Padanghalabalan**, October 44 - October 45, M **Aik Pamienke**, October 44 - April 45, M, to Siringoringo **Aik Pamienke I**, April 45 - November 45, W/C **Aik Pamienke II**, June 45 - November 45, W/C **Aik Pamienke III**, July 45 - November 45, W/C **Pakanbaru**, April 42 - June 42, M/W/C, to Padang

West coast
Padang Prison, April 42-October 43, M, to Bangkinan
Padang MP Station, April 42 – February 43, M.to Prison
        Padang KSB, April 42 – June 43, M/W/C, to Prison/Mission
        Padang MV, August 43 – September 43, M/W/C, to Prison/Mission
        Padang Mission, April 42 – October 43, W/C, to Prison
        Padang British Camp, April 42 – June 43, W/C, to Mission
        Padangpandjang, April 42 – May 42, M to Prison
        Fort de Kock, April 42 – May 42, M/W/C, to Prison/Mission

Sawahlunto, April 42 – September 43, M/W/C, to
Prison/Mission
Sungaipenuh, April 42 – august 42, M/W/C, to Prison/Mission

Indragiri
Rengat, March 42 – June 42, M/W/C, to Prison/Mission
Bangkinang, October 43 – September 45, M/B/W/C

Djambi
        Djambi, April 42 – April 44, M/W/C, to Muntok,
Palembang

Benkulen
Benkulen, April 42 – October 43, M/W/C, to
Muntok/Kepahiang
Kepahiang, October 43 – October 44, W/C, to Muntok

Palembang
Palembang Prison, April 42 – January 43, M, to Barracks
Barracks, January 43 – September 43, M, to Muntok
Pladju, April 42 – January 43, M, to Prison
Bukit Besar, March 42 – April 42, W/C, to Talang Sumut
Talang Sumut, April 42 – September 43, W/C, to Barracks
Barracks, September 43 – November 44, W/C, to Muntok
Belalau, April 45 – October 45, M/B/W/C

Lampungse
Telukbetung, April 42 – February 43, M/W/C, to Convent
Telukbetung Convent, April 42 – February 43, M/W/C, to
Muntok/Ice Factory
Telukbetung Ice Factory, February 43 – May 44, W/C, to
Palembang

Bangka
Pangkalpinang, April 42 – May 44, M/W, to Muntok
Muntok I, February 42 – March 42, M/W/C, to Palembang
Muntok II, September 43 – March 45, M, to Belalau
Muntok, October 44 – April 55, W/C, to Belalau

JAVA
Serang
Serang, March 42 – July 42 M/W/C, to Buitenzorg

Batavia
Glodok I, March 42, M, to Struiswijk
Glodok II, January 45 – September 45, M/B
Struiswijk I, March 42 – February 44, M, to Tjikudapateuh
Struiswijk II, April 42- October 43, Br./Am. W/C, to
Tanahtinggi
Struiswijk III, November 44 – October 45, W/C
Adek I, June 42 –February 44, M, Tjikudapateuh
Adek II, November 44 – October 45, W/C
Kramat I, October 42 – September 43, W/C, to Tjideng
Kramat II, September 43 – September 44, M/W/C, to Grogol
II/Tjideng
Kramat III, September 44 – October 45, W/C
      Tjideng, October 42 - October 45, W/C
Grogol I, July 43 - August 44, W/C, to Tjideng
Grogol II, September 44 - November 44, M/B, to
Baros/Tjimahi
Grogol III, November 44 - April 45, W/C, to Tjideng
Tanahtinggi, October 43 - March 44, Foreign W/C, to
Tangerang
Tangerang I, September 43 - March 44, M, to Tjimahi Army
Post
Tangerang II, March 44 - April 45, W/C, to Tjideng/Adek

Kampong Makasar, January 45 - October 45, W/C
Vincentius Convent, March 45 - October 45, M/W
 Mater Dolorosa Convent, May 45 - October 45, M

Buitenzorg
Ursulinen Convent, July 42 - November 42, M, to
Gedongbadak
Gedongbadak I, September 42 - February 44, M, to Tjimahi
Army Post **Gedongbadak II**, March 44 - October 44, W/C, to
Tjideng
Gedongbadak III, November 44 - March 45, W/C, to
Tjideng/Kampong Makasar
Kota Paris I, April 43 - May 44, M/W/C, to Gedongbadak
II/Kramat II
Kota Paris II, May 44 - November 44, W/C, to Kramat II
Kota Paris III, November 44 - March 45, M/W/C, to Kampong
Makasar

Bandung
Sukamiskin, March 42 - February 44, M, to
Purwokerto/Tjimahi Army Post **Reform School**, July 42 -
February 44, M, to Baros III/Tjimahi Army Post
Stella Maris, August 42 - February 44, M, to Baros III/Tjimahi
Army Post
Pasir Andir, August 42 - November 42, M, to Palace Hotel
Palace Hotel, November 42 - October 43, M, to Baros III
Zeelandia School, August 42 - October 43, M, to Baros III
Dick de Hoog School, November 42 - February 43, M, to Baros
III **Tjikudapateuh**, January 44 - October 45, M/B
Tjihapit, November 42 - May 45, W/C, to Batavia/Buitenzorg
Tjihapit II, December 44 - May 45, M/B, to Tjikudapateuh

346

Karees, December 42 - December 44, W/C, to
Batavia/Ambarawa/Tjihapit **Lengkong**, June 43 - October 43,
Br./Am. W/C, to Tanahtinggi
Bloemenkamp, August 43 - November 44, M/W/C, to
Tjihapit/Tjikudapateuh **Bloemenkamp**, July 44 - November 44,
W/C, to Ambarawa
Rama, December 42 - June 44, M/W/C, to Tjihapit

Tjitjalengka
　　　Tjitjalengka, May 45 - August 45, M

Tjimahi
Train Station, November 42 - December 42, W/C, to Baros I
Baros I, December 42 - July 44, W/C, to Bloemenkamp
Baros II, July 44 - October 45, M/B
Baros III, October 43 - October 45, M
Tjimahi 4 Barracks, February 44 - October 45, M to
Batavia/Buitenzorg **Hospital**, June 44 - October 45, M/W

Sukabumi
Rosalie House, January 43 - October 45, M/W
Cheribon I, March 42 - February 44, M, to
Pekalongan/Tjikudapateuh
Cheribon II, June 42 - June 43, W/C, to Kramat
Pekalongan, March 42 - September 43, M, to
School/Sukamiskin
School, December 42 - August 43, M, to Benteng
Ngawi/Tjimahi Army Post **Gudang Garam**, October 43 -
March 44, W/C, to Gedongbadak II
Tegal Prison, March 42 - June 42, M, to Pekalongan
Todan Street, October 43 - March 45, W/C, to Gedongbadak II
　　　Purwokerto Prison I, March 42 - September 42, M, to
Pekalongan

Purwokerto Prison II, August 43 - July 44, M, to Baros III
Catholic School, April 42 - October 43, M, to Benteng Ngawi

Djokjakarta
Prison, April 42 - June 42, M, to Fort Vredenburgh
Fort Vredenburgh, June 42 - February 44, M, to
Bubutan/Tjimahi Army Post

Surakarta
Hospital Ziekenzorg I, March 42 - September 43, M, to
Benteng Ngawi **Ziekenzorg II**, December 43 - June 45, W/C,
to Muntilan/Ambarawa/Halmahera

Semarang
Djatingaleh, April 42 - August 42, M, to Bubutan/Kesilir
Kalibanteng, July 42 - August 42, M, to Kesilir
Catholic School, September 42 - December 43, Br./Am. W/C,
to Tanahtinggi **Lampersari-Sompok**, November 42 - October
45, W/C
Sompok Lama, Dec. 42 - December 44, M/W IC, to
Tjikudapateuh/Lampersari   **Halmahera I**, December 42 -
June 43, M/W/C, W/C to Lampersari
Halmahera II, June 43 - January 41, M/B, to Tjikudapateuh
Halmahera III, February 44 - October 45, W/C
Bangkong I, June 43 - Sept. 44, W/C, to Gedangan/Halmahera
III/Lampersari **Bangkong II**, September 44 - October 45, M/B
Gedangan, Oct. 43 - May 45, W/C to
Bankong/Halmahera/Lampersari/ Ambarawa
Karangpanas, February 44 - Nov. 44, W/C, to Ambarawa/
Bangkong/ Lampersari
Tangsi Perlindungan, November 42 - December 42, W/C, to
Ambarawa (1) 6 **Ambarawa (1) 6**, December 42 - October 45,
W/C

Ambarawa (2) 7 I, December 42 - December 44, W/C, to Ziekenzorg/Muntilan **Ambarawa 7 II**, January 45 - October 45, M/B
    Ambarawa 8 I, June 43 - September 44, W/C, to Ambarawa 6/Banjubiru
Ambarawa 8 II, September 44 - May 45, M/B, to Ambarawa 7 II/Bandungan **Ambarawa 9 I**, October 43 - May 45, W/C, to Ambarawa 6/Banjubiru 10/11 **Ambarawa 9 II**, May 45 - October 45, W /C
Djoe Eng, September 43 - February 44, M, to Tjimahi Army Post
Sumowono, December 42 - March 44, W /C, to Ambarawa 6/7 I
Bandungan, September 44 - October 45, B
Kalitjeret, March 45 - August 45, B
Gedongdjati, September 44 - August 45, B

Banjubiru
Banjubiru 10 I, August 43 - February 44, M, to Tjikudapateuh
Banjubiru 10 II, February 44 - October 45, W/C
Banjubiru 11, December 42 - October 45, W/C
Banjubiru 12, August 45 - October 45, W /C

Muntilan
    School, September 43 - August 45, W/C, to Ambarawa 6/Banjubiru 10 II/11/12

Madiun
    Redjosari, September 43 - February 44, W/C, to Banjubiru 10 II

Ngawi

Benteng, February 43 - February 44, M, to Tjimahi
Army Post
Benteng II, January 45 - September 45, M

Kediri
Prison, November 42 - February 44, M, to Tjimahi Army Post
Sentono Pande, July 43 - February 44 M, to Tjimahi Army
Post
Galuhan, September 43 - March 44, W/C, to Banjubiru 10 II

Blitar
Kawarasan I, May 43 - March 44, W/C, to Banjubiru 10 II
Kawarasan II, September 44 - March 44, W/C, to Banjubiru
10 II

Surabaja
Bubutan I, April 42 - February 43, M, to Benteng Ngawi
Bubutan II, October 43 - February 44, Foreign M, to
Tjikudapateuh
Werfstraat I, March 42 - March 44, Br./Am. W/C, to
Tanahtinggi/Tangerang **Werfstraat II**, October 42 - March 43,
Br./ Am. M, to Benteng Ngawi **Werfstraat Prison III**, April 43
- February 44, M, to Tjikudapateuh
Darmo, January 43 - March 44, W/C, to
Muntilan/Semarang/Tangerang **Camphuislaan**, January 45 -
October 45, W/C

Malang
Navy Base, January 43 - February 44, M/B, to Tjimahi Army
Post
Wijk, November 42 - August 44, W /C, to
Solo/Semarang/Ambarawa/Banjubiru **Batu**, March 42 -
December 43, Br./Am. W/C, to Tanahtinggi

Kesilir
Kesilir, July 42 - September 43, M, to Banjubiru 10/Tangerang

BORNEO
Sandakan
Government House, January 42 - May 42, M/W/C, to Berhala
Berhala Island, May 42 - January 43, M/W/C, to Batu Lintang/Kuching

Jesselton
Jesselton House, May 42 - September 42, M/W/C, to Batu Lintang/Kuching

Kuching
Zaid Rock Road, January 42 - May 42, M, to Pandungan
Pandungan, May 42 - July 42, M, to Batu Lintangh
Batu Lintang, July 42 - September 45, M/W/C

Pontianak
Convent, February 42 - July 42, M/W/C, to Batu Lintang/Kuching

Singkawang
Prison, February 42 - July 42, M, to Batu Lintang/Kuching

Sambas
Prison, February 42 - July 42, M/W, to Batu Lintang/Kuching

Bandjermasin
Navy Base, April 42 - January 45, M/B, to Kandangan
Barracks, April 42 - February 45, W/C, to Kandangan

Kandangan
Base, January 45 - August 45, M/B, to Puruktjau
Barracks, February 45 - September 45, W/C

Puruktjau
    Barrack, August 45 - September 45, M/B

Samarinda
    House, June 43 - December 43, W, Bandjermasin

Tarakan
Base Barracks, February 42 - November 43, M, to
Bandjermasin
Base Stables, February 42, W/C, to Radiostraat
Radiostraat, February 42 - October 43, W/C, to Lingkas
Lingkas Barracks, October 43 - November 43, W IC, to
Bandjermasin

CELEBES
Makasar
    Goaweg, February 42 - September 42, M/W/C, to
Parepare/Malino

Malino
    Malino, April 42 - May 43, W/C, to Kampili

Kampili
Hospital, March 43 - September 45, W/C

Parepare
Navy Base, September 42 - October 44, M/B, to Bodjo

Bodjo
Bodjo Stables, October 44 - May 45, M/B, to Bolong

Bolong
Barracks, May 45 - August 45, M/B

Manado, Minahassa
St. Jozef School, January 42 - March 42, M/B, to Teling
Teling Base, March 42 - September 45, M/B
Prison, September 44 - October 44, M/B, to Teling

Tomohon
Convent School, January 42 - February 42, W/C, to Kaaten

Kaaten
School, February 42 - March 44, W/C, to Airmadidi

Airmadidi
Barracks, March 44 - September 45, W/C

AMBON
Boskamp, February 42, M/W/C, to Stovil
Stovil, February 42 - December 42, M/W/C, to Tantui
Tantui, December 42 - February 43, M/W/C, to Advents and
Bethanie Churches **Advents Church**, February 43 - March 43,
M, to Parepare
Bethanie Church, February 43 - March 43, W/C, to Kampili

BALI
Denpasar Prison, February 42 - July 42, M, to Makasar
Singaradja Prison, February 42 - July 42, M, to Makasar

LOMBOK
Mataram Prison, May 42 - July 42, M, to Bubutan/Surabaja
Mataram, May 42 - July 42, W/C, to Surabaja

SUMBAWA
   Bima Prison, May 42 - July 42, M/W/C, to Makasar

SUMBA
   Waingapu Prison, May 42 - July 42, M, to Makasar
   Pasang-Grahan, May 42 - July 42, W/C, to Malino

FLORES
   Ende, May 42 - July 42, M/W/C, to Malino
   Ndona Convent, May 42 - July 42, M/W, to Malino

TIMOR
Soe, February 42 - September 42, M/W/C, to Parepare/Kampili
Atambua Convent, February 42 - August 42, M/W, to
Parepare/Kampili
Dili, February 42 - June 42, M/W/C, to Soe
Liquica, February 42 - September 45, Portuguese M/W/C

DUTCH NEW GUINEA
Manokwari, May 42 - July 42, M/W/C, to Ambon
Praf River, June 44 - November 44, Indo-European and
Indonesian M/W/C **Hatam Barracks**, June 44 - November 44,
Indo-European and Indonesian M/W/C
Hollandia Barracks, February 44 - May 44, M/W

Of Interest

"Undoubtedly *Rising from the Shadow of the Sun* would be of interest to book groups, especially because de Jong's story explores how a family survives and in many ways thrives in the midst of the chaos and horror of war.

However, this book can also be incorporated into several academic curricula. History and social studies classes can use this book for primary source research in studying the Japanese occupation in Southeast Asia. Additionally, de Jong's style is so accessible that her book would be appropriate from junior high school through college levels.

An often overlooked aspect of colonialism and post-colonialism is the concept of colonialism from the perspective of the colonial. Netty's view of the Dutch and their contributions to the Dutch East Indies stands in stark contrast to the Indonesians who desire independence. Studying an opposite view may encourage energized class discussions on colonial periods.

Finally, de Jong's book reflects facets of feminist theory in action. During this time period, women around the world had not yet gained full equality. According to feminist theory women had to bond together in order to manage and even succeed in such a repressive reality. Studying and discussing exactly how the women in this book worked together to save themselves and their children would reflect "active" feminism in life and death situations."

Virginia Colangelo, MA in English, Instructor in English and Writing.

Reading Group Questions

1. How important do you think Netty's upbringing was in her moving to the Dutch East Indies? In her dealing with the Japanese occupation?

2. Describe how you think Netty felt about the Dutch East Indies.

3. How does Netty try to reassure Ronny and Paula during the air raids? Are her methods effective? Why or why not?

4. Why does mixing daily life routines with the children and preparing for war make the narrative more realistic? More poignant?

5. Netty never mentions the politics of neither Japan nor Germany. Why do you think that subject never comes up in her diary? Would that be the case today?

6. Netty goes to the dentist as the Japanese are approaching. What does this tell the reader about Netty?

7. As Fokko is being deployed Netty is sad, but not distraught. What are some possible reasons for her attitude?

8. How do the Japanese systematically break down their captives? Initially, while they are still in their own homes, then the town enclosure and finally at the camp.

9. What are some ways the women encourage one another?

10. How does Netty know that if the Allies do not win soon, she and her daughters will die soon?

11. How do the women know the war has ended? How is that the last brutal act by the Japanese?

12. Describe the reunion with Fokko.

13. What is Netty's attitude toward the extremists? How is she justified in her assessment of the situation?

14. Recount the story of the Wedding Bible.

15. Discuss Ronny's quick decision to marry Mike. Were you surprised? Why? Why not?

16. Ronny describes her life as a roller coaster ride adventure. Do you agree or disagree with her image? In a later chapter she refers to her life as whitewater rapids. Do you think that fits in? Why? Why not?

17. Discuss Ronny's return to Indonesia. What impressed her during her trip? Why was it important for her to return?

18. What was the significance of Ronny's retreat to the leper colony?

19. Including Fokko's time during the war was interspersed throughout Netty's diary and memoirs. Did you find that helpful or distracting from the narrative?

Copyright Acknowledgements

I gratefully acknowledge the use of ten official photographs from the Imagebank WW2 – NIOD in Amsterdam. NIOD is part of the Royal Netherlands Academy of Arts and Sciences.

I am very thankful to the late Roger Mansell, Founder of the Center for Research, Allied POWs under the Japanese for giving me permission to use any copyrighted information on his website. This was especially helpful in my research of the NARA files. His is a legacy to everybody who wants to know anything about the Pacific war.

Special thanks to the late Sjoerd A. Lapré, RMWO, for his earlier permission to use historical information from his book *Nederlands-Indië 1940-1950 In Kort Bestek*. My thanks also for the earlier permission from Uitgeverij Van Wijnen, the Netherlands, to use the *List of Japanese Camps in the Dutch East Indies* from a Dutch Doctoral Thesis by D. van Velden, PhD (1963) titled *De Japanse Burgerkampen* (The Japanese Camps for Civilians).

9 781609 107536